T0339657

The Art of Strategy

When it comes to strategy, how should we define victory? For centuries, Eastern and Western thinkers have grappled with this question, offering different answers. What can we learn from this difference? In *The Art of Strategy*, Moon provides a novel and systematic integration of the two dominant frameworks of the East and West: Sun Tzu's military strategy and Michael Porter's business strategy. This unlikely combination of thinking suggests an innovative extension of our understanding and practice of strategy, which will appeal to scholars, students, practitioners, and general readers with an interest in strategy. By aligning the perspectives of these two great thinkers, Moon argues that true winning is about maximizing and optimizing overall value for all engaged stakeholders, and this requires a more efficient approach to strategy.

HWY-CHANG MOON is Professor at the Graduate School of International Studies, Seoul National University. Dr. Moon has consulted many Korean and multinational companies, international organizations (e.g., UNCTAD) and governments (e.g., Korea, Malaysia, Dubai, Azerbaijan, Guangdong Province of China, and India). He has published numerous articles and books on topics covering international business strategy and economic development, including *The Strategy for Korea's Economic Success*, recently published by Oxford University Press.

The Art of Strategy

Sun Tzu, Michael Porter, and Beyond

HWY-CHANG MOON

Seoul National University

CAMBRIDGE
UNIVERSITY PRESS

CAMBRIDGE
UNIVERSITY PRESS

University Printing House, Cambridge CB2 8BS, United Kingdom

One Liberty Plaza, 20th Floor, New York, NY 10006, USA

477 Williamstown Road, Port Melbourne, VIC 3207, Australia

314-321, 3rd Floor, Plot 3, Splendor Forum, Jasola District Centre, New Delhi - 110025, India

79 Anson Road, #06-04/06, Singapore 079906

Cambridge University Press is part of the University of Cambridge.

It furthers the University's mission by disseminating knowledge in the pursuit of education, learning and research at the highest international levels of excellence.

www.cambridge.org
Information on this title: www.cambridge.org/9781108455800
DOI: 10.1017/9781108572507

First published 2018

A catalogue record for this publication is available from the British Library

ISBN 978-1-108-47030-8 Hardback
ISBN 978-1-108-45580-0 Paperback

Cambridge University Press has no responsibility for the persistence or accuracy of URLs for external or third-party internet websites referred to in this publication, and does not guarantee that any content on such websites is, or will remain, accurate or appropriate.

Contents

Figures and Tables

Preface

Sun Tzu and Michael Porter are the most frequently cited strategists in their respective fields of military and business, and their strategic philosophies have been widely applied to other areas beyond military and business. While no one disputes the authority of these two strategists, few understand how they are truly differentiated from other leaders in their own fields. It is interesting to note that despite coming from two different times and having seemingly disparate areas of focus, these two strategists share commonalities along four traits: wide perspective, insightful thoughts, systematic analysis, and easy presentation (or WISE – the initials of the four).

HOW IS SUN TZU DIFFERENT?

Wide Perspective Many leading military strategists such as Carl von Clausewitz (a famous German military strategist in the 1800s) have emphasized the military strategy for victory during a war. In contrast, Sun Tzu's philosophy encompassed military strategies "before, during, and after a war." His primary goal as a military leader was to avoid unnecessary conflicts as he understood that the ultimate goal is not simply a victorious battle but a profitable result after the battle is won. This led Liddell Hart, a British military philosopher, to praise Sun Tzu's strategy as the "grand strategy." No other military strategist or philosopher has employed such a comprehensive perspective on war.

Insightful Thoughts While other military strategists, including Clausewitz, stressed big battles as the way to win, Sun Tzu advocated small battles as a way to minimize the costs of war. Hence, Sun Tzu's ideas are more about the most efficient victory rather than just defeating the enemy. According to Sun Tzu, therefore, supreme excellence in warfare is to win without fighting; if fighting is inevitable, one has to search for ways to fight with minimum costs, in an effort to avoid casualties and the loss of other resources. This distinctive thought of Sun Tzu is highly praised by later scholars as a "complete victory."

Systematic Analysis The value of social science (natural science as well) is its ability to explain seemingly complicated real-world issues in a simple and systematic way. Sun Tzu's approach serves this purpose very well. For example, he analyzed an infinite number of possible ways to victory through the combination of two military strategies – *Cheng* (normal) and *Chi* (abnormal). Another example is that he showed how to analyze the competitiveness of oneself and one's enemy with five criteria, which include both internal and external factors. Some of his other models include six or nine variables, but all of his analytical models are systematically constructed.

Easy Presentation Despite the depth of Sun Tzu's systematic military models, they are intuitive and easy to understand. A key differentiator of Sun Tzu is his ability to simplify situations. He noted that one could create an infinite number of colors in the world through various combinations of the five basic colors of red, blue, yellow, black, and white. Similarly, Sun Tzu stressed five virtues that a competent general should have and five dangers that a general should avoid. As such, a general's strengths and weaknesses can be easily analyzed through Sun Tzu's model. Many of Sun Tzu's philosophies in *The Art of War* are easily applicable to our everyday lives today.

HOW IS MICHAEL PORTER DIFFERENT?

Wide Perspective Porter's strategic perspective is not only at the firm level but also at the industry, regional, country, society, and environmental levels. For each level, Porter provides a comprehensive perspective that is distinguished from other scholars. Other scholars' theories are generally only a subset of Porter's models – for example, the resource-based view in evaluating a firm's competitive advantage only highlights rare and inimitable resources, which is part of Porter's theory of the differentiation advantage. In contrast, Porter suggested a broader perspective in analyzing the sources of competitive advantage – differentiation and cost. He then further categorized them into a broad and narrow scope, comprised of four types of generic strategies, which allow firms to achieve superior performance relative to their competitors.

Insightful Thoughts Porter stated that there are two types of organization in the world – one (i.e., the firm) for creating values and the other (i.e., the government and nonprofit organizations) for distributing values. He further claimed that the ultimate goal of a firm is not to defeat its competitors but to create value for the stakeholders, including society. Porter then explained that there could be multiple winners in the same industry, if firms chose an appropriate and/or unique positioning. This Porterian insight shows that business is more about constructive (or positive-sum) rather than destructive (or zero-sum) competition.

Systematic Analysis Although Porter deals with a wide scope of issues, his analyses are well captured in simplified, systematic frameworks comprised of well-organized analytical tools. For example, Porter's analytical models include the generic strategy for the firm, the five forces model for the industry, the diamond model for the nation, and the model of creating shared value for the society and environment. Relative to Porter, other business scholars and strategists often make vague and disorganized arguments, such as the need to develop state-of-the-art technologies or flexibly adapt to the changing business environment.

Easy Presentation Porter's strategy models are easy to understand and applicable to various fields. While Porter's models are often criticized for lacking "sophistication," his models, although seemingly simple on the surface, are more in-depth, powerful, and practical than other complex theories. For example, while his generic strategy model looks simple, it shows several alternative ways for firms to be successful with the right positioning in the market. In contrast, other seemingly sophisticated economic models often explain the strategic choice mainly based on the cost criterion. Porter's strategy is a masterpiece of simplicity and easiness.

INTEGRATION AND BEYOND

Collaboration and integration have been rare between Eastern and Western strategies. Military and business as academic disciplines or practical fields are also far apart. Thus, the gap between Eastern military thinking and Western business thinking is very large. However, if these distant fields can be effectively integrated, we may be able to derive many useful implications. As Sun Tzu and Porter are the two most distinguished thinkers of the East and West, the purpose of this book is to learn from Sun Tzu and Porter, to integrate their philosophies, and to derive implications that go beyond each of their philosophies.

Although Sun Tzu and Porter are from different times and have different areas of expertise, the fundamental principles of strategy are the same for all areas and all times – only their applications need to be modified to specific situations. The good news is that once you thoroughly understand the fundamental principles of great lessons, you can easily be flexible with applying these principles to the real world. I hope that scholars and policy makers as well as military and business strategists will learn the important principles of strategy from Sun Tzu and Porter, build on the strengths of these two great minds, and acquire the wisdom of strategic thinking.

Acknowledgments

My research assistants spent countless hours conducting research and working on this manuscript. I would like to extend a special thanks to my lead research assistant, Wenyan Yin, whose contributions, in terms of raw research, feedback, and organizational efforts, have been crucial to the timely completion of this project. Eunice Kim provided valuable input with respect to the structure and wording of the manuscript, and Yeon W. Lee offered her assistance whenever needed. My former assistants, Jimmyn Parc, Sohyun Yim, and John Yang, also made meaningful contributions in the early stages of this book. Additionally, I have benefited from the thought-provoking questions and comments from my students who took my class on Sun Tzu and Michael Porter. Ted H. Moon and Jane J. Ng also provided very useful critiques and valuable comments. In addition, special thanks go to Seog Hwan Kim, chairman of Kunil Engineering Co., Ltd., for his strong encouragement and support for my work.

I would like to thank Valerie Appleby, my commissioning editor at Cambridge University Press, who was intrigued by the idea of this book and strongly supported its publication. My content manager Bronte Rawlings, editorial assistant Toby Ginsberg, and other staff members at Cambridge University Press, as well as project manager Rogini Pavithra, team lead Sri Hari Kumar and copy editor Ursula Acton, have also been very helpful in publishing this manuscript. Writing this book has been a very ambitious project as I aimed to integrate the strategic thinking of East and West and that of ancient and modern times. In integrating multiple strategic thoughts and developing new strategy models, I have benefited from the discussions with my colleagues in various fields. I am particularly indebted to Tom Roehl for his thoughtful advice on the comparison of Western and Asian perspectives; the late Alan Rugman and Alain Verbeke for their discerning views on Porter's work; and Dong-Sung Cho for his insightful strategic thinking. Finally, I would like to thank my family for their unconditional love and trust in me, which gave me the ability to complete this project.

Introduction

I WHY SUN TZU'S THE ART OF WAR?

This book aims to open up one of the treasures from antiquity: Sun Tzu's military guideline, *The Art of War*, which, despite being written 2,500 years ago, is still one of the most respected military strategy books in the world. It has influenced many Eastern and Western strategists not only in ancient times, but also in contemporary times. Mao Zedong and Ho Chi Minh are just two examples of modern Eastern leaders who were influenced by Sun Tzu's military philosophy. The icon of Western military history, Bonaparte Napoleon, was also a pupil of Sun Tzu (McCready, 2003; Rarick, 2009). Today, military strategists around the world continue to use Sun Tzu's philosophies in warfare and *The Art of War* remains a staple in military education (Wee, 1994).

Sun Tzu's fandom includes more than just military leaders, as his wisdom proved to be applicable to many fields outside the military (O'Dowd and Waldron, 1991; Wee, Lee, and Hidajat, 1991). Many global CEOs and managers have particularly found this ancient Chinese military book helpful in managing their businesses (Wee et al., 1991). The Chinese government has also begun to promote China's ancient cultural icons, including Sun Tzu's *The Art of War*, to enhance the appeal of Chinese culture to the global audience (Economist, 2011b).

So what is the appeal of Sun Tzu's *The Art of War*? How did this book get into the hands of today's global executives and what accounts for its sustained popularity over two and a half millennia across different cultures and fields? Comparing Sun Tzu's military strategy to Michael Porter's business strategy will shed insight to these

1

questions. Despite the generational gap and differences in culture and expertise, Sun Tzu and Porter have much in common in how they design a path toward victory in their respective fields. In the following sections, I will discuss why Sun Tzu's military strategies are applicable to business more so than others' and why I chose Porter's business theories for comparison.

2 THE FEATURES OF THE ART OF WAR

The Art of War is composed of thirteen chapters and only around 6,000 Chinese characters. Despite the short length, many readers, particularly Western researchers who are not familiar with Chinese characters and Asian cultural background, often find the text difficult to understand. Simply translating Sun Tzu's strategies word for word does not do the book justice as there are usually hidden meanings between the lines. It is necessary to capture all of Sun Tzu's subtleties to fully understand Sun Tzu's philosophies, which is rooted in the principle of *Daoism* (Yuen, 2008). Westerners, however, often find it difficult to understand Daoism because of its use of paradox.

Each of the thirteen chapters discusses different aspects of warfare in a logical order (Lee et al., 1998). The first half of Sun Tzu's book (chapters one through six) primarily discusses the strategy (or theory) of warfare, while the latter seven chapters review specific military tactics for operations (or practice) (Kim, 1999). On the other hand, the first two chapters focus on the preparations before going to war, while the rest of the book illustrates the operations for solving challenges during and after warfare (see Figure I.1).

Among many military strategies and tactics that Sun Tzu introduced in his book, I have summarized the core military thoughts below. First, despite the title, the primary message of *The Art of War* is to avoid war if possible. As previously stated, Sun Tzu's military thoughts throughout his book are rooted in the philosophy of *Daoism*, which stresses that harmony is the most

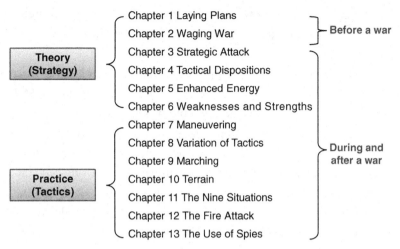

FIGURE I.I The overall structure of *The Art of War*

important goal for human activity (Sun, 1995). In order to achieve harmony, Sun Tzu's military strategies tend to avoid unnecessary conflicts. While Sun Tzu did not suggest that one runs away from conflict, he recommended that one avoids reckless warfare if there is a scarce chance of winning. Thus, Sun Tzu stated in the beginning of his book, "Warfare is a great concern of a nation as it is a matter of life and death, a road either to safety or to ruin. Hence it demands thorough comprehension and investigation." This statement suggests that warfare should be used as a last resort.

Second, Sun Tzu preferred the most efficient, low-cost approach when conflict is unavoidable. Sun Tzu said that attaining one hundred victories in one hundred battles is not the best; winning without fighting or with minimum cost is the best strategy. Therefore, according to Sun Tzu, the best form of attack is an attack on the enemy's plans, followed by their alliances, and their armies. The worst kind of attack is one on the enemy's fortified castle. However, as Sun Tzu also recognized that noncombat victory is often impossible to achieve, he introduced various military strategies on how to fight effectively in the battlefield. All of these strategies require one precondition, which is "deception."

The third characteristic emphasized in Sun Tzu's book is thus deception. In the first chapter of *The Art of War*, Sun Tzu stated, "All warfare is a game of deception." Deception is to distort the enemy's perception. A strategist who is proficient in the art of deception can create illusions to confuse, blind, or falsely convince the enemy of the ongoing situation. By commanding such illusive tactics, one can conceal one's real intentions or military dispositions, hence, depriving the enemy of decision-making capabilities on when to attack and defend, as well as forcing them to make wrong decisions. By utilizing deception, one can turn even a disadvantageous situation into an advantageous one. However, deception can be employed only after a thorough investigation of the enemy's strengths, weaknesses, and real intentions. The importance of knowing the enemy is frequently discussed throughout the thirteen chapters of his book. Sun Tzu stated, "If one knows the enemy and oneself, one will not be in danger in a hundred battles."

Last but not least, Sun Tzu taught us that the ultimate objective of war is not to simply win, but to win with profit. Sun Tzu suggested the following principles of going to war: do not move unless there is an advantage; do not use troops unless there is a gain; do not fight unless there is a danger. These general principles highlight Sun Tzu's emphasis on profitable victory. Sun Tzu paid particular attention to the aftermath of war. Even if one wins a war, if one cannot consolidate one's accomplishments, it will be very costly to maintain the victory. Therefore, winning a war is not the final goal for an army, but consolidating and profiting from the victory is more important.

3   APPLICATION OF SUN TZU'S STRATEGY TO BUSINESS

Despite their differences, business competition and warfare are often compared to each other. Figure I.2 illustrates the differences. The vertical axis (y-axis) represents the net effects on society and the

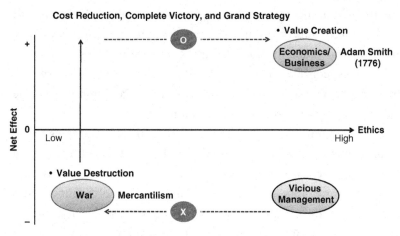

FIGURE I.2 Comparison between war and business

horizontal axis (x-axis) represents the degree of ethics. Thus, war is at best a redistribution of resources from losers to winners, and at worst, a value-destroying event. In war, one's victory is achieved at the expense of another, and even the winner can generally suffer from losses no matter how great the victory is. Hence, the net effects are always negative. Ethics is not valued in warfare, as deception is critical and an effective way to achieve victory at a lower cost.

In contrast to the zero-sum game of war, economics/business is a positive-sum game, which creates values for consumers and the society. This view traces back to Adam Smith's (1937 [1776]) *The Wealth of Nations*, in which Smith asserted that all traders can benefit if countries specialize in producing goods in which they have absolute advantages.[1] However, before Adam Smith, mercantilism was the dominant economic theory, which considered trade as a zero-sum game, similar to the logic of war. The trade surplus of one country can be attained at the expense of a trade deficit of another country, given the zero-sum assumption. However, with respect to ethics, deception or unethical business is

[1]   See Cho and Moon (2013a) for more discussion.

not allowed in today's world of business (see Figure I.2). Firms will not be able to survive if they deceive consumers with low-quality products and other immoral business operations. This is because in business, contrary to war, there is a third party which serves as an umpire (whether it be consumers or the government), while there is no such referee in the game of war.

A great number of studies that apply military strategies to the modern business environment make the mistake of neglecting these fundamental differences between war and business. With a complete understanding of these fundamental differences, Sun Tzu's advice for military battles can be a great resource for current day business leaders, especially with respect to his orientation toward cost reduction, complete victory, and grand strategy (see Figure I.2).

First, Sun Tzu argued for a profitable victory against the enemy – in other words, winning inexpensively. As war is always costly, the longer the military campaign, the more expenses one has to pay. Sun Tzu's argument, "What is important in war is a swift victory, not prolonged operations," demonstrates Sun Tzu's military thought of a "swift victory," and this message is consistent with the basic objectives of efficiency, lower costs, and profit maximization in business.

Second, Sun Tzu's philosophy teaches constructiveness over destructiveness, so that some scholars call him a pacifist. In addition to warning readers of the destructive nature of warfare at the beginning of his book, Sun Tzu continually emphasized that war should only be used as a last resort. Instead, he advocated for noncombat, blood-free victories. Winning without destroying the enemy and their resources while limiting damage to one's own resources is what Sun Tzu calls "winning the complete victory." Similarly, the goal of business is to satisfy the customer's needs by creating values, rather than destroying competitors.

Last, Sun Tzu maintained that the ultimate goal of military strategy is to ensure a sustainable victory instead of a one-time victory. Winning a war is not the final goal for an army; how to consolidate the victory is more important. Sun Tzu suggested that military leaders think long term and consider the aftermath of war instead of only focusing on short-term glory in battlefields. One may win the war and seize the enemy's land. However, if one cannot consolidate one's accomplishment, it will be very dangerous, as it would mean a drain of resources. Therefore, Sun Tzu emphasized a "grand strategy," which considers not just winning the war, but also the preparation of prewar and the effects of postwar. In business, Sun Tzu's grand strategy is comparable to creating shared value (CSV) (Porter and Kramer, 2011), the recent trend in business considerations of social interest.

4   THE INTEGRATION OF SUN TZU AND PORTER

Sun Tzu's military strategy presented in *The Art of War* has been widely adopted by scholars and practitioners of modern business management (Dalton, 2008; Douglas and Strutton, 2009). However, most existing studies are limited to only applying Sun Tzu's theories to specific business cases, and few have conducted a rigorous theoretical comparison between Sun Tzu's military strategy and business models. Most of these studies attempt to benefit from the proven wisdom of military tactics to overcome challenges in specific business contexts. However, there are risks in this simplistic application of military strategies to business contexts without theoretical substantiation and a clear understanding of the differences between war and business. Moreover, since the business environment has become increasingly interconnected and complex, military strategies optimized for a zero-sum game structure of competition have been increasingly insufficient aids for modern business strategies that must address both cooperation and competition.

Therefore, in order to use military strategies for business, one must conduct an in-depth analysis that takes out aspects of military strategy unsuitable for business context by using the filter of a business mind-set, instead of a war mind-set. In order to identify the suitable elements of military strategies, on the other hand, one needs to study the given military guidelines (e.g., Sun Tzu's *The Art of War*) and comparable business theories (e.g., Michael Porter's business models) hand in hand. By conducting a comparative study of military and business theories, one can more readily identify the strengths and weaknesses of both sides–a significant advantage considering how established business or military theories tend not to easily reveal their weaknesses. With such accurate and swift evaluation, a comparative study can generate complementary effects between the two sides and help enhance the explanatory power of both military and business theories. I chose Porter's business theories for the most appropriate comparison with Sun Tzu's military theories because of the following reasons.

First, Sun Tzu is the most reputable ancient military strategist and Michael Porter is the leading contemporary business thinker. Sun Tzu, in *The Art of War*, developed many military principles, which deal with different methods of overcoming the difficulties in warfare. Similarly, Porter also developed many business strategies on overcoming management difficulties in the modern business world. Porter has colonized the entire field of business theory (Economist, 2011a). Just as Sun Tzu's *The Art of War* is still a timeless classic and mandatory reading in major military schools (Wu, Chou, and Wu, 2004), Porter's business models and theories are contemporary classics taught at most business schools throughout the world (Adams, 2015).

Second, Sun Tzu and Porter emphasized both external and internal factors for success in military and business. Sun Tzu included two external environmental factors – terrain and heaven – in addition to the three internal factors – principle, generalship, and system – thereby proposing five determinants for victory in war. MacDonald and Neupert (2005) argued that one of the main strengths of Sun Tzu's approach is his recognition of environmental factors when formulating a strategy for dealing with the enemy. Sun Tzu said, "Knowing the enemy and oneself" is not enough to make one successful in the battle because the environment where and when the battle occurs should also be considered. Accordingly, he claimed, "Knowing the enemy and oneself, one will not be in danger, but knowing the terrain and heaven in addition to the enemy and oneself, one will obtain a complete victory."

In business, Porter has advanced the traditional perspective of the industrial organization theory. Traditional industrial organization theory emphasizes the important role that the environment has on firms' performance, implying that the firm cannot influence the industry structure. However, according to Porter, industry structure is not completely exogenous, but partly influenced by the firm's activities (Spanos and Lioukas, 2001). Porter maintained that firms' success should be attributed to both the environment and firms' managerial capabilities, which are neglected in the classical industrial organization theory. Therefore, like Sun Tzu, Porter also emphasized both environmental factors and firms' behaviors for achieving superior performance against their competitors.

Third, Sun Tzu stressed positioning in the war. According to Sun Tzu, the best military strategy is not beating the enemy through direct fighting, but winning the war without fighting or at minimum costs. With the proper strategic positioning, an army can enjoy a preponderance of power against the enemy and may even obtain the victory before the battle ensues. With a favorable position, the physically weaker army can even defeat the physically stronger army. Sun Tzu also pointed out that although the external environments are out of one's control, one can still make them controllable by exploiting favorable conditions and avoiding unfavorable conditions of terrain or heaven.

Like Sun Tzu, Porter emphasized the importance of firms' strategic positioning in the market. Porter (1980) introduced three types of generic positioning (i.e., generic strategy) – cost leadership, differentiation, and focus.[2] The firm choosing any one of the three generic strategies can achieve above average profits. Moreover, Porter (1996) emphasized that only the unique positioning with good trade-offs and fit among the firm's value activities can help firms avoid imitation from the rivals, thereby achieving a sustainable competitive advantage.

Porter introduced numerous business models since the 1980s. In this book, I selected Porter's most useful business models to compare with Sun Tzu's military strategies. These models vary in their characteristics: some are about evaluating the business environment such as the five forces model and diamond model; others are about choosing a unique positioning against the competitors, such as the generic strategy, and strategic positioning. There are also other theories and concepts, including cluster theory, and more recently the concept of creating shared value for sustainable development of both firms and the society.

In the course of my research, I was surprised to find Porter's business strategy models and Sun Tzu's military strategy models match in their numbers and characteristics. For example, Porter's diamond model of evaluating the business environment is similar to Sun Tzu's consideration of various factors of determining the victory. Porter's models on choosing firms' superior positions against the competitors are much similar to Sun Tzu's strategies, which emphasize gaining relative superiority at the point of contact, such as the military tactics of avoiding the enemy's strengths and attacking their weaknesses. These theoretical linkages of the thirteen chapters between Sun Tzu and Porter are illustrated in Table I.1.

The similarities between Sun Tzu and Porter, however, should be studied and applied with a full understanding of the fundamental difference between war and business. Victory at any cost is the nonnegotiable end in a war, but value creation

---

[2] Porter (1985) further categorized the focus strategy into two, cost focus and differentiation focus, thus four generic strategies in total.

Table I.1 *The linkages between Sun Tzu and Michael Porter for each chapter*

	Sun Tzu's Military Strategy Models.	Porter's Business Strategy Models	Linkage	Issues for Extending/Improving Sun Tzu and Porter's Strategy Models
Ch 1	Five elements	Diamond model (Porter, 1990)	Assessing overall competitiveness	**Sun Tzu:** Devising the extended five elements by including the demand conditions, and expanding the concepts of heaven and terrain **Porter:** Extending the diamond model by incorporating the concepts of generalship, the same goal, and strong internal coordination
Ch 2	Swift victory and local procurement	Value chain analysis (Porter, 1985)	Investigating the sources of competitive advantage	**Sun Tzu:** Developing the military value chain by benchmarking the firm value chain **Porter:** Incorporating speed (not just as a result but a source of competitiveness) and outsourcing (or network-based value creation system) for increasing values
Ch 3	Winning without fighting	Five forces model (Porter, 1980)	Selecting the most profitable means or areas to compete	**Sun Tzu:** Considering extended rivals in war **Porter:** Considering not just competition but coevolution with the five forces
Ch 4	Tactical dispositions	Generic strategy (Porter, 1980, 1985)	Preparing for competitive	**Sun Tzu:** Upgrading the current competitive advantage

Table I.1 (cont.)

	Sun Tzu's Military Strategy Models	Porter's Business Strategy Models	Linkage	Issues for Extending/Improving Sun Tzu and Porter's Strategy Models
			positioning before competing	**Porter:** Considering the cost of strategic mistakes and the timing for entry
Ch 5	*Cheng* (normal) and *Chi* (abnormal)	Operational Effectiveness (OE) and Strategic Positioning (SP) (Porter, 1996)	Enhancing advantages through alternative strategies	**Sun Tzu:** Not just combining *Cheng* and *Chi*, but developing a new unique strategy **Porter:** Combining OE and SP for creating higher synergy, instead of relying too much on SP for unique positioning
Ch 6	Weaknesses and Strengths	Strategies for unique positioning (trade-offs, fit) (Porter, 1996)	Making unique combination of strategies	**Sun Tzu:** Considering more unique but less risky than "deceptive" strategy **Porter:** Assessing both costs and benefits of unique-positioning strategy more closely
Ch 7	Turning the devious into the direct	Creating shared value (CSV) (Porter and Kramer, 2011)	Turning the disadvantageous position into advantageous one	**Sun Tzu:** Developing a win-win perspective between the army and the society **Porter:** Providing guidelines for enhancing the efficiency of intra- and interorganizational communication
Ch 8	Variation of tactics	Consistency and changes in strategy (Porter, 1979, 1996)	Deciding what to do and what not to do for effective changes	**Sun Tzu:** Being careful of the risks of an extreme variation of tactics **Porter:** Considering both favorable and unfavorable factors for changes in strategy

Table I.1 (cont.)

Sun Tzu's Military Strategy Models	Porter's Business Strategy Models	Linkage	Issues for Extending/Improving Sun Tzu and Porter's Strategy Models
Ch 9 Moving troops and investigating the enemy	Extended generic strategies (Porter, 1980, 1985, 1996; Moon et al., 2014)	Expanding the scope of tactics and competitive targets	**Sun Tzu:** Deepening internal capabilities first before designing fancy strategies **Porter:** Incorporating environmental factors into the generic strategy when serving the BOP (bottom of the pyramid) market, in particular
Ch 10 Tactics for dealing with six types of terrain	Cluster theory (Porter, 1990, 1998, 2008)	Exploiting location advantages for increasing synergies	**Sun Tzu:** Enhancing synergies by clustering terrains and other related factors **Porter:** Investigating the asymmetric performance of firms within the cluster and incorporating the concept of international (or global)-linking clusters
Ch 11 Strategic attack by an expeditionary force	Configuration-Coordination model (Porter, 1986)	Extending and integrating strategies in foreign locations	**Sun Tzu:** Coordinating more between expeditionary forces **Porter:** Investigating foreign location factors more closely

Table I.1 (cont.)

Sun Tzu's Military Strategy Models	Porter's Business Strategy Models	Linkage	Issues for Extending/Improving Sun Tzu and Porter's Strategy Models
Ch 12 Fire attack	Innovation (Porter, 1990)	Creating superior power through innovative means	**Sun Tzu:** Putting more emphasis on created advantage than inherited advantage **Porter:** Considering costs of innovation and a wider range of stakeholders for successful innovation
Ch 13 Using spies	Information technology (Porter and Millar, 1985; Porter, 2001)	Utilizing information for enhancing competitive advantage	**Sun Tzu:** Reassuring the limitation of information advantage compared to core competence **Porter:** Analyzing and adapting to local institutional environment for success in international business

by keeping ethics and rules is the purpose of business. In this perspective, while Sun Tzu's military strategies give valuable insights to business, applying them to business without careful modification will mislead business managers. For this reason, this book also discusses critical differences between Sun Tzu's military principles and Porter's business ones. Hence, in each of the following thirteen chapters, I will discuss which of Sun Tzu's strategies can be applied and which cannot be applied to business. In addition, I will also suggest possible extensions for both Sun Tzu and Porter's strategy models by borrowing useful concepts from each other. Therefore, these comprehensive and systematic approaches will provide useful guidelines for both managers and scholars in the military and business fields.

I Getting Started: Overall Assessment

Sun Tzu: Five elements for laying plans
Porter: Diamond model for analyzing competitiveness

While seamlessly organized, each of the thirteen chapters in *The Art of War* is an independent set of military strategies and theories on warfare. Thus, a comparison of Sun Tzu to another theoretician must cater to each of Sun Tzu's chapters, rather than the whole book as a single unit. This chapter selects Sun Tzu's five elements framework from the first chapter of *The Art of War* and Porter's diamond model for theoretical comparison. The five elements are used to compare one's own competitiveness with that of one's opponent to assess the probability of winning in war. Similarly, the diamond model was developed to evaluate the competitiveness of nations, but it has also been widely applied to industry- and firm-level analysis.

A careful analysis of Sun Tzu's five elements and Porter's diamond model reveals a surprising level of congruence between the core thoughts of two masters, cutting through more than 2,500 years of history. Sun Tzu's five elements are compatible with three endogenous factors of the diamond model. This chapter demonstrates that by adding Sun Tzu's overarching strategic theme – knowing the enemy – to the five elements and extending the elements of terrain and heaven (two of the five elements), Sun Tzu's extended five elements can better estimate the probability of victory in war. On the other hand, if Porter's diamond model adopts some of Sun Tzu's elements (i.e., the generalship, the same goal, and the system of internal coordination), related to firm-specific advantages, it becomes a more useful framework for analyzing a firm's competitiveness.

This chapter first presents an overview of Sun Tzu's five elements and Porter's diamond model. It then examines the linkages between the two models, and finds that each model's strengths can be used to extend the other to improve their explanatory power in the real world. This chapter then applies the extended five elements and diamond model to respective military and business cases (i.e., Japan's attack on Pearl Harbor and Sony's experience with the Walkman). Finally, the chapter concludes by summarizing contributions and provides useful implications by addressing the similarities and differences between war and business.

I.I   SUN TZU: FIVE ELEMENTS FOR LAYING PLANS

The opening thesis of Sun Tzu in *The Art of War* is, "Warfare is a great concern of a nation as it is a matter of life and death, a road either to safety or to ruin. Hence, it demands thorough comprehension and investigation." *The Art of War*, conceived to guide rulers and generals on how to manage and win a war, has at its core the consideration of the destructive nature of war that entails huge economic losses and other harmful effects. In fact, Sun Tzu stressed extremely careful deliberation before deciding to engage in a war. To this end, he proposed five fundamental elements for consideration – *principle, heaven, terrain, generalship*, and *system*.[1] Sun Tzu then claimed that by comparing one's own competitiveness against that of the enemy, one could calculate the prospects for victory before going to war and make prudent decisions on how to approach the conflict. According to Sun Tzu, the more advantages one has in the five elements, the more likely one is to win the war.

Principle is explained as the shared purpose or common cause between a ruler and the public (Chen, 1994; Tung, 1994; Wong, Maher, and Lee, 1998). In order to motivate the public and gain their support, the ruler must be able to lay out a convincing, justified cause to his people on why they must march to the battlefield

---

[1]   The Chinese characters are: 道, 天, 地, 將, 法.

and risk losing their lives. A widely supported cause and trust in their ruler promise stronger loyalty of the people, making them willing to follow their ruler into perilous battlefields. *Heaven*, on the other hand, signifies things such as *yin* and *yang*, cold and heat, and times and seasons. This concept is concerned with all of the interactions between natural forces (Griffith, 1963), not just the climate or weather conditions. *Terrain* represents things like far or near distances, danger or safety to march, open or narrow passes, and the circumstances of life or death. Terrain can be classified into the geographical features of the battlefield and the chosen ground for fighting (Chen, 1994; MacDonald and Neupert, 2005). While the geographical features of the battlefield are hard to change, one can still choose the most favorable ground for oneself or lead the enemy into unfavorable ground. *Generalship* refers to the five necessary virtues for good military leadership – intelligence, trustworthiness, benevolence, courage, and sternness. It is worth noting that Sun Tzu emphasized the basic qualities and cultivations of generalship over a general's military training and career background (Chen, 1994). Lastly, *system* refers to the structure of military organizations, regulations for controlling forces, and logistical support.

As opposed to the superstitious methods relied on to predict the likelihood of winning the war before Sun Tzu, his objective, comprehensive, and systematic five elements provide valuable guidelines for assessing the relative strengths of one's enemy and oneself. Among these five elements, there are two exogenous (or uncontrollable) elements – heaven and terrain – and three endogenous (or controllable) elements – principle, generalship, and system. As briefly mentioned before, while heaven and terrain cannot be controlled, they can still be strategically managed. According to Sun Tzu, a capable strategist can manage even the climate and terrain, by taking advantage of favorable situations or avoiding disadvantageous situations. Hence, in a broad sense, the five elements account for the created competitive advantage of a military force, similar to Porter's four determinants of the diamond model.

1.2 PORTER: DIAMOND MODEL FOR ANALYZING COMPETITIVENESS

Porter's (1990) diamond model is a useful framework for analyzing national competitiveness. This model is composed of four endogenous variables – *factor conditions; demand conditions; related and supporting industries;* and *firm strategy, structure, and rivalry* – and two exogenous variables – *government* and *chance. Factor conditions* represent the factors of production necessary to compete in a given industry. They are distinguished into basic factors that are inherited (e.g., cheap labor and natural resources) and advanced factors that are created (e.g., skilled labor and technology). *Demand conditions* describe the nature of domestic demand for the industry's products and services, and include the size and sophistication of the market. *Related and supporting industries* refer to the availability of internationally competitive related and supporting sectors and the close interaction and synergy creation among them (i.e., cluster effect). *Firm strategy, structure, and rivalry* represent the business strategy, the structure of firms' creation and organization, and the nature of domestic rivalry. Since this variable is mainly about the national circumstance and context that influence the firm's strategy and structure, it will be referred to as *business context* hereafter for simplicity.[2]

Government and *chance* affect the firm's competitiveness through influencing each of the four determinants of the diamond model, but they are beyond a firm's control. Like Sun Tzu's five elements, the diamond model is a comprehensive model that incorporates useful ideas of earlier scholars (Sledge, 2005; Cho

---

[2] Porter later renamed it as the context for strategy and rivalry (Porter, 1998; Porter and Kramer, 2002; Porter et al., 2008), and this book refers to it as *business context* for conciseness. In fact, other studies (e.g., Cho, Moon, and Kim, 2008; Rugman and Oh, 2008) also refer to firm strategy, structure, and rivalry as "business context."

and Moon, 2013a). Porter defined national competitiveness as a nation's capability to create a productive business environment that facilitates firms' innovation and value creation. According to Porter, a country's competitiveness is more likely to be determined by the key competitive industries, which are further influenced by firm activities.

However, Porter's diamond model concentrates on the home-based diamond and does not fully account for international activities. The central idea of Porter's diamond is that firms' competitiveness is subject to the competitiveness of the home country. This is why international business scholars tried to improve Porter's diamond model to explain the competitiveness of small and open economies (e.g., Singapore, Hong Kong, and Korea) in particular, whose competitiveness depends much on the international activities of multinational companies. To this end, scholars introduced extended models, such as the double diamond model (Rugman and D'Cruz, 1993), the generalized double diamond model (Moon, Rugman, and Verbeke, 1995, 1998), and the dual double diamond model (Cho et al., 2008).

In addition to analyzing competitiveness at the national level, the diamond model has also been applied at the industry level (Jin and Moon, 2006; Mann and Byun, 2011) and firm level (Moon and Lee, 2004). Porter (1990) claimed, "It is the firms, not nations, which compete in the international markets." The central question Porter raised to study national competitiveness was why firms in a particular nation gain superior competitiveness. To deal with this research question, Porter performed a firm level analysis by selecting the representative firms in the internationally successful industries of ten countries. Thus, Porter's research on national competitiveness actually represents the firm and industry competitiveness of the relevant nations, although Porter's diamond seems to be conceptually confined to a national level analysis.

This chapter presents an extended version of Porter's diamond model by incorporating some of Sun Tzu's military strategies to better analyze firm competitiveness in particular. With sub-variables borrowed from Sun Tzu's military concepts – characterized as firm-specific factors – the extended diamond model can fill the gap for evaluating firm competitiveness in practice. This chapter also extends Sun Tzu's five elements by incorporating some determinants of the diamond model, including demand conditions and related and supporting sectors.

1.3   THE INTEGRATION OF SUN TZU AND PORTER

Porter's diamond model and Sun Tzu's five elements share certain similarities. First, the purposes of the two models are similar. Sun Tzu's five elements are used to explain the probability of winning in warfare by assessing the strengths and weaknesses of the competing rivals. Similarly, Porter's diamond model is used to evaluate the competitiveness of nations (as well as industries and firms) in relation to their competitors. Second, both models have achieved comprehensiveness by incorporating most of the key determinants in one framework. Just as Sun Tzu stressed thorough examination of the military capabilities and conditions of one's enemy and oneself based on the five elements, Porter emphasized that competitiveness is determined by the four factors of the diamond model.

1.3.1   *Principle versus Business Context*

In business, Sun Tzu's *principle* can be interpreted as the establishment of the same goal between the firm and employees, so that employees will be responsible and loyal to the firm (Chen, 1994). Wong et al. (1998) extended Chen's (1994) concept to a broader scope, including the consensus between firms and the society. Internal consensus refers to the consensus between managers and employees, while external consensus refers to the consistency between the firm's goals and social interests. Therefore, the key objective of this element is to share the same vision and values within the firm as well as between the firm and the society.

The internal and external consensus can be placed under the variable of *business context*. Porter (1990) particularly pointed out that firms tend to succeed when their goals are in line with the sources of a nation's competitive advantages (e.g., ownership structure and capital market conditions) because they can then gain sustainable capital investments and talent inflows. This implies that Porter's business context variable emphasizes the importance of external consensus (i.e., the firm's goal and the needs of nations) more than the influence of internal consensus within the firm on firm performance. Therefore, the concept of business context can gain greater relevance and applicability, by explicitly incorporating the importance of internal consensus characterized in Sun Tzu's *principle*, and considers both internal and external consensus with equal weights. This consideration will further the understanding of a firm's competitiveness that Porter pioneered.

1.3.2   Heaven and Terrain versus Related and Supporting Industries

Existing studies on Sun Tzu from a business perspective interpret *heaven* as the economic and business climate, such as business cycles, government policies and incentives, cultural and social norms, the state of technology and its changes, market structure, and other general economic and social factors (Wee, Lee, and Hidajat, 1991). On the other hand, *terrain* is read as local, physical, and infrastructural variables, including supplies of industrial and raw materials, access to the capital markets, technology and R&D centers, and infrastructure services (e.g., transportation, telecommunication, and water and power supply) (Chen, 1994).

However, these interpretations are too subjective and lack strong theoretical support for validation. As noted earlier, among the five elements, heaven and terrain are the uncontrollable yet manageable variables, if a leader possesses the proper skills and strategic mind-set. A renowned strategist of ancient China, Zhu Geliang, for example, utilized the changing direction of the wind to defeat his enemy through a fire attack. Similarly, Han Xin strategically deployed his army in front of a river, which did not offer his troops an option to retreat. Han Xin used geography and psychology to motivate his army to "fight to the death" and ultimately emerged victorious. As such, both variables of heaven and terrain can play an important role in enhancing one's competitive position in warfare.

In a similar vein, related and supporting industries can reinforce firm competitiveness and help create new advantages. In this respect, heaven and terrain can be linked to Porter's related and supporting industries. However, Sun Tzu overlooked the interaction between the enemy and other indirectly involved parties, which in fact could also influence the military strengths of counterparts. Thus, Sun Tzu, too, could learn from Porter's business theory. In this case, Sun Tzu's heaven and terrain variables can be extended by adding the concept of the enemy's relationship with third parties when analyzing an enemy's competitiveness.

1.3.3   Generalship versus Factor Conditions

Generalship can be equated to a CEO's leadership in business. Wee et al. (1991) reinterpreted Sun Tzu's five attributes of generalship in the business context as follows: *intelligence* as wise decision-making in the face of various business opportunities and threats; *trustworthiness* as the trust placed upon the leadership; *benevolence* as being sympathetic and kind to subordinates; *courage* as the boldness of making decisions and willingness to take necessary risks; and *sternness* as being highly principled.

Porter (1990) did not explicitly define leadership as a separate determinant of the diamond model, because although business leadership is indeed important for competitiveness, it does not function independently from the other four determinants of the diamond. However, in the diamond model, Sun Tzu's generalship can find its place in advanced factor conditions (i.e., skilled human resource). Porter defined business leaders as those who have an excellent understanding of and belief in the critical factors. They have the ability to recognize and incorporate the national advantages to enhance their business competitiveness. Leaders must also have a strong willingness and courage to change and be prepared to sacrifice the easy life for difficulty in order to achieve desired results. Therefore, Porter (1990) stressed three out of the five virtues of a competent general suggested by Sun Tzu – *intelligence, courage*, and *sternness*.

On the other hand, there is an interesting difference between Sun Tzu and Porter on defining leadership. Sun Tzu placed a greater emphasis on the basic qualities and cultivations of generalship instead of military and technical pedigree. This distinction is important because knowledge and skills can be improved through training, but the qualities of generalship are not easy to acquire (Chen, 1994). Therefore, Sun Tzu's requirements for good leadership tend to revolve around innate or inherited characteristics. On the other hand, Porter (1990) stated that the birth of heroes in an industry is a result of the national environment – thereby emphasizing the role of the national system in nurturing the leadership.

1.3.4 System versus Business Context

Sun Tzu's *system* refers to organizational structure and regulation. Wong et al. (1998) explained this element as the organizational structure facilitating efficient coordination among various business functions within the organization. Each of these business functions should then be designed not only for its own purpose but also for the support of other functions. Therefore, Sun Tzu's system can be compared to firm structure under the business context of the diamond model. For this variable, Porter (1990) stressed that there is no single, universally appropriate management system for a firm to follow, and he downplayed the role of firms' internal organization, particularly the creation of synergies through internal coordination and cooperation among different divisions and businesses within the firm. However, firms tend to be successful if the management system favored by the national environment is well suited to the sources of competitive advantages in the industry. Therefore, Porter eventually came to emphasize the influence of external factors on the formation of competitive firm structure and performance.

The interaction between external and internal factors has become increasingly important in today's globalized economic environment, as firm competitiveness is no longer the function of home-based resources alone. Instead, firms disperse their value activities to different nations that can most productively perform their operations, thereby maximizing profits. The capability of configuration and coordination of various activities (Porter, 1986) in the value chain on the global scope is critical to enhance a firm's overall competitiveness (Moon, 2016a). Furthermore, a firm's competitiveness is not limited to a single firm but subject to the holistic business ecosystem, the interaction among the involved firms and institutions in the global value chain (Moon, 2016b). Hence, a firm's system should be considered more comprehensively when analyzing its competitiveness.

1.3.5   Knowing the Enemy versus Demand Conditions

The above analysis shows that the five elements of Sun Tzu match the key determinants of Porter's diamond model except for the demand conditions. The match for this factor can be found in Sun Tzu's overarching tenet, "knowing the enemy." However, what is included in this tenet reaches beyond the scope of the five elements, which are concerned with tangible military strengths and conditions. In knowing the enemy, one must also know the enemy's intention, which is intangible and more related to psychological operations. In fact, Sun Tzu placed a greater importance on the latter, as it is difficult to observe from the outside.

Throughout all thirteen chapters of *The Art of War*, Sun Tzu stressed the strategy of knowing the enemy. Sun Tzu famously advised, "If one knows the enemy and oneself, one will not be in danger in one hundred battles; if one is ignorant of the enemy but knows oneself, one's chances of winning or losing will be equal." This implies that one is less likely to be successful if one merely knows the enemy's physical strengths, but not their real intentions. Therefore, knowing the enemy is another important factor to consider along with the five elements.

In business, many interpret *knowing the enemy* as knowing the competitors. However, in business, a comprehensive interpretation should include all the relevant stakeholders, particularly business customers. The customers make the final judgment for the products and services produced by companies. Even if a company introduces a high-quality product, it will fail if there is little market demand for that product. The orientation to customer needs is critically important, particularly for global managers in order to maintain success in the global market (Richey et al., 2011). Therefore, while knowing the enemy is a precondition for winning a war, knowing the consumers (or the market) is a key to success in business. In practice, there are many failed business cases, even among the renowned companies (e.g., Kodak, Hewlett-Packard, and Nokia), because they ignored the changing patterns of consumer demand.

By combining the idea of knowing the enemy with the five elements, all of the four endogenous factors of the diamond correspond nicely to Sun Tzu's elements for laying plans. Although Porter's original diamond model is comprehensive for analyzing national competitiveness, some firm-specific elements borrowed from Sun Tzu's five elements (i.e., the generalship, the same goal, and the system of internal coordination) can enhance the explanatory power of the diamond model for application at the firm level. On the other hand, Sun Tzu's five elements can also be improved by borrowing certain concepts from diamond model factors – demand conditions and a subfactor (i.e., the interaction among related parties) of related and supporting industries (see Figure 1.1). The following section will show how the extended analysis can better explain real military and business cases.

1.4   MILITARY CASE: JAPAN'S ATTACK ON PEARL HARBOR

The attack on Pearl Harbor was a surprise military strike conducted by the Imperial Japanese Navy. This attack was aimed to prevent the

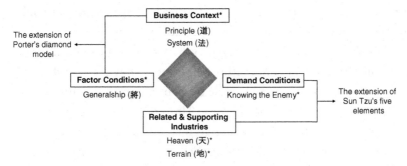

FIGURE I.I Sun Tzu's five elements and Porter's diamond model
Note: * represents the variables improved by borrowing the concepts from either Sun Tzu's five elements or Porter's diamond model.

US Pacific Fleet from interfering with the military actions that Japan was performing in order to expand its power in Southeast Asia and the Pacific. Yamamoto Isoroku, the commander of the Japanese fleet, designed the attack plan. He and other officers concluded that the attack could only succeed if it met the following conditions: (a) the attack must catch the Americans by complete surprise, (b) it must be done early Sunday morning when the American defense would be least prepared to respond, (c) the Imperial Japanese Navy must commit all six of its best aircraft carriers, and (d) the attack must be performed by the best airmen (Bowen, 2007).

After extensive preparation and training, the Japanese launched two waves of heavy bombing against the US military on the morning of December 7, 1941. The first wave, which was the primary attack, targeted capital ships; the second wave was focused on destroying whatever was left. During the two-hour attack, both the US Navy and Air Force were heavily damaged, and thousands of US servicemen were killed or wounded while Japanese casualties were quite low. However, this attack precipitated America's entry into World War II. Although Japan's attack appeared temporarily successful, it served as the catalyst to ending the Japanese empire. Sun Tzu's five elements and the extended model can be applied to analyze both Japan's initial success and eventual failure.

Principle The decision was made by a small group of senior officials of the Imperial Japanese Army and the Imperial Japanese Navy. Although there were some disputes between the army and navy regarding the timing and methods of attack, they all regarded the United States as the main obstacle to their territorial expansion and objected to any concessions to the United States (Record, 2009). In other words, there existed a high level of consensus in terms of national interest and goals among the Japanese decision makers.

Heaven and Terrain Japan deliberately chose Sunday morning to attack. Most US soldiers had Sundays off, making it the perfect time for the Japanese military to make a surprise attack (i.e., heaven). Japan chose Pearl Harbor as their target, because it was a very important strategic base of the US military power in the Pacific. Japan trained its forces in a place in Japan that geographically resembled Pearl Harbor, and redesigned and upgraded its weapons and transportation methods for more effective completion of the mission (i.e., terrain).

Generalship Yamamoto was an expert in leading the operations of aircrafts and aircraft carriers. He and his colleagues conducted a thorough study, assessed the feasibility of the attack, designed the entire battle plan, and eventually achieved what initially appeared to be a great success (i.e., intelligence). In the early stages of the plan, Yamamoto initially expressed doubt and apprehension, reluctant to push Japan into a war against the United States. However, upon being appointed as the commander-in-chief of the Pearl Harbor assault, he withdrew his personal disagreements and dutifully carried out his assignment (i.e., courage). Yamamoto then proceeded through intensive planning and training of soldiers for the attack (i.e., sternness). However, because many officers regarded the attack as a gamble, the Japanese Imperial General Staff initially rejected Yamamoto's strategy. Yamamoto threatened to resign if his plan was not approved. The Imperial General Staff finally agreed considering his reputation and credit as a capable military leader (i.e., trustworthiness). Yamamoto was also a benevolent commander. For example, he shook hands personally and emotionally with each of his pilots before they left for the mission (Barrett, 1989), which was a very strong gesture of giving deep affections at that time in the Japanese military (i.e., benevolence). Yamamoto was indeed a leader with the rare combination of all the virtues that Sun Tzu suggested for good generalship.

System Yamamoto and his staff conducted extensive research on the UK air attack on the Italian fleet at Taranto in 1940. Japan's strike on Pearl Harbor at the time was an air strike of unprecedented scale. Japan strictly controlled the use of radio messages to avoid alerting the US forces prior to the attack. Moreover, a successful implementation of the plan required multiple waves of attacks and involved the systematic targeting and demolition of specific ships, airfields, aircraft, and dry-docks. The immediate result of the Pearl Harbor raid attested to the efficiency of the organizational structure and operation of the Japanese military.

On the other hand, although Japan achieved its immediate military objectives through a comprehensive plan that incorporated Sun Tzu's five elements, it eventually failed because the Japanese leaders misunderstood the intentions of the United States. According to Sun Tzu's term, Japan failed to know its enemy. Japan expected that the Americans would negotiate with Japan after the attack, but instead they made an immediate declaration of war. Yamamoto once stated, "I am afraid we will awaken a sleeping giant." He predicted that despite a successful attack on the US fleet, Japan could not win an extended war against the United States due to the vast gap in military and economic capabilities. On a similar note, the US failure to repel Japan's initial attack can also be explained by its negligence in knowing Japan's real intentions. The United States did not anticipate that Japan would attack Pearl Harbor.

This case also illuminates the shortcomings of Sun Tzu's theories. In terms of heaven and terrain, Sun Tzu emphasized the physical or natural conditions of the battlefield, but overlooked the interaction between the enemy and other indirectly involved parties. In the case of Pearl Harbor, although the United States publically resisted involvement in war in the beginning, it indirectly supported Western European countries with weapons, ammunition, and other resources. Moreover, at the time, the United States and the United Kingdom shared close ties at the national as well as personal levels. Therefore, the attack on Pearl Harbor provided the US government a legitimate reason to engage in war. Although Sun Tzu's theories provide very useful insights into this case, the negligence of interactive activities in competition has somewhat limited their explanatory powers.

This shortcoming is where Sun Tzu can also benefit from Porter's insights. While Sun Tzu emphasized the evaluation of the enemy only, Porter emphasized the importance of interaction among all the related parties (e.g., the United States and the United Kingdom in this case), as an independent explanatory variable of enhancing competitiveness. Therefore, Sun Tzu's five elements can borrow some of Porter's concepts (i.e., demand conditions and related and supporting industries) to better explain why Japan succeeded in performing the immediate mission but failed in correctly predicting the US response after the attack on Pearl Harbor.

1.5   BUSINESS CASE: SONY'S EXPERIENCE WITH THE WALKMAN

Sony's Walkman was first released in Japan on July 1, 1979, and it became a big hit in the Japanese market. It also received much attention in international markets, including the United States and Europe. However, Sony had been falling behind its competitors since the late 1990s, taking an especially large blow when the iPod was launched in 2001. In order to challenge the iPod, Sony introduced a new digital Walkman in 2004. However, it turned out to be a disappointment. Why did Sony's portable music player succeed in the 1980s and 1990s but not in the 2000s? In the following section, the diamond model will be used to compare Sony's strategies in these two different periods and explain the reasons behind Sony's success and failure.

Porter's diamond model is useful for explaining the early superior performance of Sony compared to other international counterparts. The unique characteristics of Japan explain why Japanese firms including Sony could succeed in the international market of music players. Japan's lack of natural resources and land prompted Japanese firms to develop compact, energy-saving products like the Walkman (i.e., factor conditions). Sony also benefited from a sophisticated Japanese domestic market. This can be seen from the fact that expensive and sophisticated products were produced domestically, pressured by the sophisticated Japanese consumers (i.e., demand conditions). The continuous upgrade of products was possible with the support of competitive suppliers of parts and components (i.e., related and supporting industries). Lastly, the competition among rivals in the Japanese electronics industry was fierce, and the Japanese firms were very good at imitating their competitors' products. This made market leaders like Sony speed up their development of new models through incremental innovation (i.e., business context).

In addition to the strengths of the home-based (Japanese) diamond, the sources of Sony's competitiveness were extended to the international sphere of resources, particularly in demand conditions and related and supporting industries. More than 80 percent of Walkman sales were made in the US and European markets. Moreover, Sony enhanced competitive advantages by establishing foreign design centers, which helped it adequately localize the designs and specifics of its products. The extended diamond model encompassing the firm's international activities (Rugman and Verbeke, 1993; Moon et al., 1995, 1998; Verbeke, 2013) is thus useful in explaining the success of Sony. The diamond model can be further extended to fully explain Sony's transition from success to failure in the field of media players over the past decades. To this end, some of Sun Tzu's elements (i.e., the generalship, the same goal, and the system of internal coordination) can be used for a better analysis.

First, later Sony CEOs gradually lost strong generalship or business leadership. In the beginning, the launch of the Walkman was initiated by Sony's founders, who provided strong support and saw substantial market potential for the product. Therefore, Sony could exploit the first-mover advantage, because of the founders' early recognition of the new market and their roles in energizing the firm to innovate continuously. However, the absence of such strong leadership and appropriate corporate goal-setting since the 1990s increasingly degraded Sony's competitiveness. The succeeding Sony CEOs failed to find the new growth engines for creating sustained competitive advantages.

Second, the strategy for sharing the same goal (i.e., principle) was lacking among different departments within Sony. When the first Walkman was being developed, strong unity existed in the firm, in terms of goal orientation. Right after launching the original Walkman, although the media were clearly unimpressed with the device, the marketing department pursued various innovative promotion strategies with a strong conviction on the potential of the new products. For example, the company combined various strategies of word-of-mouth and promotions, in addition to the conventional television advertisements to gain publicity. Therefore, in addition to the competitiveness of the product itself (i.e., Walkman), the strong goal orientation among different divisions within the firm added to the success of the Walkman. However, since the late 1990s, as the firm expanded into software and media contents businesses, different divisions pursued divergent interests of their own, instead of a unified strategy to maximize the synergies among them.

Third, the system of internal coordination was weakening because of its conflicting interests among different business divisions. When the company was founded, a well-unified corporate culture existed. At the time when the Walkman was introduced, for example, the founders (the control tower) directed the R&D and production sectors to closely coordinate with the marketing department.

However, the later CEOs failed to wield the same influence as before. Different divisions did not cooperate or share their strengths as closely; they rather expanded the resources and focused on making their own, incompatible products (e.g., conflicts between the software and hardware divisions). As a result, although Sony still possessed the capability to develop competitive products to the iPod, it failed to introduce new products to satisfy consumers' real needs because of strong resistance from Sony's software division. Therefore, the independent divisional culture became a critical obstacle to the company's sustainable growth.

1.6   CONCLUSION AND IMPLICATIONS

The strategic guidelines and analytical tools of Sun Tzu and Porter are widely cited in their respective fields for their usefulness. Mindful of the devastating effects of engaging in a war, Sun Tzu introduced five elements to diagnose the power parity between one's enemy and oneself. On the other hand, Porter's diamond model explains how firms (or nations) can gain competitive advantage. This chapter found that Sun Tzu's five elements cover most of the key factors of the diamond model for determining the competitiveness, except for demand conditions and a sub-factor of related and supporting industries. Reorganizing Sun Tzu's pre-war evaluation criteria, by adding knowledge of the enemy and extended interpretation of heaven and terrain to the existing five elements, allows an enhanced comprehension of military cases, such as Japan's attack on Pearl Harbor. Similarly, by incorporating some of Sun Tzu's variables such as the generalship, the same goal, and the system of internal coordination, the extended diamond model can better explain the changing competitiveness of firms. The cross-disciplinary utilization can augment the explanatory power of both military and business strategies in the real world.

Despite these similarities, there are also critical differences between the two approaches. First, the four determinants of Porter's diamond model are interrelated and self-reinforcing, but there is no such relationship among the five elements of Sun Tzu, which are rather independent. For example, *principle* does not directly affect the conditions of *heaven* or *terrain*. Second, unlike in war, competition in business is often accompanied by cooperation. As a firm engages in diversified business areas, it can have a competitive relationship with other firms in one area, but a cooperative relationship in another area. For example, Apple is Samsung Electronics' major rival in the smart phone business, but at the same time, it is an important buyer of Samsung's displays. Therefore, the relationship between business players can result in a win-win situation for all when the ultimate goal is to create value for all stakeholders. In contrast, warfare emphasizes competition with the adversary, and the relationship between competitors is a zero-sum situation. This means that the gains of one side will come at the loss of the other.

When a businessperson reads *The Art of War*, he may think of a "competitor" as the equivalent of "enemy." However, in business the customers should be a greater concern. This is because the company's ultimate goal is not to beat its competitors, but to create profits, which can be achieved only when its products or services satisfy the needs of the consumers. In Sony's case, the company failed in the music player business because it focused on competing with its rival (i.e., Apple) with its proprietary technology, rather than trying to figure out the consumers' real needs. Therefore, there is a fundamental difference between why one must "know the enemy" in war and why one must "know the consumers" in business. Sun Tzu defined warfare as a game of deception: comprehensive information on the enemies is needed to deceive them effectively or to avoid being deceived by them. However, this deception strategy is incompatible with business because the ultimate goal of business is not to get rid of the enemy or the consumers. Instead, business can flourish when both the firms and the enemy-equivalent (rivals and/or consumers) are well off.

A firm strives for value creation based on a win-win strategy. The deception strategy in the world of business may offer temporary success, but not a sustainable one. Unlike in warfare, characterized by the prevalence of anarchy, business has governments and consumers to act as regulators and referees to enforce fair play and ethics. Many of Sun Tzu's strategies in warfare have proven to be insightful and applicable to today's business world. Nevertheless, it is critically important to aptly modify Sun Tzu's teachings to reflect the fundamental differences between war and business. Managers should remember the differences, and employ the military strategy as a complementary tool, rather than giving it unwarranted trust to render one's management style in a strictly militaristic manner.

2 Economic Consideration

Sun Tzu: Swift victory and local procurement in waging war
Porter: Value chain analysis in aligning activities

The second chapter of Sun Tzu's *The Art of War* focuses on warnings against the high economic costs of a war and the importance of preparing properly, before further discussing how to win a war. Indeed, a strong economy that can support military costs is a must for any nation going into war. Montecuccoli, an Italian military general, explained this simply: "To wage a war, you need first of all money; second money, and third, you also need money" (Kósa and Porkoláb, 2009).

One of the distinctive characteristics of Sun Tzu's military strategy is that the goal of war is not simply to win a war, but to win at the lowest cost with maximum gains (Handel, 2000). In other words, Sun Tzu argued that a military victory should not just be in name, but should have positive effects on the economy and other sectors. This is why Sun Tzu discussed the economic concerns of war early on, immediately after the introduction of *The Art of War*. Clausewitz also mentioned the economics of military action when he said, "Every unnecessary expenditure of time, every unnecessary detour, is a waste of power, and therefore contrary to the principles of strategy" (Clausewitz, 1968[1832]). All wars are expensive to fight; and they become the more expensive, the longer they last. Sun Tzu was aware of the financial strains that a war could put on a nation, especially on a small nation like the one (i.e., Wu) in which he served as a general.

Considering the catastrophic costs of war, Sun Tzu suggested two strategies in the second chapter "Waging War" of *The Art of War*: avoiding lengthy campaigns and utilizing the enemy's resources for reducing one's economic burden. This chapter links Sun Tzu's two strategies of cost reduction in war to Porter's (1985) value chain analysis, which is a tool for analyzing the sources of competitive advantages – cost and differentiation. Despite its wide use in both academia and actual practice, Porter's value chain is often criticized for being static and thus not fully explaining the sources of competitiveness in the turbulence of a rapidly changing environment. Accordingly, through a theoretical comparison of Sun Tzu's strategies in "Waging War" and Porter's value chain, this chapter aims to improve the theories of both Sun Tzu and Porter. The proposed theoretical extension is followed by an analysis of the military case – Napoleon's invasion of Russia – and the business case – Hyundai Motor Company's global strategy – to show how the extended models of Sun Tzu and Porter can be utilized to better explain success and failure in real life.

2.1 SUN TZU: SWIFT VICTORY AND LOCAL PROCUREMENT IN WAGING WAR

When engaging in warfare, one should not only consider the possibilities and benefits of winning, but also the possibilities of losing and the potential damages. If the costs are greater than the benefits of winning the war, the victory will not be as satisfactory. Therefore, it is important to obtain victory while minimizing costs. With this goal in mind, Sun Tzu first discussed the economic costs of war before suggesting two principles for reducing economic burdens. This section will focus on Sun Tzu's two strategies of reducing the financial costs of a war: swift victory and local procurement.

2.1.1 Swift Victory: Avoiding Long Campaigns

Sun Tzu claimed, "Although we have heard of haste in war despite the lack of perfect preparation, no nations have benefited from long delays in war."[1] This rhetorical remark points a finger at the various problems that come from a lengthy war. Sun Tzu's strategy of prioritizing a quick end to a war reflects his outstanding insights on military

---

[1] The Chinese characters are: 兵聞拙速, 未睹巧之久也.

strategy. In general, people prefer perfectly designed strategies and complete preparation to swiftness. However, Sun Tzu opposed the pursuit of perfection at the expense of time. Even though preparations may seem insufficient, speed is paramount and good timing should not be sacrificed.

A swift victory is top priority because of the following four kinds of damage a prolonged war will cause. First, if a campaign is extended, the country's resources will be depleted; Sun Tzu claimed that the cost of fielding a hundred thousand soldiers was a thousand ounces of gold a day.[2] Resources are also required to maintain equipment and weapons. Thus, it would be difficult for a country to maintain a protracted war. Second, lengthy wars decrease the morale of soldiers, who lose the will to fight when supplies become inadequate. Third, depletion of a country's resources will force it to conduct additional conscriptions and taxation. This will increase public dissatisfaction with the war, which might even result in social disturbances. Last, when resources, morale, and arms have been depleted, the country will be vulnerable to rebellions by feudal lords. Therefore, Sun Tzu's avoidance of lengthy campaigns is not only important for victory, but also for social order and national survival.

The significance of agility has not diminished over two and a half millennia. Since the 9/11 terrorist attacks, the US defense budget has skyrocketed to levels unprecedented since World War II. Senior defense department officials define the biggest threat to US security as none other than the national debt, because the United States can no longer afford to fight two large land wars overseas (Korb and Rothman, 2011). The Iraq War is a case of excessive military spending by the United States, mainly due to the prolonged war. The Congressional Research Service estimated that the United States spent $805 billion on the war from 2003 to 2011. However, the real long-term cost including veterans' benefits is estimated to reach $4 trillion over the next fifty years (Hinton, 2012).

---

[2]   "A thousand ounces of gold" is the direct translation of Chinese characters of "千金," but this may mean just a large amount of money (Minford, 2008).

Sun Tzu's strategy of pursuing a swift victory is indeed ideal for a strong, superior force. However, for weak forces without enough resources to aptly overwhelm the enemy, a protracted engagement (i.e., reversing Sun Tzu's strategy) may be necessary. This way, even with fewer advantages, the weaker army can cause the enemy to exhaust their energy during the extended campaign, while the weaker army can earn more time to build up their strengths and ultimately seek an opportunity to counterattack the enemy. For example, during the Second Sino-Japanese War, Mao advocated a strategy of attrition and protracted the war, thereby exhausting the Japanese while buying the Chinese forces time to recover and rebuild their military power. A similar strategy was employed in the Vietnam War when the Viet Cong dictated a drawn-out form of guerrilla warfare that exhausted US troops and bought time until the war-weary American people at home finally raised demands against the war. The supporting evidences behind the efficiency of reversing Sun Tzu's swift victory strategy will be further explored in the later parts of the chapter, by using the example of Russia's victory against Napoleon's invasion in 1812.

2.1.2 *Local Procurement: Using Enemy's Resources*

Sun Tzu stated, "A wise general does not conscript the people twice nor transport provisions a third time; he obtains the equipment from the home country and relies on seizing provisions from the enemy."[3] In other words, Sun Tzu advocated the exploitation of enemy's resources or local procurement in enemy territory as much as possible.

Note here, however, that the range of items to be procured from the enemy does not include military equipment. Three key reasons exist for obtaining military equipment from the home country. Unlike provisions (i.e., food and forage), military equipment can be utilized repeatedly and is relatively easy to transport. Second, the

---

[3] The Chinese characters are: 善用兵者, 役不再籍, 糧不三載; 取用于國, 因糧于敵, 故軍食可足也.

characteristics of the arms and equipment (e.g., size, function, and weight) need to be customized to locational specifics and strategic requirements. This means that the foreign equipment would also have been tailored to the enemy's needs and often incompatible with the needs of one's own army. Third, weapons and other equipment are often strictly controlled by the enemy. Hence, a practical limitation exists in obtaining enemy equipment, making home production a more effective and reliable method.

In contrast, there are good reasons to procure provisions locally. Strong armies constantly require a large supply of food, which is a heavy financial burden on the home country to provide, and the quality of food is relatively consistent across different areas. In addition, Sun Tzu's era was one with underdeveloped transportation and road systems, which meant most of the provisions were lost to natural causes or consumed by the transporters themselves during transport. In Sun Tzu's estimation, "One unit of foodstuffs taken from the enemy is worth 20 units of your country resources."[4] In other words, 19 units of foodstuffs are lost for every one unit transported from the home country successfully. This is not an exaggerated figure. For example, in one anecdote in *Shiji*, the king of Qin (Qin Shi Huang) dispatched the general Meng Tian to fight against the Northern Xiongnu. He sent 190 *shi* (an ancient unit for weight) of food, but when they arrived at the battlefield, only one *shi* was left. Therefore, procuring food from enemy territory is more effective for reducing the economic burdens on the home country and economizing the expenditure for transportation.

In addition to foodstuffs, Sun Tzu listed other items that can be effectively obtained from the enemy. Human resources are included in this list as captive enemy soldiers can be persuaded to join one's army. In order to take away resources as much as possible from the enemy, Sun Tzu suggested offering noticeable incentives to the soldiers to capture the enemy. If the rewards are not noticeable, soldiers may consider them not worth their efforts. Moreover, Sun Tzu stressed

---

[4]　The Chinese characters are: 食敵一鐘, 當吾二十鐘.

that the captive enemy soldiers should be treated kindly. This was to coax the enemy soldiers into providing useful information or even converting to serve one's own army. In this manner, one can use the enemy's military equipment and forces to increase the strength of one's own army. These suggested augmentations show how one can strengthen one's forces by using the enemy's resources rather than increasing the burden on people back home. This is one of the many points whereon the value of Sun Tzu's strategy can be seen for its consideration of both economic and psychological factors in warfare.

2.2   PORTER: VALUE CHAIN ANALYSIS IN ALIGNING ACTIVITIES

In 1985, Porter introduced the concept of the value chain in his book titled *Competitive Advantage*.[5] The value chain is a basic tool for examining how discrete activities contribute to a firm's competitive advantage. It is a widely accepted tool for assessing business activities and identifying competitive advantage (McPhee and Wheeler, 2006). The activities are divided into two broad categories – *primary* and *support activities*. *Primary activities* are those involved in the physical creation of the product, as well as its sale and transfer to the buyer and post-sale service. *Support activities*, on the other hand, support the primary activities and the entire value chain. Primary activities are divided into five categories and support activities into four categories. The following section briefly explains each activity.

2.2.1   Primary and Support Activities of Porter's (1985) Value Chain

Primary Activities
Inbound logistics: Activities related to receiving, storing, and disseminating inputs to the product (e.g., material handling, warehousing, and inventory control).

---

[5]   The business concept of value chain was first conceptualized by McKinsey & Company in 1980 (Lütolf-Carroll, 2009), and Porter (1985) improved the concept and linked it to the competitive advantage of firms.

Operations: Activities related to transforming inputs into the final product (e.g., machining, packaging, and assembly).

Outbound logistics: Activities related to collecting, storing, and physically distributing the product to buyers (e.g., finished goods warehousing, material handling, and delivery vehicle operation).

Marketing and sales: Activities related to providing a means for buyers to purchase the product and inducing them to do so (e.g., advertising, promotion, and sales force).

Service: Activities related to providing service to enhance or maintain the value of the product (e.g., installation, repair, training, and parts supply).

Support Activities
Procurement: Activities related to purchasing inputs used in the firm's entire value chain, not just the purchased inputs for manufacturing the final product.

Technology development: Activities related to improving the product and the production process.

Human resource management: Activities involved in recruiting, hiring, training, development, and compensation for all types of personnel.

Firm infrastructure: Activities including general management, planning, finance, accounting, legal and government affairs, and quality management.

      Porter claimed that each activity within the value chain has an interdependent relationship with the others. The connections between the activities are defined as the relationship between the method of performing one value activity and the performance of another (Porter, 1985: 48). For example, if a company invests more into product design, production materials, and in-process inspection, it will improve the product quality and decrease the rate of defective products, which in turn is likely to reduce the costs of after-sales service. Therefore, optimizing resource allocation and improving coordination within the value chain allows a firm to add more value to the product and ultimately generate a larger margin than its competitors. Porter argued that efficient management of interconnected activities in the value chain is central to achieving competitive advantage.

2.2.2   Extension of Porter's Value Chain Analysis

The activities in the value chain are highly interdependent, because each activity plays an important role in delivering products or services to end users. Furthermore, collaboration with other firms is often more efficient for creating consumer values because a single firm rarely, if ever, possesses all of the up-to-date knowledge and technologies. On the other hand, through outsourcing, a firm can concentrate resources on its core competences (Prahalad and Hamel, 1990). In one of Porter's later works, Porter and Rivkin (2012) also suggested that it is more desirable to maintain the sophisticated, skill-intensive activities at home (e.g., R&D, sophisticated manufacturing, and skill-intensive traded services), while outsourcing or relocating low-end activities (e.g., simple assembly and routine remote customer service) to the low-cost, developing countries.

Hence, Porter's conventional value chain model has evolved into a network-based value creation system, due to the emergence of "network economy" (Moon, 2016b). The central idea of a network-based value creation system is that values are created by a cluster of various players, in a competitive and cooperative relationship (Moon, 2016b). Accordingly, the sources of competitive advantage are beyond each value activity or traditional value chain linkage of a single firm, and shift to how the members involved in the network could be best coordinated to maximize synergy. Similar logic can be found in other terms, such as global value chains (Gereffi et al., 2001), business ecosystem (Moore, 1996), value creating network (Kothandaraman and Wilson, 2001), value network (Peppard and Rylander, 2006), and value constellation (Normann and Ramirez, 1993).

On the other hand, even though Porter mentioned speed as a contributing factor to improving firms' performance in some cases (e.g., Japan's just-in-time (JIT) system), he did not directly list speed as a critical factor in raising firms' competitive position in the value chain. The value of speed in Porter's work is more concerned with smooth linkage among value chain activities. Therefore, speed is viewed as the result of efficient conduct of value chain activities, not as the source, or separate factor of competitive advantage. However, in the current fast-changing business environment, keeping an agile pace with technological development and consumers' taste has become more important than ever and is actually a necessity for sustaining and gaining competitive advantage. In this regard, some scholars have introduced concepts such as manufacturing agility (Gunasekaran, 1998, 1999; Koste and Malhotra, 2000), value chain flexibility (Zhang, Vonderembrse, and Lim, 2002), value chain agility (Swafford, Ghosh, and Murthy, 2006), and overall process agility (Moon, 2016b). Swafford et al. (2006) defined the concept of value chain agility as the speed with which the value chain can improve its competitive position regarding cost, quality, flexibility, innovation, and so on. Agility is influenced by the flexibility in the value chain; yet it is different from flexibility in that agility concerns the length of reaction times, while flexibility is the capacity to react and change.

2.3 THE INTEGRATION OF SUN TZU AND PORTER

The main goal of a firm is to maximize profit margins in the value chain, whereas the ultimate objective of war is to win. In order to raise margins, firms can either increase values or decrease costs. The former is associated with the differentiation strategy, while the latter is related to the cost strategy. However, the nature of war is not to create value, but to redistribute existing value at its best. More often, war is a value-destroying activity (McCormick, 2001). Therefore, in war, a winner's gains are not created but often obtained at the expense of the losers. In order to obtain the net gains, one should calculate the costs of war to see whether or not a war is necessary. Thus, cost is a critical concern in analyzing competitive position in war. Despite these critical differences, Sun Tzu's strategies and Porter's value chain do have things in common which will be shown in the following.

2.3.1   The Cost Drivers: War versus Business

In order to examine the sources of costs in business, Porter disaggregated firm activities into five primary and four support activities. On the other hand, Sun Tzu, in his second chapter (see Figure I.1), also mentioned many activities which incur military costs: "In war operation, where there are a thousand swift chariots, a thousand heavy chariots, and a hundred thousand soldiers, with provisions enough to carry them a thousand *li*, and other expenses, including entertainment of guests, materials for repair and maintenance such as glue, the cost will be a thousand ounces of gold per day. Such is the cost of raising an army of a hundred thousand men." The following paragraphs explain how Porter's value chain activities can be compared to Sun Tzu's military activities.

Inbound logistics are the activities of supplying inputs to operations. They can be compared to receiving, storing, and disseminating the necessary equipment, provisions, and solders for fighting in the battlefield. A thousand swift chariots, a thousand heavy chariots, a hundred thousand soldiers, and the expenditures for carrying the provisions a thousand *li*" mentioned by Sun Tzu can be classified as costs related to inbound logistics. Because of the underdeveloped road systems and poor means of transportation at the time, long-distance transportation was extremely costly. Therefore, Sun Tzu said, "A wise general does not conscript the people twice nor transport provisions a third time." In other words, a battle should be won in the first attempt, in order to reduce expenditures on inbound logistics.

Operations refer to the process of transforming inputs into final products. Firms need to produce quality products to win against their rivals. In a war context, operations can be compared to training an army for victory; an army should be properly fed, trained, and equipped with superior weapons in order to increase their performance when fighting against the enemy.

Outbound logistics determine the allocation of business assets for the efficient delivery of products to the end user. The management of outbound logistics can be compared to the proper alignment of an army in order to achieve victory. Sun Tzu proposed that the overwhelming disposition (or *Hsing*) of the army is more important than the mere size of the army.[6]

Marketing and sales, the promotional activities encouraging customers' consumption, can be compared to the creation of enhanced energy (or *Shih*).[7] In order to magnify sales in business, firms often research and analyze psychological factors of the consumers and introduce a series of promotional events to stimulate their interests. Similarly, in war, a general must create *Shih* to induce soldiers to concentrate all their efforts toward a single goal. This enhances the effectiveness of fighting against an enemy.

Service, which entails maintaining or enhancing the value of products and services, can be compared to the maintenance of chariots, weapons, and army strength. These expenditures account for a large portion of the total costs, and Sun Tzu similarly estimated the expenditures of war to amount to 60 percent of the government's total revenue.

Procurement in business is like the method of procuring military equipment and provisions. On this matter, Sun Tzu said that equipment should be obtained from the home country, while provisions should be seized from the enemy. This strategy will not only help reduce a large amount of the cost incurred by war, but also lead to "more effectively conquering the enemy and growing stronger."

Human resource development, which includes recruiting, hiring, training, development, and compensation for all types of

[6]   See Chapter 4 for details about this concept.
[7]   See Chapter 5 for details about this concept.

personnel, is just as critical in military management as it is in business management. For an army, human resource development entails the system of treatment, management, and compensation for the soldiers. It plays an important role because the performance of soldiers is associated with their happiness and productivity, which directly influences the result of war. Sun Tzu claimed a general should not only be fair and kind to his own soldiers but also to the captive enemy soldiers. Compared to mobilizing more civilians from one's own country, integrating the enemy's soldiers into one's army is a more economical way to enhance one's military strength.

Firm infrastructure, which refers to organizational structure and its management, can be equated to the general administration, budget planning, and military regulations that assure the effective management of warfare. Sun Tzu included various types of expenditures such as entertainment of guests and administration costs of the home government in this category.

Table 2.1 illustrates the similarities in activities between Porter's firm value chain and Sun Tzu's military value chain. Although the military value chain activities are abstracted from Sun Tzu's concepts and thoughts, Sun Tzu did not align them in a systematic way into a framework like Porter's firm value chain. The military value chain can be developed by borrowing the concepts of Porter's firm value chain. This value chain is helpful in determining different types of costs associated with war, in addition to identifying synergistic effects among military activities in war. All of which are critical to achieve victory.

As demonstrated above, military activities listed in *The Art of War* overlap with most activities of Porter's firm value chain. Thus, by reorganizing Sun Tzu's military activities into the structure of Porter's firm value chain, we can derive a military value chain. However, missing from Sun Tzu's ideas is technological development (see Figure 2.1). Lack of attention given to technology can be understood by considering the historical context. During Sun Tzu's time, weapon systems were underdeveloped and not differentiable. As such,

Table 2.1 *Comparison of Porter's firm value chain and Sun Tzu's military value chain*

	Nine Activities of Firm Value Chain (Porter)	*Eight* Activities of Military Value Chain (Sun Tzu)
Inbound Logistics	Supplying inputs to operations	Supplying equipment, provisions, and soldiers to operations
Operations	Transforming and assembling inputs into final products	Training soldiers to increase their performance in the battlefield
Outbound Logistics	Efficiently delivering products to the market	Efficiently sending an army to the battlefield
Marketing & Sales	Encouraging customer demand through promotional activities	Creating enhanced energy (or *Shih*) through effective combination of *Cheng* and *Chi*
Service	Maintaining the value of products and services	Maintaining military equipment, weapons, and the strength of soldiers
Procurement	Purchasing inputs for the activities of the firm	Providing provisions and weapons for the army
Technological Development	Creating new products and improving existing products and process	Not available because there was little technological development at the time of Sun Tzu
Human Resource Management	Recruiting, training, and compensating personnel	Recruiting, training, and managing soldiers
Firm Infrastructure	Managing organizational structure and finance	Managing general administration, budget planning, and regulations

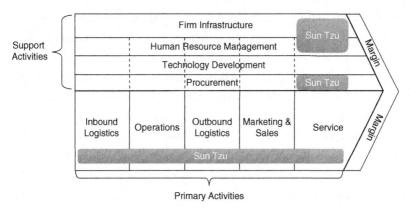

FIGURE 2.1 Sun Tzu's cost drivers and Porter's value chain

they were not considered an important factor in the cost reduction of war. However, in the current era, technological development plays a large role in improving a nation's competitiveness and diversity of strategic options in security. The world has seen a considerable rise in R&D expenditure and modernization of weapons and related facilities. For example, some countries like North Korea and Iran develop their own nuclear weapons, which can significantly alter their military position and bargaining power in the international arena. By incorporating the technological development aspect of Porter's firm value chain, we can obtain a more complete framework of the military value chain in the modern era. On the other hand, Porter's firm value chain can be further enriched by incorporating Sun Tzu's concepts of swift victory and local procurement, which will be discussed in detail in the following sections.

2.3.2 Swift Victory versus Connectivity within the Firm's Value Chain

Sun Tzu regarded time as an important factor that affects the cost occurred in war, because prolonged war not only results in the rise of inputs, consumption, and expenditures, but also other indirect harmful effects to the whole nation. Therefore, war should be completed as quickly as possible. For business, time management can be better understood using the concept of value chain. Porter claimed that activities in the value chain stand as parts of an integrated system, and are thus dependent on each other. Therefore, it is natural for firms to strengthen the linkages internally between divisions and externally with their partners for smoother coordination to reduce the process time in the value chain. Toyota's JIT system is a good example. In order to reduce overall manufacturing time, suppliers transport and provide the exact amount of parts and components required to the right users in the right place at the right time. This not only eliminates the need for expensive storage space but also improves quality by reducing the ratio of defective products. Nowadays, the overall firm performance through the agile and efficient coordination among different divisions can be further enhanced with advanced information technology systems across countries globally (e.g., cooperation between Silicon Valley and Bengaluru[8] in India).

Although Porter mentioned the role of linkage, which contributes to reducing the process time across the value chain and ultimately enhances competitive advantage, he did not explicitly mention specific business strategies for enhancing the speed of each value chain activity. However, in the emerging business literature on firm competitiveness, speed is acknowledged as an important source of competitive advantage (Moon, 2016b). Particularly, facing the period of "quality inflation," there is a decreasing gap in the (commercially meaningful) quality of products or services among competitors; thus, a speedy response to the market (e.g., timely introduction of new products and quick response to consumer feedback) becomes more important for gaining competitive advantage (Gertner, 2013). Moreover, in the quickly changing market environment, it is also important for firms to adapt flexibly to changing consumption patterns. Therefore, agility – which Sun Tzu identified as a core strategy

---

[8]   It was renamed from Bangalore in 2006.

in managing war – needs to be applied to the value chain (i.e., value chain agility; Swafford et al., 2006) to create firms' additional competitive advantage. Thus, Sun Tzu's ideas can be usefully incorporated into the value chain analysis.

2.3.3 Using the Enemy's Resources and Interfirm Linkages in Global Value Chains

Sun Tzu suggested using the enemy's resources as an effective way to avoid depleting one's economic and financial resources. Similarly, Porter introduced the concept of international coalition, which refers to the global dispersion of value chain activities to exploit economies of scale and country-specific advantages. However, despite Porter's proposition of global strategy (Configuration-Coordination framework; Porter, 1986), Porter preferred the concentration of value activities in one location to exploit the synergy effects of local clusters because of the additional cost of coordination between different locations. This tendency to concentrate on local clusters can also be observed in Porter and Rivkin (2012), which illustrated the example of a recent trend of American firms' reshoring to the United States. On the other hand, Sun Tzu advocated dispersing different activities (or different input materials) across different locations (i.e., home and enemy territories). Therefore, Sun Tzu's military thoughts of using the enemy's resources 2,500 years ago, ironically, may be more relevant to today's international business in terms of the global spread of value chain activities and interorganizational linkages.

Porter's concept of a globally dispersed value chain, on the other hand, is more related to vertical integration, which may be less flexible in responding to external changes. As products that converge different technologies are trending, even the most competitive firms cannot meet the diversity of consumer needs without cooperating with other firms, unless they somehow master *all* the required input technologies to produce the final goods and services. Coordinating within the network is no longer an option but a necessity. The firms and institutions involved in network-based coordination include not only the main firms bound by long-term agreements, but also other members and partners connected through looser relationships (e.g., sales, licensing, and other nonequity modes). In such a network, the participants engage in complementary relationships, as all participants not only contribute to an increase in the size of the profit but are able to have a piece of it. Therefore, the current competitive multinational firms no longer internalize all of their activities, but establish a platform for other partners and suppliers to enrich their global value chains and together create more value.

Therefore, based on the above discussion, Porter's value chain can be improved in two ways to better explain the sources of competitive advantage in the changing global business environment: first, by incorporating the speed of each value chain activity and flexible response to external changes instead of just the reduction of process time through enhanced linkages across value chain; and second, by incorporating interfirm linkages globally instead of just the coordination of intrafirm linkages. If a firm is to sustain its competitive advantage over its rivals, it must be able to respond quickly and flexibly to the changing business environment by maintaining a dynamic and efficient network with various partners.

On the other hand, in addition to the construction of the military value chain, Sun Tzu's two strategies for cost reduction in war can also be extended as follows. First, Sun Tzu emphasized the importance and benefits of swift victory, but did not specify strategies for dealing with unexpected events, which may even interrupt well-designed plans. Hence, Sun Tzu's swift victory strategy can be extended by incorporating a flexible response to external changes. Second, in order to reduce one's economic burden, one can exploit not only the enemy's resources, but third-country resources as much as possible as well. This procurement strategy is particularly important when unexpected events occur. These linkages, and the extension of both Sun Tzu's and Porter's models, will be discussed in detail through the following case study section.

2.4 MILITARY CASE: NAPOLEON'S INVASION OF RUSSIA

In order to compel Russia to maintain its embargo on England and to protect Poland from Russian invasion, Napoleon declared a war against Russia in 1812.[9] Napoleon formed an extremely large European army and made extensive preparations to supply his massive army with food and armor for up to forty days. In addition, he established warehouses near the border as a supply line. As he did not intend to step deeper into Russian territory, these provisions seemed to be sufficient.

The invasion into Russia started on June 24, 1812. Initially, the French army encountered almost no resistance as the outnumbered Russians decided to retreat from their first line of defense. In pursuit, Napoleon decided to move at forced march, deviating from his initial plan. Eventually, the supply line failed to maintain pace with the army's movements. Upon careful deliberation, the Russian general decided to retreat after executing the so-called scorched earth policy of burning warehouses and bridges. As a result, when the French arrived, they could not find any food or provisions to capture. To make things worse, the supply line was already extended beyond its limits so it could not keep up with the speed of the army.

Napoleon expected Alexander to negotiate for peace at this time, but the Russian emperor would not do so. Napoleon then ordered his forces to march into Moscow as quickly as possible, which made the supply line problems even worse. The governor of Moscow decided to evacuate the city and destroy as much of the supplies as possible. When Napoleon entered the city on September 14, nothing was left for his forces to use. With insufficient food and a long supply line constantly attacked by Russian troops, Napoleon had no choice but to retreat.

---

[9] Information for this case study is abstracted and modified from library.brown.edu/cds/ napoleon/time6.html, research.omicsgroup.org/index.php/French_invasion_of_Russia, and www.newworldencyclopedia.org/entry/French_invasion_of_Russia.

Winter was coming and the temperature dropped rapidly. When Napoleon's forces arrived in Moscow, it was empty. Meanwhile, the Russians kept harassing Napoleon's army until they crossed the border back to Poland. Of the 700,000 men initially comprising Napoleon's forces, only 27,000 to 80,000 made it back; 380,000 were killed and an additional 100,000 were taken as prisoners by the Russians. Because of the broken supply line, Napoleon's army suffered from starvation throughout the campaign. Many starving troops resorted to surrendering to Russian forces. There were even reports of cannibalism.

It is widely believed that the harsh Russian winter was the main reason for Napoleon's demise. However, the winter in 1812 was in fact milder than average. The fundamental reason should instead be found from the internal mistakes rather than the external uncontrollable factors. Napoleon's invasion of Russia exemplifies expected outcomes of failing to adhere to Sun Tzu's two strategies: completing the war as quickly as possible and exploiting the enemy's resources to solve one's supply problem. In contrast, the Russians succeeded by using the counterstrategy, pursuing a drawn-out war because they knew they could not defeat Napoleon's army in an open battle. The Russian generals lured the French deeper and deeper into Russian territory, and with Napoleon's eager cooperation, they secured a decisive victory.

However, even though the failure to follow Sun Tzu's two strategies shows why Napoleon was defeated, the question remains why Napoleon was unable to adhere to Sun Tzu's advice when he had every intention of following it. In the beginning, Napoleon actually did plan to avoid a lengthy campaign. His initial plan was to quickly march into Russia, defeat the Russian army in a series of decisive battles, and return across the Polish border before the onset of winter. Napoleon also established supply depots along the border and secured enough supplies for his army for forty days.

To solve this riddle, we can borrow some concepts from Porter's value chain analysis and its extended model. Napoleon had envisioned and prepared for a swift victory but failed to consider alternative courses of action when facing a series of unexpected developments. Evidently, Napoleon failed to display agility and flexibility in responding to external changes. Furthermore, the breakdown of linkages within the military value chain also prevented Napoleon from properly executing his military plans, and the decision to enter Moscow made the French army in the forefront unable to obtain help from their own support line. Moreover, when the French army retreated from Russia, its flanks and rear guard faced constant attack from the Russian army. This implies the lack of an efficient communication and coordination system among different divisions, which can be compared to the linkages in the value chain Porter suggested. In addition, even though Napoleon failed to exploit Russia's local resources, he could have leveraged resources from neighboring countries, if he carefully planned to do so before his invasion. Thus, in retrospect, Napoleon could have avoided failure if he properly responded to unexpected changes and utilized third-party resources. By incorporating Porter's extended framework of the value chain, one can see how Napoleon could have turned failure to victory if he appropriately prepared for unexpected occurrences and procured assistance from other neighboring countries.

2.5 BUSINESS CASE: HYUNDAI MOTOR COMPANY'S GLOBAL STRATEGY

Hyundai Motor Company (hereafter named as Hyundai), a Korean automaker, was established in 1967 as a small, domestic company. However, during the past fifty years, it has improved multiple activities in its value chain and became the world's fifth largest automobile manufacturer in 2014 (Ludwig, 2015). In particular, Hyundai has achieved remarkable success in the US market over the years by pursuing continuous efficiency in its value chain. In the early 1990s, the predominant perception of Hyundai cars was low-class cars at a cheap price. However, since the 2000s, its popularity soared and Hyundai experienced extraordinary growth in the US market, especially after the opening of its first manufacturing plant in Alabama in 2005. Hyundai had several reasons for making this investment decision: increasing trade conflicts between Korea and the United States, profit loss due to exchange rate fluctuations, a need to change its image as a cheap carmaker, a low level of union presence in Alabama, and heavy financial incentives offered by the Alabama government (Jo and You, 2011). Hyundai's analysis of the situation and calculations behind investing in Alabama proved effective and contributed to developing a competitive advantage in the United States.

This is what Porter called exploiting additional opportunities with the geographic expansion of the value chain, and this can also be explained by Sun Tzu's second strategy of cost reduction – exploiting the enemy's resources while improving your own strengths. However, there are differences between war and business. In war, a general uses enemy resources to reduce his costs. When a general uses the enemy resources from the enemy's land, it is a unilateral exploitation of resources. Due to the unilateral exploitation and negative effects of such a move, it is likely to result in retaliation from the enemy country. In international business (e.g., foreign direct investment), however, both the investors and host countries can gain benefits. This is why many countries around the world actually compete to attract investment from abroad, offering various incentives to investing companies. This is what the United States did when Hyundai showed interest in investing in the United States in the early 2000s.

In the meantime, we must also understand how Hyundai was able to create competitive advantage through cost reduction and differentiation. Hyundai America's value chain is a stellar realization of Porter's value chain concept, in which activities are conducted internally and vertically integrated. The level of Hyundai's vertical integration is rare in the automotive industry (Holstein, 2013), from supply of raw materials (e.g., steel, engines, and parts) to assembly, logistics, design, and marketing. Hyundai is the only carmaker in the world procuring its own steel (Holstein, 2013).

Regarding the value chain in the United States, although Hyundai outsourced some parts of value activities to other independent local companies, the majority of the value activities were conducted by its subsidiaries or associated firms. For example, parts and components are supplied by Hyundai Mobis, steel by Hyundai Steel, the inbound and outbound logistics by GLOVIS America, manufacturing operations by the Alabama plant, financing by Hyundai Capital, and technology development by its California Design and Technology Center. Such value chain structures can also be seen in other regions, such as Europe and China. The overseas production sites are often accompanied by Hyundai-owned suppliers, R&D centers, and marketing offices. Therefore, Hyundai's global strategy is to move the entire value chain of its own brand across different regions.

Hyundai's many parts suppliers accompanied it to the United States and located their factories around the Alabama manufacturing plant, reducing transportation and inventory costs. In addition, the established relationship between Hyundai America and its affiliates allowed for greater flexibility and speed, further reducing cost and increasing efficiency. Due to the better coordination among activities in the value chain, Hyundai America was able to achieve additional cost advantage. On the other hand, investment in the United States also contributed to improving the quality and design of Hyundai cars through employment of highly skilled local engineers and designers (human resource development), establishment of R&D centers, and learning from the local market (technology development).

Hyundai, as the world's fifth largest automaker, produced almost eight million vehicles in 2014 (Ludwig, 2015). Its overseas production surpassed domestic production, with little room left for further expansion in Korea. The only way to achieve its mid-term goal of manufacturing ten million cars (Ludwig, 2015) would be more aggressive global expansion. However, the *Wall Street Journal* (Nam, 2015) reported that Hyundai showed a fifth consecutive decline in net quarterly profits since 2014, struggling to compete with Japanese counterparts such as Toyota. Although some argued that the strength of the South Korean won relative to the Japanese yen contributed to the slower growth of export markets, more fundamental and internal problems need to be identified for continued growth.

Sun Tzu's military strategies shed light on the two reasons for Hyundai's falling sales. First, Toyota's mass recalls in 2010 showed that quality could not be sacrificed to expand market share. Since then, Hyundai has put more effort into quality control, while being reluctant to expand capacity, although most of its global plants have already been running at full capacity. Hyundai's UK executive stated, "We have a constrained production situation in 2013. We just cannot get enough vehicles [to maintain growth rates]" (Madslien, 2013). Financial Times (Mundy, 2013) commented that Hyundai seemed to be too cautious when it came to global expansion. Sun Tzu emphasized the importance of speed in achieving victory. He said that speed should not be sacrificed in order to seek perfection. Even if the preparation seems to be suboptimal, the general should not delay his campaign but rather make all efforts to end it as quickly as possible. This military thought can also be applied to the Hyundai case: Hyundai must not shy away from the speed of global expansion in pursuit of mythic security.

The second issue concerns Hyundai's vertically integrated value chain. The current structure is unlikely to withstand fast-growing global competition and achieve sustainable growth. Hyundai should incorporate more internationally competitive suppliers and firms, nonaffiliated or nonassociated firms, into its network (i.e., Sun Tzu's local procurement strategy). On the other hand, Hyundai's affiliated firms of supplies and logistics should also diversify and enlarge their sources of revenue. For example, more than 70 percent of GLOVIS revenues are from Hyundai Group business (Ludwig, 2015). Therefore, instead of performing most of the activities internally, they need to expand their business ecosystem to include non-Hyundai firms for further growth. However, this requires the implementation of an open platform where involved firms openly share advanced information. In this regard, the traditional Korean aversion to information sharing and open communication may be obstacles.

2.6 CONCLUSION AND IMPLICATIONS

The chapter "Waging War" in *The Art of War* discusses the economic cost of waging war – that is, minimizing the cost while maximizing the chances of winning. War, by default, is expensive and a burden on the nation's economy. To minimize the damage and economic costs, Sun Tzu advised against prolonged campaigns and recommended using the enemy's resources as much as possible. However, swift victory is more appropriate for the stronger army, which has the capability to dictate the process of war. In contrast, drawing out the war to deplete the stronger army's resources may be more advisable for the weaker side. Therefore, Sun Tzu's strategy should be applied flexibly depending on the relative competitive situations of the opponents.

For the business model, I selected Porter's value chain for comparison. The comparative analysis not only helps examine similarities between Sun Tzu's and Porter's strategy models, but also finds ways to extend both models. The effectiveness of a swift victory is similar to the synergy of linkages among activities within the value chain, because both emphasize time reduction and greater efficiency to reduce cost (in war and business) or increase value (in business). However, Porter viewed *speed* as the result of effectively operating the linkages of firm value chain instead of the source of competitive advantage, which is actually important in the fast-changing environment. Hence, Sun Tzu's strategy of swift victory can complement Porter's value chain. On the other hand, using the enemy's resources is similar to a coalition with other firms to enhance the performance of value chain activities. Although Porter acknowledged the benefits from international coalition, he preferred to exploit domestic clusters. In this respect, Sun Tzu's strategy of exploiting the enemy's (or international) resources to enhance one's competitive edge can complement Porter's value chain.

In the military case study, Napoleon failed because he could not adhere to Sun Tzu's two strategies: swift victory and exploitation of the enemy's resources. This case can then be more systematically explained by the breakdown of linkages within the military value chain. On the other hand, in the business case, Hyundai significantly enhanced its competitive advantage with its investments in the United States by quickly establishing its global presence and utilizing the US resources. However, its recent experience of declining position in the global market can also be explained by Sun Tzu's concept of swiftness and further by the extended perspective of Porter's value chain (i.e., the network-based integrated value chain). Therefore, a company can gain further competitive advantage by using the strategic ideas of Sun Tzu's swift victory and external coordination on each component of Porter's value chain; and a military leader can also gain further insights by utilizing a military value chain, which can be developed from the systematic structure of Porter's firm value chain.

3   Avoiding Competition

Sun Tzu: Complete victory by strategic attack
Porter: Five forces model for selecting an attractive industry

Fighting is a means of winning, not an end in itself. As we have shown in Chapter 2, violent campaigns inevitably hurt both winners and losers with lives lost and money spent. In particular, if the campaign is prolonged, even the winner is likely to be in need of expensive rehabilitation to restore prewar levels of stability and welfare. Therefore, a wise leader should do his best to resolve a conflict or gain what he wants through nonviolent means instead of diving headlong into a battlefield. Even if one has a well-organized war management system – a large army, and bountiful resource supplies well over those of the enemy – winning without exhausting such capacity would be the ideal situation, actually for both one's opponent and oneself. In the chapter "Strategic Attack," Sun Tzu called subduing the enemy without destroying them a "complete victory" and asserted the achievement of complete victory should be the goal in all conflicts.

Formulating strategy comes after assessing economic costs and available resources. Only when one knows one's own capacities, one can decide what kind of strategy to employ. Both capacity assessment and strategy formulation, however, are part of the same process designed to achieve the single goal: achieving victory at a minimal cost. On the other hand, the renowned war theorist Clausewitz advocated dominating force and defeating the enemy through combat operations. To Clausewitz, the ultimate goal of a war was the destruction of the enemy's army and occupation of its territory, as exemplified by the bloodshed of World War I (Clausewitz, 1968[1832]). Scholars such as Hart (1954), however, commented that Sun Tzu's strategy of winning a complete victory is superior to Clausewitz's strategy of winning at all costs. While the idea of benefiting both one's opponent and oneself may seem an

61

extraordinary proposition in the politics of war, in business, as I have been emphasizing throughout the previous chapters of this book, the win-win situation between a firm and its competitors and other stakeholders has been an all-time goal. Thus, Sun Tzu's complete victory strategy is a good example that can be applied to business, which is the central topic of this chapter.

In the business world, the strategy of winning without fighting can be analogous to Porter's strategy of finding an attractive industry, characterized by his five forces model. However, the convergence of technologies and industries has spread throughout the economy, particularly since Apple introduced the iPhone to the market. Because of the converging phenomenon, firms tend to rely more on the partnership or cooperative relationship for providing more competitive products and services to the customers. This thus raises questions on Porter's competition-based five forces model, when selecting an attractive industry, which I will discuss in more depth later. In this respect, Sun Tzu's concept of complete victory can complement Porter's five forces model to better explain the changing competitive landscape, from sole competition to both competition and cooperation for coevolution. On the other hand, this chapter will also extend Sun Tzu's concept of "enemy" in a war to a wider scope by incorporating Porter's concept of extended rivals (i.e., five competitive forces) in business.

In the following sections, I will first explain the military ideas in Sun Tzu's chapter "Strategic Attack." Then I will introduce Porter's five forces model. In the subsequent section, I will compare and combine Sun Tzu's military thoughts with Porter's five forces model and apply them to military and business cases: Genghis Khan's terror strategy and Apple's entry into the smartphone industry. With the aid of the case studies, readers can better understand the distinctions between Sun Tzu and Porter and how the respective models complement each other when explaining real world cases.

3.1 SUN TZU: COMPLETE VICTORY BY STRATEGIC ATTACK

3.1.1 *Winning without Fighting*

Sun Tzu said that fighting a hundred battles and winning in all hundred battles do not demonstrate supreme excellence, but winning without fighting is the true representation of supreme excellence in warfare. The use of physical force raises strong resistance from the enemy, leading to large wartime expenditures and sacrifice of many lives. Hart (1954) gave a good description of the disadvantages of resorting to the use of force:

> The more brutal your methods the more bitter you will make your
> opponents, with the natural result of hardening the resistance
> you are trying to overcome ... If you concentrate exclusively on
> victory, with no thought for the after-effect, you may be too
> exhausted to profit by the peace, while it is almost certain that the
> peace will be a bad one, containing the germs of another war.
>
> (Hart, 1954: 357, 366)

The evidence can be found from the two World Wars, which took millions of lives, devastated the entire European continent and much of Asia, and left the winners weaker and poorer than before the wars (McNeilly, 1996).

On the other hand, winning without fighting is much less costly. Sun Tzu's principle of winning without fighting, or a "complete victory," involves capturing the enemy soldiers alive and their assets intact. Winning without fighting might be more difficult than winning through a direct battle because it requires extensive and accurate knowledge of the enemy's situation, characteristics, and all kinds of related factors that allow one to manipulate the enemy's thinking and minds. Therefore, winning without fighting is more akin to psychological warfare (Cheng, 2013). However, winning without fighting does not mean one should ignore military preparations or abandon all military options but to avoid fighting if possible. Complete victory is one of the core military principles of Sun Tzu's entire book of *The Art of War*. The strategic thinking behind complete victory has positively influenced the military thinking of later scholars such as Liddell Hart's indirect approach.

Under the military thought of complete victory, Sun Tzu classified types of strategies into four ranks from the best to the worst: the best type of strategy is to defeat the enemy's plans; the second best is to defeat their alliances; the third is to defeat their army; and the worst is to defeat their fortified castle.[1] The order of the four strategies corresponds to the increasing size of costs. The first two of the four involve defeating the enemy without fighting, while the latter two require direct fighting. However, bloodless victory requires good preparation of arms and supplies as well as a strong domestic economy as the backbone; otherwise, one will be vulnerable to retaliation. On the other hand, attacking the enemy's fortified castle not only requires the largest input but is also the most difficult way of achieving victory in warfare. Moreover, despite the heavy preparations for such an attack, failure to take it will result in tremendous disaster. Therefore, Sun Tzu suggested that one should attack an enemy's fortified castle only when there is no other option.

Sun Tzu's recommendations are not limited to advocating the strategy of winning without fighting but also include ideas pertaining to reducing the burden of resources for physical battles. Sun Tzu gave the following tactical advice when attacking the enemy's army: "If one's army is ten times the enemy's, surround them; if five, attack them; if double, divide the enemy; if equal to the enemy, engage them; if fewer, circumvent them; and if out-matched, avoid them."[2] Therefore, one should flexibly adopt tactics and decide whether to engage in the war or not after comparing one's strengths with the enemy's strengths. Otherwise, one will become the enemy's captives.

---

[1]   The Chinese characters are: 故上兵伐謀, 其次伐交, 其次伐兵, 其下攻城.

[2]   The Chinese characters are: 十則圍之, 五則攻之, 倍則分之, 敵則能戰之, 少則能逃之, 不若則能避之.

3.1.2 *Knowing the Enemy and Oneself*

Whether it is winning with or without fighting, the prerequisite is to know the enemy and oneself. To quote one of the most famous lines of *The Art of War*, Sun Tzu said, "If one knows the enemy and oneself, one will not be in danger in a hundred battles. If one knows oneself but not the enemy, one will win one and lose the other. If one knows neither the enemy nor oneself, one will lose in every battle."[3] "Knowing" here means understanding the relative strengths and weaknesses of oneself and of the enemy, in terms of both physical and psychological attributes.

Regarding the physical aspects of the enemy, a commander should be informed of the enemy's size, location, number and types of equipment available, readiness for battle, an extent of logistics, and so on. Commanders often find it difficult to maintain a clear picture of operations that may be taking place hundreds of miles away. The more accurate one's view of the enemy, the more readily and effectively one can prepare operational plans, array one's own forces and assets, and anticipate the course of future events. Having accurate information on the capabilities, limitations, and location of one's own forces is as important as knowing those of the enemy; overestimation or underestimation of one's own capacity can happen at any time.

Sun Tzu placed greater emphasis on knowing the *will* of the enemy and oneself. The "will" here refers to the national will. If the objective of the war (i.e., political interest) is consistent with the national will, one will have a reasonable chance of victory (Desutter, 1994). The national will is consistent with the factor of "principle," which was introduced in Chapter 1 of this book. In order to achieve victory, the ruler or king should first obtain public support within his own country. Knowing the enemy's will refers to knowing the enemy's intentions, with a thorough understanding of the enemy, for example, by using human intelligence (e.g., spying) (Phua, 2007).

---

[3] The Chinese characters are: 知彼知己, 百戰不殆; 不知彼而知己, 一勝一負; 不知彼不知己, 每戰必殆.

If understanding the enemy's intention and their capacity is one of the keys to winning, withholding one's information and not giving away one's intention are the goals of almost any military force. As a result, it is crucial for a commander to skillfully gather as much accurate information about the enemy as possible. Throughout the history of war, there have been numerous disasters and failures due to the lack of precise information on the enemy. For example, the United States launched into the Vietnam War without a clear understanding of the enemy's intentions, and the war ended in failure. Collins (1978) warned about the danger of underestimating the significance of understanding the enemy while simply relying on one's superior physical strengths, by referring to the failure of the United States in the Vietnam War: "We oriented on opposing armed forces, not opposing strategies, a fatal failure in that (Vietnam) war. We overrated ourselves and underrated opponents. Technological strengths and superior numbers consequently conferred no advantage on the United States. Finally, we forgot that armies are not the only weapons in the counterinsurgent's arsenal, nor even the most important."

Sun Tzu's concept of "knowing the enemy and oneself" is also reflected in Clausewitz's work, *On War*. Clausewitz (1968[1832]) defined war as an act of violence intended to compel one's opponent to fulfill one's will. Clausewitz (1968[1832]) further said, "If we desire to defeat the enemy, we must proportion our efforts to his powers of resistance. This is expressed by the product of two factors which cannot be separated, namely, the sum of available means and the strength of the will" (p. 30). Clausewitz thus emphasized that in order to conquer the enemy, one should not only physically outcompete the enemy, but also be coercive psychologically. However, it should be noted that knowing the enemy and oneself can alleviate danger but not completely guarantee a victory. In the chapter "Terrain" of *The Art of War*, Sun Tzu said, "If one knows *Heaven* and *Terrain*, the victory can be complete." Therefore, in addition to knowing the enemy and oneself, environmental factors (i.e., heaven and terrain) should also be considered for a complete victory. A detailed discussion regarding this issue will be given in Chapter 10 of this book.

3.2 PORTER: FIVE FORCES MODEL FOR SELECTING AN ATTRACTIVE INDUSTRY

Porter first introduced the five forces model in his 1979 article, which later became popularized in his 1980 book. Although it has been more than decades since its introduction, the five forces model is still one of the most widely used tools for strategy formulation in academia and in practice. According to Porter (1979, 1980), the industry structure determines both industry and firm profitability. Although industries are seemingly different from one another, the underlying drivers of industry attractiveness are largely homogenous and can be described by the five forces – suppliers, buyers, potential entrants, existing competitors, and substitutes. Porter claimed that industry competition, which influences firms' profitability, goes beyond the direct competitors and that the five competitive forces should be considered as the extended rivals.

3.2.1 Five Competitive Forces (Porter, 1980)

Bargaining Power of Suppliers If the number of suppliers is limited and competing firms are reliant on their suppliers, the bargaining power of suppliers will increase. Thus, suppliers can call for premium prices, thereby deteriorating the attractiveness of the industry.

Bargaining Power of Buyers Greater bargaining power is handed to the buyers when their number is limited or when the supply is greater than demand. Powerful buyers can force down prices and demand better quality or more services, thereby decreasing industry attractiveness.

Threat of New Entrants New entrants to an industry typically increase the intensity of competition among firms and decrease the industry attractiveness. Therefore, existing companies try to increase entry barriers by controlling resources, realizing economies of scale/scope, and raising capital requirements.

Rivalry among Existing Players The internal competition among companies is an integral determinant of the attractiveness of an industry. The higher the intensity of the rivalry is, the lower the attractiveness of an industry is. Price competition for rivalry is particularly unstable, which worsens the industry attractiveness while diminishing firms' profitability.

Threat of Substitutes Substitutes are products or services provided by other firms that offer roughly the same function as one's own and thus lure the customers away. If the threat of substitution is high, the industry profitability will decrease.

These forces are interdependent. A change in one force will affect the others. The collective strength of the five forces determines the attractiveness or profitability of an industry. If the bargaining powers of five forces are high, it will be difficult for a firm in the industry to earn a high rate of return on investment (e.g., airlines and textiles). On the other hand, if the forces are kept at favorable levels, many firms in the industry will earn high profits (e.g., software and soft drinks). Therefore, it is critical for a firm to find an attractive industry where it can better defend against the competitive forces or minimize their threats.

Although in the short run some industries may appear susceptible to factors outside the five forces such as weather and business cycle, in the long run, the five forces will be able to succinctly and sufficiently explain any industry structure and its attractiveness (Porter, 2008). Therefore, managers should pay close attention to the changes in the five competitive forces, and shift their competitive strategies or positioning in the industry accordingly.

3.2.2   Extension of Porter's Five Forces Model

Porter's five forces model is a good framework for firms to pick an attractive industry and earn high profits. However, it can be extended to better explain the current competitive landscape, which mainly derives from two issues – the convergence of technologies, products, and industries; and the growing importance of an interfirm collaborative relationship.

Porter emphasized the critical role of industry structure on determining the profitability of firms. Indeed, it is crucial for firms to choose an appropriate industry. However, when choosing an industry, firms should be careful *not* to define the boundary of what an "industry" comprises at too broad nor too narrow scope. According to Porter (2008), the industry boundary is determined by two criteria – the scope of products or services, and geographic scope. However, due to the emergence of convergence of technologies, products, and industry, it becomes difficult to define the industry boundary. Teece (2007) also argued that industry boundaries are fading, at least in technologically progressive environments.

The evidence of fading industry boundaries can also be found in the changing trend of the process of invention. Youn et al. (2015) argued that the process of invention has changed since the nineteenth century, around the time of Edison's invention of the light bulb. According to their findings, in the nineteenth century, about 50 percent of US patents were single-code inventions, but after the nineteenth century, it has become more popular to introduce a new patent by combining two or more codes (i.e., technology convergence) –amounting to about 90 percent of US patents for inventions combining at least two codes. Therefore, due to the emerging technology convergence, a product, which had strictly belonged to a specific industry, now has a higher probability of being a part of another new product creation. Accordingly, firms are trying to find a new growth engine for the future business apart from their existing industries. For example, the leading information technology (IT) firms (e.g., Apple and Google) are expanding their businesses to non-IT industries, such as automobile, watch, and so on. In this respect, these firms' profitability depends less on their selection of one particular industry. With convergence, firms that used to belong to the unrelated industries can now arise as new competitors (Hacklin, Battistini, and Krogh, 2013). This change of game thus requires a firm to consider not only the industry where it currently competes, but also related or seemingly unrelated industries, which can be incorporated to create a new competitive advantage. Therefore, Porter's single-industry analysis unit needs to be extended to incorporate the multi-product and multi-industry level.

Second, regarding the drivers of firm profitability, Porter mainly focused on the competitive relationship with competitive forces. Therefore, in order to maintain their competitive position, firms have to augment their bargaining power by lowering the threats of the extended rivals. However, this argument holds true only for the closed system of production and innovation, in which firms internalize all the value activities for the final products and services. When a new type of smart, connected product (Porter and Heppelmann, 2014) comes to the market, which encompasses a cluster of related products (e.g., iPhone), traditional single-product providers (even the market leader) might become one of the suppliers for the creation of new products. Although firms can internalize these activities by expanding into the relevant areas, this method would be less effective because no firm can master all areas of the integrated business.

Therefore, the platform strategy by the ecosystem aggregators has become popular. These firms, rather than directly participating in the production, establish the platform and connect the complementary products and services. One of the important advantages of this strategy is that it allows a firm to avoid direct competition with the established providers by incorporating them into the platform. For example, Apple's operating system connects two different groups of users: application developers and smartphone users. More application developers will attract more smartphone users, and vice versa. The competitive forces or high bargaining powers of suppliers and buyers do not always threaten firms' profits, but they can also be the sources of enhanced innovation and competitiveness. In this case, firms' profitability and sustainability depend on whether they can continuously and efficiently attract the participation of a broad range of contributors, including their competitors.

Therefore, in addition to the competitive relationship suggested by Porter's five forces, the cooperative relationship should be considered as a critical factor for maintaining a healthy business ecosystem to increase benefits, because the weakening of any specialized participant might disrupt the whole system.

3.3 THE INTEGRATION OF SUN TZU AND PORTER

3.3.1 Complete Victory versus Entering an Attractive Industry

Sun Tzu declared that the ideal strategy is to subdue the enemy without fighting, and "winning without fighting" is also an ideal outcome in business (Ma, 2003). However, in the real world, firms always compete against each other in the same business, through either direct confrontation or indirect competition. On the other hand, the fast-changing environment and fast catch-up make the market competition more intensive than ever before. Even brand new inventions entice followers and future competitors and often fail to hold their dominant position very long (McNeilly, 1996). For example, not long after Apple's introduction of the iPhone, Samsung Electronics launched similar smartphone products (i.e., the Galaxy models) and changed the competitive landscape in the global smartphone business.

In business, direct fighting involves face-to-face competition using similar products or services (e.g., price war), but avoiding fights with rivals entails firms focusing on value creation by satisfying different customer groups or providing different product features for the same group of customers (e.g., differentiation). Since both "fighting" and "nonfighting" involve some degree of competition with rivals (i.e., competing for the market share), selecting an attractive industry is very important for gaining profits. From this perspective, the industry structure described by Porter's five forces model can have a substantial influence in deciding the competitive environment.

However, Porter's strategy of "entering an attractive industry" seems to be rather transitory, particularly in the era of a fast-changing and turbulent environment. As the industry matures, the attractiveness decreases due to the increasing bargaining power of the competitive forces. For this reason, Porter's five forces model can be improved by borrowing Sun Tzu's concept of "complete victory" from the following two aspects for sustaining a firm's profitability.

In contrast to the traditional one-product producer, the producers of a new type of multi-technology or multi-function products can have alternative solutions. By creating a platform, firms can incorporate the complementary products and services, absorbing them into a new type of product. This strategy can reduce the threats from the existing competitors. Rather than searching for new attractive industries, firms can reshape or expand the industry boundaries by producing smart, connected products. These products are likely to exhibit better performance because they add new features, which are not found in the traditional products. The iPhone's entry into the mobile phone industry is a good example. On the other hand, firms producing a single product can utilize other firms' (or the platform creators') value chain and create a new platform or ecosystem. For example, some IT firms (e.g., Google) make alliances with the automakers for developing self-driving cars. Recently, we see that many globally competitive firms (e.g., Google, Apple, and Samsung) have been simultaneously pursuing both strategies (i.e., creating their own platform and joining others' platform to create a new platform).

3.3.2 *Competitors in War versus Business*

In war, Sun Tzu stressed knowing one's enemy in order to achieve a complete victory. Similarly, in business, Porter claimed that firms should know a broad set of five forces. Sun Tzu's concept of enemy emphasizes the enemy within the terms of direct conflict. Therefore, by borrowing the concept of Porter's five forces model, Sun Tzu's concept of enemy can be extended to a broader perspective to include existing enemies, potential enemies, alternative solutions, soldiers and generals, and the public. If the five industry forces determine the attractiveness of an industry, the five military forces determine the potential cost of waging war. The enhanced models of military and business analysis (i.e., the five military forces model and five industry forces model) are illustrated as follows (see Figure 3.1).

Existing Players (Business) versus Existing Enemies (War)
Firms are constantly pressured to improve their relative positions in the industry. Therefore, a firm's strategic move will always incite other firms' efforts to counter or move. Price competition is particularly destructive, since it diminishes the whole industry's profitability. Similarly, in a military context, countries attack or conquer other countries in order to pursue their own national interests. The opponent countries can be compared to the existing competitors in business.

Potential Entrants (Business) versus Potential Enemies (War)
The threat of new entrants relies on the barriers to entry and the reaction from the existing competitors. If the barriers are kept high or the likelihood of sharp retaliation from existing competitors is known to potential new entrants, the threat of entry will be low, keeping the industry attractive. The entry barrier in business is comparable to the relative military strength of a country or the cost of offense. As lower industrial entry barriers attract the entry of the industry contenders, a weaker country is more likely to be a target of being attacked by the potential enemies. Sun Tzu said that prolonged campaigns impair one's strength and deplete one's resources, giving feudal lords a chance to take take advantage of the country's weakness to attack. As Winston Churchill once said, there are no permanent enemies, only permanent interests. Diplomatic and military relationships among countries change frequently, depending on the military strengths of nations and their mutual interests. The current friends might become enemies in the future.

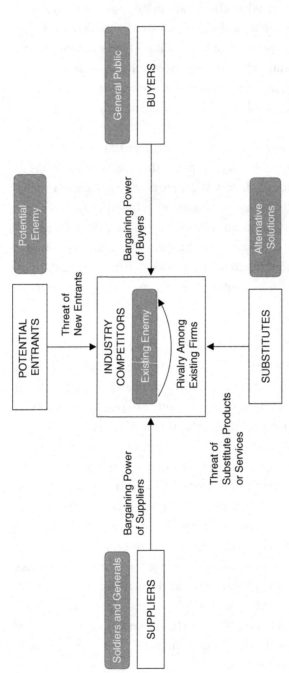

FIGURE 3.1 Sun Tzu's five military forces and Porter's five forces model

Substitutes (Business) versus Alternative Solutions (War)

In business, substitutes refer to products with similar functions that may be used in place of one's own products. According to Porter, if the substitutes have lower prices or better quality, they will be threats to the existing products. In particular, firms earning at high rates of profitability may induce the creation of substitutes, which in turn will threaten to change the overall industry structure and profitability. In war, alternative solutions or the strategy of winning without fighting could change the relative benefits of winning the war by decreasing the destructive effects and expenditure of war, thereby achieving victory at lower cost and risk.

Suppliers (Business) versus Soldiers and Generals (War)

The significance of suppliers in the process of value creation varies according to the industry structure. The supplier bargaining power may raise prices or reduce the quality of input goods and services, imposing a direct threat to the competitiveness of the final product. An equivalent of suppliers in warfare would be the soldiers and generals who directly affect the probability of victory in war. The size and quality of the army are very important to determine the overall competitiveness of the military. The role of a general is particularly important, as Sun Tzu said, "The general is the supporting pillar of the country. If the general is all-encompassing, the country will invariably be strong. If he is deficient, the country will invariably grow weak."

Buyers (Business) versus General Public (War)

Buyers are the final judges of the products or services that firms provide. Powerful buyers may force down prices, demand higher quality or services, and pressure the firms to compete against each other. Similarly, although they are not as influential as the buyers in business, the public judges the moral legitimacy of waging war. They do not participate in direct fighting, similar to how buyers are often not directly involved in business operations, but they take very important positions in the military campaign. Without the public's support, it will be very difficult to achieve a complete victory, as Sun Tzu argued in his chapter 1.

3.4 MILITARY CASE: GENGHIS KHAN'S TERROR STRATEGY

Temujin, known as Genghis Khan (meaning "Oceanic Ruler"), was born around 1162.[4] He founded the Mongol Empire, which at its peak in the thirteenth century stretched over substantial parts of China, Central Asia, the Middle East, and Europe. The territory he conquered totaled to more than half the known world at that time and was larger than the sum of the territories conquered by Alexander the Great, Napoleon, and Hitler. Due to the sheer size of the Mongol Empire, one might easily imagine the tremendous size of an army sweeping through those lands. However, at the time, the Mongol population was only 1.5 million, and the number of soldiers was only around 100,000.

With a relatively small army, the Mongols rose as conquerors through the ingenious strategies they employed on the battlefield, utilizing both direct confrontation and subduing the enemy without fighting. Particularly noteworthy tactics of Genghis Khan's army are the ones that did *not* involve direct fighting. A good example is the terror strategy. The Mongols spread terror and destruction where they arrived, and as a result, many were overwhelmed with fear just from hearing their very name – weakening the troops psychologically. Hence, the use of terror strategy became a very effective method for the Mongols to achieve their objectives without great costs.

Gruesome and tragic fates often awaited the people who received the Mongols. A well-practiced example was the decapitation and impaling of defeated enemies' heads for public display. Mercy was an antonym to the Mongols' treatment of people who resisted them:

[4]   Information of this case study is abstracted and modified from Barnes (2010) and Moon (2013).

women were raped; young men were enslaved as laborers or soldiers; older males were executed; and artisans were sent to Mongol camps. The Mongols were, however, not unreasonable to those who voluntarily surrendered. This strategy made surrender the more appealing for terror-stricken people rather than betting successful defense against the war-gods-like conquerors. Indeed, when a city did not resist, the Mongols readily exhibited mercy and spared the people, as they had done for the ancient city of Herat. The people of Herat, however, underestimated the determination of the Mongols to maintain their rule – peace upon surrender and complete destruction upon resistance – and revolted after the Mongols' departure. The price of this mistake was high. Genghis Khan subsequently sent his army back to Herat and slaughtered everyone.

The terror strategy is not the evidence of the bloodthirsty barbarism of the Mongols, but of their excellent understanding of how to use a psychological weapon just as well as physical ones. The basic message of the Mongolian terror strategy was that resistance was futile and that the same terrible fate awaited anyone who resisted. News of the Mongols' destruction often arrived much sooner than the Mongols themselves and many cities surrendered without a fight, saving the need for costly battles. Paradoxically, through the display of brutal deaths and suffering, the Mongols were able to avoid unnecessary bloodshed. Moreover, being well aware that news would disperse faster through written words, Genghis Khan requested 100,000 sheets of paper from *Goryeo* and had his scribes record their brutal activities over any praise of their achievements.

In the short run, the Mongol strategy was definitely effective for letting them gain those vast territories; it allowed the Mongolian army to stick in their flags on numerous cities without having to always engage in a wasteful direct confrontation with the enemy. At the same time, however, the victories earned through the terror strategy amounted to only half the complete victory as defined by Sun Tzu. Complete victory of Sun Tzu entails two parts: resources of one's own must be saved through winning without fighting; and the resources of the defeated enemy must be preserved at large for one's own use. However, the Mongols carried out excessively brutal tactics, needlessly wasting the enemy's human and nonhuman resources. The exercise of brutality also brought them similar treatments by the enemies. When Mongol soldiers were captured by Muslim forces, they were deliberately killed by various brutal means, such as driving a nail into heads and crushing bodies with elephants. Moreover, the brutal strategy resulted in numerous revolts after the Mongols' departure. This shows that the Mongols' terror strategy was not sustainable in the long run because the enemy did not surrender by their own free will but by their fear of the Mongol's brutal image.

Porter's five forces model also sheds lights to understanding the causes behind the Mongol Empire's eventual decline. The Mongol Empire's fall was the result of various internal factors (Morgan, 2009). In the Mongol Empire's later years, the entire empire was divided into four independent khanates, ruled by members of the Mongol royal families. The internal disintegration (i.e., soldiers and generals) further weakened their military capacity. In addition, the loss of harmony among different ethnic and religious groups (i.e., the public) caused greater internal turbulence. Although soldiers, generals, and the public were not the direct enemies engaged in war, the inappropriate treatment of them affected the competitiveness of the empire, which further determined the potential weakness of defending against the direct or potential enemy in war. Thus, Sun Tzu's concept of enemy can be extended for more preciseness and greater breath by borrowing the concept of Porter's extended rivals in business. This extension will strengthen the explaining power of Sun Tzu's "knowing the enemy" concept if Porter's extended model of rivals is applied to military cases.

3.5 BUSINESS CASE: THE CHANGING ATTRACTIVENESS OF THE MOBILE PHONE INDUSTRY

Smartphone sales in 2014 accounted for two-thirds of the global mobile phone market (Gartner, 2015), and Apple had the lion's share of the industry profits.[5] Apple used to be a manufacturer of personal computers and entertainment equipment. However, it has since become a major player in the smartphone industry. How did the company successfully enter the mobile phone market, without facing severe resistance from existing players? The following section will detail the changing industry structure of the pre- and post-smartphone market using Porter's five forces model, and then analyze Apple's entry strategy with the extensions of Porter and Sun Tzu.

Rivalry among Existing Players Before the introduction of the smartphone, the competition was fierce among existing mobile phone manufacturers. The product life cycle was very short and buyers' tastes changed frequently. As a result, companies had to continuously introduce new mobile phones with better features. In order to do this, firms needed to invest heavily in R&D to meet the customers' needs. However, since the introduction of the iPhone, the number of players in the smartphone industry has dramatically entered a bipolar order with Apple and Samsung as the industry's hegemons. In addition, the smartphone market has changed from a niche to a mass market, and the competition has become fiercer than ever. The intensity of the rivalry in the smartphone industry is far from being extreme, but neither is it mellow, since the two major players, namely Apple and Samsung, continue to fiercely compete against each other. Therefore, the degree of rivalry can be considered to rank medium.

Threat of New Entrants In the pre-smartphone era, it was hard to maintain customer loyalty, since the switching cost to another mobile phone was low. It was also easier for firms to enter the market, especially low-end product markets, due to the homogenization of hardware. However, the initial costs of entering this industry was very high in terms of R&D investment and marketing to compete with established companies. Therefore, the threat of new

---

[5]   This case study compares the structure of the mobile phone (or feature phone) industry and that of the smartphone industry in its early stage when there were only a few players in the industry right after the Apple's introduction of the iPhone.

entrants was medium. However, since the introduction of the iPhone, the threat of new entrants has become lower. First, it was difficult for new entrants to convince customers to switch to another brand. Second, it was very difficult to produce a better smartphone at an affordable price than those produced by existing manufacturers.

Threat of Substitutes A device equipped with wireless capability was considered a must with the emergence of Wi-Fi standardization, so handheld emailing devices might be considered substitutes for mobile phones. However, since the introduction of the iPhone, the threat of substitutes has become very low, as the smartphone combined many of the functions of other electronic devices such as cameras and music players. It became impractical to purchase and carry all of these devices at the same time, except for highly specialized and professional purposes. Therefore, the threat of substitutes has decreased from medium to low.

Bargaining Power of Suppliers As there were many suppliers for different parts and components of mobile phones, they did not have much power to seriously affect the decision-making of mobile phone manufactures. As a result, the bargaining power of suppliers was low, since manufacturers could easily switch to other suppliers for desirable price and quality. However, as the platform came to be dominated by a few players providing operating systems, the core software system for smartphones (e.g., Android and iOS), and the device design became increasingly customized for a particular operating system by a specific supplier, it became very expensive to switch suppliers. Therefore, the bargaining power of suppliers has changed from low to medium since the introduction of the smartphone.

Bargaining Power of Buyers Customers had high bargaining power because of the great number of choices in the mobile phone industry. The loyalty of customers was very low, and it was usually determined by quality instead of the brand. As a result, leading manufacturers strove harder to meet customer demands as much as possible in order to keep and attract new customers. However, the entrance of Apple into the mobile phone market decreased the bargaining power of buyers dramatically through generating an unprecedented fandom for the company products with the appeals of an eye-catching design, high quality, and robust software capability.

Before the introduction of the iPhone, the overall mobile phone manufacturing industry did not appear very attractive or profitable. However, the Apple case shows that an industry's threat of substitutes is subject to changes over time and can sometimes overturn the whole industry structure. The revolutionary entry of Apple changed the industry structure from less attractive to very attractive, as the threats from most of the five forces (except suppliers) have decreased (see Figure 3.2).

Porter (2008) claimed that substitutes become a great threat under two conditions. The first is when they are improving the price-performance trade-off with the current industry's products. In other words, when consumers have become less price sensitive to the higher price because of the improved value of products. Although the price of the iPhone is higher than the older feature phones, customers prefer to pay the extra price for better performance of the product. Therefore, the trade-off between product price and performance is improving. The second is when the cost of switching to a substitute is low. Traditional cell phones (or feature phones) are capable of voice calls, text messages, and occasional photos, but do not include many other functions. In contrast, smartphones are essentially handheld computers. Users can check their email, search the Internet, watch video, and so on. As the smartphones offer new user-friendly and valuable functions, consumers are easily persuaded to switch from their old phones to smartphones. Smartphones satisfied both of these conditions.

However, Apple's success was due to more than Porter's five forces, and could be better explained by referring to some of Sun Tzu's military strategies of this chapter. Porter emphasized the determining

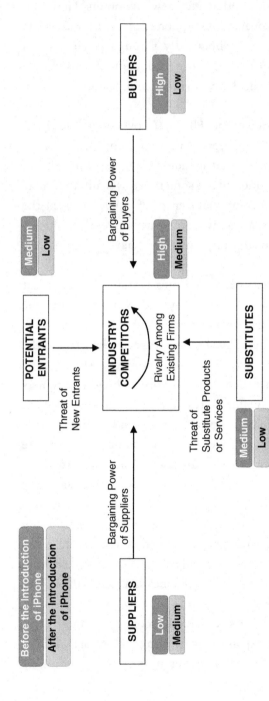

FIGURE 3.2 Five forces of the mobile phone industry

role of industry characteristics on firms' high profitability. However, the previous mobile phone industry was hypercompetitive and not so profitable. In the case of the iPhone, Apple's achievement of high profitability is actually more about creating a highly profitable market segment, rather than entering and sharing the existing market. Therefore, the five forces can explain why the iPhone achieved higher profits than mobile makers by comparing the five forces of mobile phone and smartphone, but do not fully explain why the iPhone could so quickly and easily dominate the smartphone market in such a short time.

The iPhone market share in the smartphone was only 4 percent in 2007, but it reached 30 percent in 2009. Two factors explain iPhone's fast domination of the market. The first factor was Apple's coevolution with the involved partners. Upon the introduction of the iPhone, Apple found numerous new business opportunities for the market. Apple controlled and coordinated the core portion of the value chain, leaving the other parts to the third parties, such as the network provider (AT&T) (Laugesen and Yuan, 2010). Moreover, it even cooperated with its major smartphone competitor – Samsung Electronics, the supplier of key iPhone components such as display and memory. Thanks to the new sources of profit earning, Apple could enter the market with relatively fewer market obstacles. This can be explained by Sun Tzu's military principle that the best strategy is not to destroy the enemy but to subdue it while keeping it intact. Apple's success strategy is thus more about constructive rather than destructive evolution.

The second success factor was Apple's complete understanding of the consumers' needs. In the beginning, Apple offered only one model for the entire global market. Yet this extreme case of specialization was possible because it correctly targeted the right consumer segment – male of 25–34 years old, college educated, and earning relatively higher income (ComScore, 2008). This consumer group pursued a higher degree of sophistication in terms of technology, information, and adoption of new products. While hardware design alone may not have been a perfect one-size-fits-all since aesthetic appreciation differs across cultures, the software's technological superiority certainly possessed a universal appeal. Moreover, the kaleidoscopic array of applications, which consumers of almost any taste could choose from, allowed the one-product policy to be successful. It is embedded by advanced software and various applications to serve different consumer demands. Because of its highly effective functions at a reasonable price, Apple could take a large portion of market share in a short period. This success reflects the significance of understanding the enemy as Sun Tzu advocated.

In sum, Apple's success embodies both aspects of Sun Tzu's complete victory. Apple minimized its costs of entry through a speedy and effective elimination of major obstacles, while successfully grasping a large market share. On the other hand, Apple did not destroy the ecosystem of the industry for its success by abusing its bargaining power, but rather generated more vitality into it by actively cooperating with other firms in the value chain. In addition, through providing better quality products at reasonable costs, Apple has also benefited its consumers. Thus, Apple's increased profitability qualifies as a business case of complete victory, because it maneuvered around obstacles to reduce costs and left "its enemies intact," to quote Sun Tzu.

3.6 CONCLUSION AND IMPLICATIONS

In the chapter "Strategic Attack," Sun Tzu proposed a military concept of complete victory. Sun Tzu claimed that keeping the enemy's country or army intact was better than destroying it and he preferred a noncombat victory, which leads to lower retaliation and cost. Attacking the enemy's plans and their allies are the two typical strategies for a noncombat victory. Regardless of winning with or without fighting, one important precondition is to know the enemy and oneself. Knowing the enemy's intention is particularly important to achieve a noncombat victory.

In this chapter, I provided an overview of Sun Tzu's concept of complete victory along with Porter's five forces model, and the extended military and business models combining the two. Sun Tzu's complete victory entails less consumption of resources and unnecessary sacrifices compared to winning through violent means. Similarly, Porter's five forces model suggests that a firm enters an industry in which it can exert a higher bargaining power over competitive forces. In this way, the firm can save resources from unnecessary competition and obtain greater profits. Both strategies have the same goal of achieving maximum output using minimum input. Another linkage between the two strategies is Sun Tzu's concept of "enemy" and Porter's extended rivals encompassed in the five forces model. Despite these similarities, however, there are still some differences between the two. Sun Tzu mainly focused on the current enemy or those confronted in battles, while Porter incorporated a more comprehensive scope of rivals in business. In this respect, this chapter extended Sun Tzu's concept of enemy and introduced five types of extended enemies in war, by borrowing the concepts of Porter's five competitive forces.

In the military case, Genghis Khan's terror strategy proved to be effective for conquering a vast territory with his relatively small army. However, there is an important difference between the terror strategy and Sun Tzu's concept of "winning without fighting": the Mongol strategy was too cruel to achieve a sustainable victory. This chapter also showed that the Mongol Empire's rise and fall can be better explained by using the concept of extended enemies. In the business case, I analyzed the change in the industry structure of the mobile phone market with Apple's introduction of the iPhone. Apple's revolutionary product (i.e., iPhone) avoided stiff competition and achieved great success. However, Apple's success was not achieved simply through choosing an attractive industry or reducing the competitive forces as the five forces model suggested. It was through creating a new attractive industry where all the involved partners could co-develop. Therefore, the profitability model shifts from competition-only to both competition and cooperation. In this respect, Apple's success model can be better explained with the help of Sun Tzu's conception of complete victory, winning without fighting or subduing the enemy without destroying them.

4   Competitive Positioning

Sun Tzu: Easy victory through tactical positioning
Porter: Generic strategy for advantageous positioning

"War is a rational activity of the last resort that correlates the end and means to enhance the vital interests of the state" (Bartley, 2005). Therefore, one should engage in war only when it is in the best interest of the country, and war activities must cease when the costs outweigh the benefits. This utilitarian philosophy of war engagement is the very foundation of Sun Tzu's military strategies as embodied in every chapter of *The Art of War*. The previous chapter illustrates Sun Tzu's military strategy of winning without fighting, and the chapter "Tactical Disposition" of *The Art of War* is concerned with obtaining victory at the lowest cost when confrontation is unavoidable. Sun Tzu advised generals to arrange their army in a particular *Hsing* (形) or a domineering tactical disposition, for both defense and offense, when military confrontation is unavoidable.

Sun Tzu claimed that one should first prepare a good defensive disposition to secure oneself from an unexpected enemy attack. The match for defensive disposition among Porter's theories is the generic strategy, which also purports to defend against the threats of five competitive forces and obtain above-average profits. On the other hand, the Porterian twin of Sun Tzu's offensive disposition is to upgrade competitive advantages in order to secure a better position.

However, despite their similarities, Sun Tzu and Porter show visible differences that I have been highlighting in previous chapters of this book. Unlike Sun Tzu, Porter emphasized the influence of external factors on the erosion of competitive advantage. Sometimes, however, firms' internal factors – such as strategic mistakes in decision-making or failing to upgrade properly due to complacency – can also lead to ruin. Sun Tzu alluded to this idea when he claimed, "Making no mistakes establishes victory." By complementing Porter's strategies with Sun Tzu's ideas, one can better explain the reasons behind a firm's success or failure in the real world. In this chapter, I add Sun Tzu's consideration of internal threats to Porter's business model (i.e., generic strategy) in order to better analyze Toyota's successful entry to the US market; then I extend Sun Tzu's original arguments by borrowing Porter's ideas to analyze the Soviets' victory in the Battle of Stalingrad.

4.1   SUN TZU: EASY VICTORY THROUGH TACTICAL POSITIONING

Sun Tzu said, "When a battle is won, everyone says that is good, but it is often not the best of all good outcomes." This statement purports to highlight the cost that diminishes the sweetness of victory. Instead, Sun Tzu stressed, "A clever fighter is one who not only wins, but excels in winning with ease." In order to achieve an easy victory, one has to create conditions that ensure the enemy's defeat before going to war. Sun Tzu called them the domineering conditions, *Hsing*.

Hsing literally means "form" or "shape" and refers to the appearance of a subject or situation. In Sun Tzu's chapter "Tactical Disposition," it is defined as the disposition of defense and offense. An effective disposition plays a determining role in the outcome of military campaigns. Sun Tzu claimed that victory results from the arrangement and effective positioning of the army rather than simply the number of soldiers. To formulate a "domineering disposition" that can generate exponential magnification of military power, Sun Tzu emphasized deploying the troops at the right time and place. Clausewitz reflected a similar view saying, "as many troops as possible should be brought into the engagement at the decisive point ... This is the first principle of strategy."

Furthermore, Sun Tzu claimed, "A good fighter first puts himself beyond the possibility of being defeated, and then waits for an opportunity to defeat the enemy." The first half refers to the "disposition of defense," whereas the latter half relates to the "disposition of offense." The following section will discuss the details behind proper defensive and offensive dispositions.

4.1.1   Tactical Disposition of Defense and Offense

Before attacking the enemy, one should first assess one's ability to fight. If one is fully prepared, one can intimidate the enemy enough to prevent them from attacking, and even if they attack, one can stave off defeat (Gang, 2011). To Sun Tzu, defense is more than passive resistance and is actually the precondition for attacking or even defeating the enemy. Therefore, the power of being unconquerable lies with oneself. However, a good defense can only stave off defeat and cannot guarantee victory. In order to win, one must attack the enemy.

As for offensive disposition, Sun Tzu singled out attacking the enemy's weak points as the most efficient method. If the enemy has no weakness, one has to create the conditions for the enemy to make mistakes, otherwise, there is no way of defeating the enemy. However, the enemy also has their own will and way of thinking, and one cannot guarantee that the enemy will act according to one's plans. It is for this reason that Sun Tzu said one cannot anticipate the enemy to be conquerable. In addition, when attacking the enemy, one should concentrate one's military strength in the appropriate place at the right moment in order to create an overwhelming advantage.

If the disposition of offense is aligned with a weak disposition of defense, the enemy can exploit one's weaknesses and conquer one's forces instead. Therefore, in order to achieve victory, an army must be able to maintain both good defensive and offensive dispositions; there can be no room for error. Sun Tzu said, "One wins battle by making no mistakes. Making no mistakes establishes the victory." However, all the conditions for an easy victory should be prepared before the war, rather than during the war. Sun Tzu said that, "Winners only go to war when they are fully prepared and certain of their victory. On the contrary, losers go to war blindly without adequate preparation."[1] Good generals are those who excel in winning with ease.

4.1.2 Two Factors of Creating an Overwhelming Tactical Disposition

Strong physical support is required to formulate effective tactical disposition. Sun Tzu compared a victorious army to pent-up water crashing a thousand fathoms into a valley.[2] The strong physical support of the military force is compared to the weight of water. The weight combined with the speed results in great power. Without massive weight, water will hit the ground with relatively less force even if it is positioned thousands of fathoms high. Similarly, without a strong military force, the threat posed to the enemy will have limited effects. Therefore, to use dispositional strategy to its best effect, one must first strengthen one's army as a precondition.

Sun Tzu argued that the strength of a nation's military force is largely determined by its national resources. Specifically, the size of a nation's land determines the amount of resources it can devote to war, such as the number of soldiers, weapons, and other equipment. Then, the military strength largely influences the chance of victory in war. The comparison of military strength between one and one's enemy helps the general decide whether to defend or attack and then establish the appropriate defensive and offensive dispositions. Sun Tzu said, "Standing on the defensive position indicates insufficient strength; attacking requires overwhelming strength." This is because an attack usually requires more military force than defense. In the previous chapter, we saw how Sun Tzu estimated that "if one's army is ten times the enemy's, surround them; if five, attack them; if twice, divide one's army into two; if equal to the enemy, engage them; if fewer, circumvent them; and if outmatched, avoid them." Therefore,

---

[1] The Chinese characters are: 勝兵先勝而後求戰, 敗兵先戰而後求勝.

[2] The original Chinese text expresses the height of the valley as 1,000 ren, a traditional Chinese unit, and this is approximately equal to one fathom. 1 fathom = 6 feet = 1.8 m.

one should make all efforts to enhance military strength, rather than pursuing victory by chance.

However, Sun Tzu's emphasis on military strength does not mean that it is the sole determinant of victory, but an important factor that should not be neglected. The effective use of military force is another important factor in determining victory in war. In the chapter "Tactical Disposition," Sun Tzu emphasized the location and allocation of one's forces. Even if one possesses an inferior military force in absolute terms, one can still achieve victory if one can ensure that one's force at a key position is superior to that of the enemy. For example, a well-positioned army, proportioned and concentrated in appropriate focal points, can obtain an upper hand over the enemy, even if the enemy is numerically and quantitatively greater.

4.2 PORTER: GENERIC STRATEGY FOR ADVANTAGEOUS POSITIONING

A firm's profitability may rise over, fall below, or stay around the industry's average level, depending on its strategic positioning in the industry. A firm in a good position may earn high rates of return, even if the industrial structure is unfavorable (Porter, 1980, 1985). In order to yield a superior return on investment, firms have to take defensive action to secure their advantageous position in the industry by skillfully coping with the five competitive forces (i.e., the five forces model) (Porter, 1980, 1985). Porter said the fundamental basis of above-average long-run performance is a sustainable competitive advantage. He then identified two basic types of competitive advantage: cost and differentiation. These two combined with the scope of activities lead to three generic strategies – cost leadership, differentiation, and focus. These strategies give rise to three alternative industry positionings to outperform rivals. Porter (1985) later subdivided the focus strategy into two variants – cost focus and differentiation focus – thereby producing a total of four generic strategies. In the following paragraphs, each strategy will be explained in detail.

Cost Leadership Cost advantage comes from different sources depending on the industry structure. However, a cost leader cannot ignore the bases of differentiation, which Porter named as parity or proximity in differentiation (Porter, 1980). It means that the firm pursuing cost leadership should also be able to meet the minimum quality standards of products in order to satisfy consumer needs. In addition, since the firm's breath of activities is also important for maintaining cost advantage, firms often retain a broad array of activities and participate in more than one industrial segment or even in different industries. If there is more than one cost leader in an industry, the competition will become fierce and profitability will decrease.

Differentiation By differentiating themselves from other competitors within the industry (e.g., enhancing product quality), firms can charge a premium price. In order for a differentiation strategy to be sustainable and effective, the price premium must exceed the cost of differentiation. Similar to cost leadership, firms that carry out differentiation strategy also provide a variety of products or services. In addition, a differentiator cannot ignore its cost position, otherwise premium prices will be nullified by excessively high cost position. Porter (1980) called this parity or proximity in cost. In contrast to cost leadership, more than one successful firm with differentiation strategy may coexist in an industry.

Focus Unlike cost leadership and differentiation strategies, firms employing this strategy limit their participation to a narrow competitive scope within an industry. A firm with differentiation focus pursues a differentiation advantage in its target segment, and a firm with cost focus strategy pursues a cost advantage in its target segment. Therefore, focus strategy aims to exploit the special needs of buyers in certain segments. Both differentiation focus and cost focus strategies depend on the differences between the firm's capabilities of meeting their target segments in the industry. Competitors targeting a broad range of industry segments would have difficulty competing against firms with focus strategy in the segments.

Porter warned that unless carefully designed to be sustainable, implementing generic strategy would make the firm vulnerable to different types of attacks and fail to yield above-average performance. For example, as the industry grows, the industry competitive forces may change, and the bargaining power of firms may decrease. Firms are always vulnerable to attack from new entrants into the industry or established competitors seeking reposition. These changes will threaten the firms' competitive position of the existing generic strategy. Porter (1980, 1985) listed potential risks that may result from using generic strategies as shown in Table 4.1. On the other hand, by understanding the risks or weaknesses of each generic strategy listed in Table 4.1, a firm may gain insights on how to attack its competitors.

Thus, to avoid challenges from other firms and generate a sustainable competitive advantage, a firm should prevent other firms from imitating its strategy by building barriers, which can be created by partaking in continuous investment to improve its current position. On the other hand, for successful implementation of the offensive strategy, the challenger should satisfy the following three requirements (Porter, 1985). First, the challenger should possess competitive advantages, either cost or differentiation, against a leader. For example, if the leader's advantage is low cost, the challenger should provide an even lower price than the leader. Second, the challenger should be able to neutralize the leader's other advantages. For example, when offering a product at a lower cost than the existing leader, the challenger should maintain the product quality at the same or higher level than that of the competing products; otherwise, the leader will easily counter by simply lowering the price. Third, the challenger should also have some means to constrain the leader from retaliating; if not, it may have to suffer from potentially overwhelming retaliation by the existing industry leader.

Over time, however, firms may change their strategic positionings as they grow. To explain this evolution, I extended Porter's generic strategies in a more dynamic way (Moon, 1993), suggesting two alternative ways for firms to upgrade their current competitive positions and

Table 4.1 *Risks of generic strategies*

Risks of Cost Leadership	Risks of Differentiation	Risks of Focus
Cost leadership is not sustained • Competitors imitate • Technology changes • Other bases for cost leadership erode	Differentiation is not sustained • Competitors imitate • Bases for differentiation become less important to buyers	The focus strategy is imitated The target segment becomes structurally unattractive • Structure erodes • Demand disappears
Proximity in differentiation is lost	Cost proximity is lost	Broadly targeted competitors overwhelm the segment • The segment's differences from other segments narrow • The advantages of a broad line increase
Cost focusers achieve even lower cost in segments	Differentiation focusers achieve even greater differentiation in segments	New focusers sub-segment the industry

Source: Porter (1985), p. 21.

sustain their competitive advantages (see Figure 4.1). When a new firm enters an industry, it usually cannot effectively compete with its established competitors on the grounds of technology, capital, management skills, and experience. Therefore, the new firm will usually choose cost focus as its initial competitive strategy. As the new entrant gradually accumulates additional capital, experience, professional knowledge, and

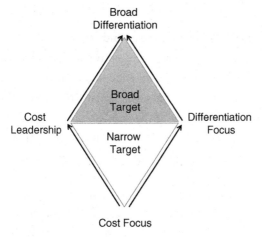

FIGURE 4.1 Dynamic model of Porter's generic strategies
Source: Moon (1993).

other necessary resources, its strategy will then move on to either a differentiation focus or cost leadership. After this stage, firms will further step into broad differentiation. Hence, this framework (i.e., dynamic evolution of generic strategies) has extended Porter's generic strategies by explaining how one strategy shifts to another as the firm develops from a lower to higher stage.

4.3   THE INTEGRATION OF SUN TZU AND PORTER

Sun Tzu's "easy victory" strategy is about taking a domineering disposition for defense and offense to subdue the enemy easily. Porter's generic strategy is concerned with securing an attractive position in the industry to effectively compete against the industry competitive forces, thereby obtaining a high rate of return. There is a similarity between these two strategies as they both aim to effectively penetrate a target (i.e., an enemy or a market) or defend oneself from outside attacks, through a strategic positioning. In the following sections, I will further explore the linkages between Sun Tzu and Porter's strategies.

4.3.1 Disposition of Defense versus Four Generic Strategies

Sun Tzu distinguished between defense- and offense-related tactical dispositions for easy victory. What is interesting is that Sun Tzu gave higher priority to the disposition of defense. He believed that before concerning oneself with offense plans, one must first ensure that one will not be defeated by the enemy. If the defense is strong enough, the enemy will not dare to attack. Even if the enemy attacks, one will still be able to protect oneself. For this reason, Sun Tzu repeatedly emphasized the importance of sufficient preparation in his chapter "Tactical Disposition." Especially, Sun Tzu suggested that one should make sure that one's defensive weaknesses are not exposed to the enemy. Defense, unlike offense, has little to do with what the enemy does; thus preventing defeat is entirely one's own responsibility.

In the business field, firms have to possess a particular competitive advantage in order to survive in severe competition. Competitive advantage can also be viewed as the firm's core competence and is the precondition for the firm to earn profits. According to Porter, the four types of generic strategy reflect firms' ability to achieve competitive advantages against competitors. This is because by gaining a competitive position in the industry, firms can exercise market power and earn monopoly rents (Spanos and Lioukas, 2001). Therefore, Sun Tzu's defense disposition strategy and Porter's generic strategies share the common core idea.

Yet one point of deviation lies in Sun Tzu's emphasis on concealing one's disposition of defense, which is not considered in generic strategies. Nevertheless, when faced with pressure from numerous competitors on various occasions, firms will experience difficulty in countering every attack. Thus, it would be important for firms to discourage other firms from attacking them by making the industry appear less attractive or highly retaliatory, as short-term prescriptions. For long-term survival and prosperity, however, a firm must continuously commit to upgrading its competitive advantage. This long-term strategy can be linked to Sun Tzu's disposition of offense, which will be further explained in the next section.

4.3.2 Disposition of Offense versus Sustaining Competitive Advantage

Sun Tzu said in order to defeat the enemy, one has to attack the enemy. Thus, strategy of tactical disposition is comprised of both defense and offense strategies. However, Sun Tzu pinpointed that the attack should never be the product of an impulse. Instead, he asserted that a successful attack requires the possession of two things: a well-trained, robust military force and a thorough understanding of the enemy's weaknesses. A strong military force is required because successful offense requires greater military capabilities than defense. Therefore, before initiating the attack, one should check whether one possesses the capability and necessary resources to fight. Yet, no matter how strong one's army is, if the enemy is not a complete weakling, engaging in an open battle with them would be a dangerous and wasteful act. If one has not yet found the enemy's weaknesses, one should wait for the enemy to make mistakes or induce the enemy to do so. However, one cannot entirely rely on or expect the enemy to make mistakes as one hopes. Therefore, according to Sun Tzu, it is the enemy who determines the certainty of one's victory, as one's successful attack depends on the conditions and strategies of the enemy.

A choice of generic strategy in business, on the other hand, provides only a temporary cure against vigorous attacks from competitors and does not guarantee a sustained competitive advantage in the long run. Continuous upgrade is necessary for a firm to achieve sustained predominance in the industry. Sometimes, a firm will have no other choice but to duel the industry's incumbent leaders. However, industry leaders are likely to have a strong defense system of their own and the capability to mobilize resources for retaliation against challengers. Therefore, posing a direct challenge against a leader is a risky strategy. Similar to how Sun Tzu advocated attacking the enemy's weak points, Porter suggested entering the market underserved by the incumbent leaders, instead of directly confronting them, to increase one's chance of winning.

However, there is one fundamental difference between business and war in terms of pursuing an aggressive strategy. Sun Tzu emphasized defeating the enemy by creating favorable conditions for attack (i.e., finding the enemy's weaknesses or inducing mistakes). If collapse of the enemy is one's goal in war, one should find the enemy's weaknesses by inducing their mistakes and losses. However, bankrupting competitors is not the goal in business. There is a fine line between pursuing one's own prosperity by not hurting a rival firm and pursing the destruction of a rival firm by taking away its profits. This distinction is possible, because in business one is not fighting over a narrowly defined trophy, such as land, but an expandable pie of values.

Therefore, even though Sun Tzu is quite revolutionary in his considerations of making the war profitable, Porter's ideas of offenseive strategy are far more constructive, as he suggests tackling the market by increasing one's own competitiveness through providing better quality and better priced goods and services to the consumers, instead of ripping them off or depriving them by destroying rival firms. In fact, when a firm strives to enhance its competitiveness, it may eventually fill the gap between previously offered goods and new goods for better serving the consumers while not necessarily exploiting other firms' weaknesses. Therefore, firms compete not to force their rivals out of the market, but to pursue a better position in an industry, where market players can prosper simultaneously. This is particularly true for firms competing with differentiation strategy, since there could be more than one winner in an industry or an industry segment.

4.4   MILITARY CASE: SOVIETS' VICTORY IN THE BATTLE OF STALINGRAD

The battle of Stalingrad took place between July 17, 1942, and February 2, 1943, during Germany's invasion of the Soviet Union.[3] Following the failure of Operation Barbarossa in the spring of 1942,

[3]   Information for this case study is abstracted and modified from www.jewishvirtualli brary.org/jsource/ww2/Stalingrad.html, and www.2worldwar2.com/stalingrad.htm.

Germany ordered its Army Group South to head toward Baku's rich oil fields. However, at some point during the progression, Hitler divided the Army Group South into two subgroups, with the first still heading toward Baku and the second aiming for Stalingrad (the Sixth Army). There were two main reasons for targeting Stalingrad: it was a key communication network center, and its factories produced a large number of weapons for the Soviet army.

The Germans' attack began with aerial bombardments of defensive fortifications along the Volga River. Between July 25 and July 31, 1942, thirty-two Soviet ships were sunk and nine were seriously damaged. Approximately a thousand tons of bombs were deployed, which damaged about 80 percent of the city's structures. The Soviet air force was driven away and forced to withdraw its control of the skies. However, Stalin disallowed civilians from leaving the city with the hope that their presence would encourage greater resistance from the city's defenders. Some factories survived and continued to produce military supplies while the workers joined in the fighting. Civilians, including women and children, were mobilized to build trenches and protective fortifications. Germany's ground forces reached the River Volga on August 23, 1942, and launched their first ground assaults on the city on September 13. German forces battled their way through the city to reach the banks of the river Volga, and by the beginning of November, they were able to control 90 percent of Stalingrad.

However, the Germans were then running critically short of ammunition and food. Despite these problems, General Paulus (Sixth Army commander) decided to order another major attack on November 10. The German army took heavy casualties for the next two days as the Soviet army launched a counterattack. Paulus was forced to retreat southward, but when his army reached Gumrak Airfield, Hitler ordered them to stop and stand fast despite the danger of encirclement. To make matters worse, General Paulus had committed most of his best troops to the city, leaving his flanks defended by Romanian, Hungarian, and Italian troops. The Soviet army recognized the vulnerability of the German flank and launched a counterattack on November 19, 1942.

By December, Germany's incoming supplies decreased to around 70 tons a day, when the encircled German army actually needed a minimum of 300 tons a day. Recognizing that the Sixth Army was in danger of being starved to death, Hitler ordered Field Marshal Erich von Manstein and the fourth Panzer Army to launch a rescue attempt. Manstein managed to get to within 30 miles of Stalingrad but was brought to a halt by the Red Army. In Stalingrad, over 28,000 German soldiers died in just a month. On January 30, 1943, Hitler promoted Paulus to field marshal and sent a message reminding him that no German field marshal had ever been captured. Hitler was clearly suggesting Paulus to commit suicide, but he refused and surrendered to the Red Army on the following day. The last German troops surrendered on February 2. The battle for Stalingrad ended in the Soviets' victory, leading to over 91,000 Germans being captured and an additional 150,000 deaths from the siege.

The Germans' defeat in the Eastern Front became a turning point in World War II, as it marked the end of Germany's legend of invincibility. It was also one of the bloodiest battles during the whole course of the war, with total casualties reaching up to two million people. How did the Soviets defeat the German troops, who had been so successful until the Battle of Stalingrad? We can analyze the Soviet victory by using Sun Tzu's strategy of tactical disposition.

Recall Sun Tzu's teachings that securing oneself against getting defeated lies in one's own hands, but the opportunity of defeating the enemy depends on the enemy's conditions and capabilities. Faced with the unexpected attack from Germany, the Soviets lacked time for preparation. However, the Soviet troops did not simply evacuate. Stalin gave an order to defend the city at all costs, down to the last man. Sun Tzu also said that generals win the battle by making no mistakes and making no mistakes establishes the victory. In order to maintain the initiative in Stalingrad, the Germans poured more and more troops into the city, leaving their flanks covered by weak Romanian and other foreign forces. Thus, the Soviet army was able to exploit the weakness and launch a counter attack on the weak point.

Furthermore, Hitler made a fatal mistake when he promoted the Sixth Army's general. Although the intention was to force him to fight to the death, the disappointed German commander surrendered to the Russians shortly thereafter. Another serious mistake was that Germans did not adequately prepare for winter battle, as they were overly confident about their ability to end the war and return before long. They lacked much of the necessary equipment and foods to survive the winter. One can easily see how the Soviets took advantage of Germany's mistakes and crushed the invasion successfully.

However, the Soviet victory was not just a product of chance, bestowed by the enemy's mistakes. They purposely prolonged the campaign to wear down their superior foes and build up their strengths to respond with a strong counterattack. These activities can be better explained by Porter's concept of upgrading current competitive advantages to sustain the firm's attractive position. Although Sun Tzu also mentioned the importance of military strength when initiating an attack against the enemy, Sun Tzu's concept is relatively passive and dependent on inherited factors such as the endowment of natural resources.

In addition, business competition offers more room for flexibility than war situations. In business, one must calculate the cost and benefit from investment. If the cost exceeds the benefit, the best strategy is disinvestment. Therefore, in business, the CEO has options for maintaining the business or giving it up when he is attacked by a challenger. However, warfare sometimes simply leaves no alternative, but to defend to the death. For example, in the battle of Stalingrad, due to the strategic position and symbolic importance of the city, the Soviets had to protect their territory without the option of surrendering.

4.5   BUSINESS CASE: TOYOTA'S CHANGING POSITION IN THE AUTOMOBILE INDUSTRY

The Toyota Motor Corporation is a global company headquartered in Japan.[4] Toyota was founded in 1933 as a division of Toyota Automatic Loom Works and was reorganized as an independent company in 1937. Toyota began to penetrate into foreign markets in the late 1950s, and after sixty years, it has emerged as the world's largest automobile manufacturer in terms of sales volume. Porter's generic strategies and offensive strategy well explain Toyota's success, particularly in the US market.

Toyota launched its first prototype model, the AA passenger car, in 1936 in the Japanese market, by applying the manufacturing process adopted from Ford Motor Company. For many years, Toyota continued to focus on small-sized cars with low-cost productions. Until the 1950s, the production scale of Toyota was much smaller than that of US automakers. For example, the number of cars manufactured by Toyota was only one-twentieth of the US company, General Motors (GM). However, due to the two oil crises in the 1970s, US consumers suddenly turned to small cars with better fuel efficiency. US car manufacturers had previously viewed small economy cars to be entry-level products that entailed relatively lower quality to maintain low prices. Although they began downsizing their products after the first oil crisis in 1973, US carmakers still mostly focused on producing large cars. Moreover, US automakers did not pay much attention to quality and design improvements, because they were able to maintain high profits without them. Furthermore, the US mass-production system made it expensive to invest in innovation for new models.

In contrast, Toyota continuously invested in improving the quality and efficiency of its production system. Toyota attributed its success in cost leadership to some operational techniques such as the

---

[4]   Information for this case study is abstracted and modified from Moon (2010), Toyota USA Newsroom, Automotive News, and BBC news.

just-in-time (JIT).[5] The JIT production system was a revolutionary movement and substantially increased the productivity of the automobile industry. By significantly reducing the time and cost of production, and differentiating its products in quality and features, Toyota was able to occupy a substantially enhanced position in the market. US carmakers did not expect that small, fuel-efficient Japanese cars could be produced at good quality and a reasonable price. Hence, when the US market itself shifted its demand to small and fuel-efficient cars, US carmakers could not respond quickly enough, thereby opening the way for Japanese firms to dominate the market. In the 1980s, imports of Japanese cars increased dramatically. US carmakers eventually benchmarked Toyota's lean production system but were unable to achieve the success of Japanese automakers. Womack, Jones, and Roos (1990) remarked, "Lean production: it is easy to say you will do it, but harder to actually implement it."

Toyota further improved its product quality, and as a result, it received its first Japanese Quality Control Award in the 1980s. In the 1990s, Toyota began to branch out by adding several larger and more luxurious vehicles to its lineup, including Lexus in 1989. Toyota also began producing the world's best-selling hybrid car, the Prius, in 1997, and ever since then the company has been the leader in hybrid passenger cars. Toyota further developed its own fuel-efficient and clean energy technology. In 2012, it introduced the Prius Plug-in Hybrid, which combined the benefits of the standard Prius' hybrid vehicle operation with extended electric vehicle at a more affordable price than pure electric vehicles. As a result, while sustaining its competitive advantage of low cost, Toyota was able to continuously create an additional value for the buyer.

---

[5] JIT is a set of techniques to improve manufacturing efficiency by reducing inventory and associated carrying costs. A finished automobile consists of about 30,000 parts, and therefore, it is necessary to create a plan for firms to know "which part is needed, when it is needed, and how many are needed." Toyota borrowed the idea from the "supermarket method," which uses product control cards to collect information such as a product's name, code, and storage location. Similarly, Toyota adopted the *kanban* signs in their production processes to communicate which parts have been used (Toyota Motor Corporate website).

On the other hand, US automakers ignored environmental concerns with increasing oil prices in the 1980s and 1990s, focusing on the production of sport utility vehicles to counter Japanese threats. At that time, the sport utility vehicles were protected by high import tariffs and less regulated by government rules on carbon emissions. The US firms' strategic mistake again caused them to lose ground in the hybrid car market, with further losses in the US and global market shares.

The US firms' failure and Toyota's success in the US auto market can be well explained using Porter's generic strategy model. Before the oil crisis, US firms enjoyed high bargaining power against market competitive forces and exploited high profits. However, as Porter suggested, the firms had to face the risks of external factors eroding away the advantages of generic strategy. In this case, it was the changes in consumer demand that reshaped the industry structure of large cars, facing the oil crisis, less attractive. On the other hand, Toyota successfully attacked the vulnerable small and fuel-efficient car market. Toyota's production system was able to fend off US firms' imitation attempts. Furthermore, rather than being complacent with these series of successes, Toyota also continued to expand over the years from a cost focus to broad differentiation strategy.[6] Toyota not only defended, but also continuously penetrated into new markets in order to upgrade its competitive position. In particular, Toyota's early environmental concerns allowed it to gain a competitive advantage in hybrid cars, successfully transforming it from a follower to a leader.[7]

However, there are other explanatory factors, which can be found from Sun Tzu's strategies. The first is "timing." Porter suggested attacking the vulnerable leader, but did not elaborate on "when" to attack. The oil crisis in 1973 was an opportune moment

---

[6] This strategic change can be better explained by the dynamic evolution of generic strategies (Moon, 1993).

[7] Porter's generic strategy is also helpful for explaining the US firms' failure in responding to the industry change.

for Japanese carmakers to enter the US market. Before the oil crisis, small Japanese cars were not taken seriously and mainly purchased for high school graduation gifts. For example, in 1969 Honda's first automobile sold in Hawaii was the N600. In 1970, the car was exported to California and other areas, but its tiny 600cc engine and very small dimensions were unpopular among the US public.[8] However, as the oil price jumped dramatically, the US consumers began to seek more fuel-efficient cars. Had the oil crisis not occurred, Toyota would have had to wait even longer to enter the US market. Toyota and other Japanese carmakers also benefited from the economic boom in the 1980s by introducing luxury cars that offered lower prices than their European counterparts and better technology than their US counterparts. Hence, the 1970s oil crises and the US economic boom in the 1980s can be regarded as "the opportunity for defeating the enemy" mentioned by Sun Tzu.

The second is "eliminating mistakes." Sun Tzu said, "Making no mistakes establishes the victory." Although the oil crises and shifting demand for smaller cars contributed a large portion of Toyota's success, the US firms still made several mistakes in improving quality and seizing small car market segments. If the US firms had learned a lesson after the first oil crisis in the mid-1970s and improved their production systems, the results would have been much different.

4.6 CONCLUSION AND IMPLICATIONS

In the chapter "Tactical Disposition" of *The Art of War*, Sun Tzu emphasized winning with ease. Two key points to remember are, first, in order to achieve such a victory, one must first prepare invincibility. A good fighter then puts himself into a position that makes being defeated impossible. Hence, if one is defeated by the enemy, it is not because of the enemy, but because of oneself. Then second, one should attack the enemy's weaknesses. If there is no weak point to be found from the enemy, one needs to create the conditions for the

---

[8]   The information is abstracted and modified from www.anythingaboutcars.com/1960s-foreign-cars.html.

enemy to make mistakes and wait for the appropriate time and place to attack. Therefore, one can anticipate but not absolutely guarantee a victory, as the second condition is determined by the enemy's will, which is not controllable by oneself.

Sun Tzu's strategy for an easy victory through well-designed defensive and offensive dispositions can be linked to Porter's strategy. Specifically, Sun Tzu's defensive dispositions match Porter's generic strategies, as both share the similarity in emphasizing the defense perspective – defending against the rivals and surviving from severe competition. However, in contrast to Sun Tzu's warnings against the internal factors concerning the possibility of defense failure, Porter pointed fingers toward external risks, which can erode a firm's competitive positioning. On the other hand, Sun Tzu's offensive disposition is linked to Porter's strategy for upgrading one's competitive advantages.

Porter's concept of upgrading one's competitive advantages (or dynamic perspective) can complement Sun Tzu's strategy for tactical disposition of offense, as Sun Tzu's strategy mainly emphasizes the mistakes of the enemy. The concept of upgrade is particularly useful in explaining the Soviet victory in the military case. In addition to prolonging the battle and exhausting the enemy, the Soviets made efforts to build up their military strengths. On the other hand, Sun Tzu's strategy also provides meaningful implications for business strategy, as shown in the case of Toyota's success and the US firms' loss of market share in the US auto industry. The declining competitive position of the US automakers was not only due to the changing business environments (e.g., the entrance by Toyota and changing the US consumer needs), but also to the US firms' own mistakes (e.g., late response to the market change). Along with continuous investment to upgrade a competitive position in the market (as suggested by Porter), the timing of entering a market segment or attacking competitors is also important (as suggested by Sun Tzu).

5　Enhanced Advantage

Sun Tzu:　Synergies from the combination of *Cheng* (normal) and *Chi* (abnormal)

Porter:　Distinguishing Operational Effectiveness (OE) and Strategic Positioning (SP)

The Chinese word, *Shih*, the title of the chapter "Enhanced Energy" in Sun Tzu's book, can be interpreted as "situation" or "power." Sun Tzu gave a poetic description of what he means by *Shih*: "the rush of a torrent, which rolls stones along its course" and "the momentum of a round stone, which rolls down a mountain from thousands of feet in height." The symbols of "the rush of a torrent" and "the momentum of a round stone" are strongly suggestive of enhanced energy, which does not get exhausted, but only grows, when it is used. A more tangible example of *Shih* would be the power of psychological unity created by raising the morale of the army; and the psychological unity reinforces the heightened morale to a higher level, turning the generation of *Shih* into a self-intensifying system much like the torrent rolling heavy stones on its course. When one's army is able to form *Shih*, one can defeat the larger and seemingly stronger enemy.

The chapter "Enhanced Energy" of *The Art of War* revolves around *Cheng* and *Chi* – two forces that create *Shih*. *Cheng* refers to the normal, regular, or general military methods for handling the enemy, whereas *Chi* refers to special, unusual, or irregular methods, aimed at confusing the enemy's understanding of one's disposition and intentions. One must appropriately combine the two to create and exploit the vital force of *Shih* in order to win the war. Sun Tzu's *Cheng* and *Chi* can be compared to Porter's operational effectiveness (OE) and strategic positioning (SP). Unlike the military theory of *Shih*, in which Sun Tzu emphasized the combination of *Cheng* and *Chi* by giving the same weights for both, Porter's business version has the limitation of favoring one element (i.e., SP) over another (i.e., OE) – thus overlooking the crucial effect of the two working in tandem. In this chapter, I will demonstrate the significance level of OE and SP for different development stages and the effectiveness of combining them for the creation of strategic advantage, similar to how Sun Tzu's *Shih* is generated through the combination of *Cheng and Chi*. The military case of the Vietnam War and the business case of Walmart will be used as examples to show why both elements must be used in combination.

5.1 SUN TZU: SYNERGIES FROM THE COMBINATION OF CHENG (NORMAL) AND CHI (ABNORMAL)

Shih is like one side of the coin with *Hsing* on the other side. *Hsing*, the title of the chapter "Tactical Disposition," pertains to physical capability maximized by adroit and timely arrangement of troop disposition. *Shih* is about enhancing military performance by utilizing the psychological element to maximum effect. *Hsing* and *Shih* are also interdependent. *Hsing* refers to the object that is moving, whereas *Shih* is its movement. *Hsing* is the basis of *Shih*, and *Shih* is the revealed power and effects of moving *Hsing*. Yet, the creation of *Shih* depends on the general's ability to combine and exploit the advantages of *Cheng* and *Chi*. Sun Tzu claimed that an army can gain a victory by properly maneuvering *Cheng* and *Chi*. In the following section, I will explain the definitions of *Cheng* and *Chi* as well as the relationship between the two.

5.1.1 *Definition of* Cheng *and* Chi

As Daoism is the philosophical base of Sun Tzu's military thinking, his theories often stem from the concepts of paradoxes and counterbalances (also known as *yin* and *yang*). Sun Tzu's theory of *Cheng* and *Chi* is a good example. Scholars throughout history have had numerous versions of interpretations regarding *Cheng* and *Chi* (see Table 5.1). Sawyer's (2005) translation of *Cheng* as "orthodox" and *Chi* as "unorthodox" is widely used but not universally accepted (Bartholomees Jr., 2008). According to the Oxford dictionary,

Table 5.1 *Explanations of* Cheng *and* Chi

	Study	Explanations	Translation (*Cheng* vs. *Chi*)
1	Li Ch'uan	Facing the enemy is *Cheng*; whereas making lateral diversion is *Chi*.	Straight forwardness vs. lateral diversion
2	Chia Lin	In presence of the enemy, your troops should be arrayed in normal fashion, but in order to secure victory abnormal maneuvers must be employed.	Normal vs. abnormal
3	Mei Yao-ch'en	*Chi* is active, whereas *Cheng* is passive; passivity means waiting for an opportunity	Passive vs. active
4	Ho Shih	We must cause the enemy to regard our straightforward attack as one that is secretly designed, and vice versa; thus *Cheng* may also be *Chi*, *Chi* may also be *Cheng*	Straightforward vs. secret (unexpected)
5	Wei Liao Tzu	Direct warfare favors frontal attacks, whereas indirect warfare attacks from the rear.	Direct vs. indirect
6	Cao Cao	Going straight out to join a battle is a direct operation; appearing on the enemy's rear is an indirect maneuver.	Direct vs. indirect
7	Sawyer (2005)	"Orthodox" tactics employ troops in normal, conventional, and therefore predictable ways; "unorthodox" tactics stress flexibility, imagination, and surprise.	Orthodox vs. unorthodox

Source: Machiavelli (2007), Sawyer (2005).[1]

[1]   The explanations for numbers 1 to 6 were provided by Chinese ancient scholars on Sun Tzu's *The Art of War*: Li Ch'uan and Chia Lin (Tang dynasty), Mei Yao-ch'en (North Song Dynasty), Ho Shih (Song Dynasty), Cao Cao (Three Kingdoms). For more details about them, refer to Minford (2008). Wei Liao Tzu is a military classic of ancient China, written during the Warring States Period but the author is unknown.

"orthodox" refers to "a person or the view of religious or political ones, or other beliefs or practices," conforming to what is generally or traditionally accepted as true, established, and approved. On the other hand, "unorthodox" refers to the extraordinary – the opposite of the word orthodox.

As suggested by many notable commentators on Sun Tzu's *The Art of War*, *Cheng* operations can be best described as straightforward, direct, or expected action. On the contrary, *Chi* operations involve extraordinary, unexpected, or creative maneuvers. Therefore, it would be more appropriate to translate *Cheng* as "normal," which means conforming to standard, usual, typical, or expected, and *Chi* as "abnormal," which refers to deviating from what is normal or usual (Oxford dictionary).

Each of *Cheng* and *Chi* strategies has its own strengths and weaknesses. The systematic characteristic of *Cheng* strategy offers greater stability than *Chi* strategy, but it is also limited by its easy predictability. As most *Cheng* strategies, or normal strategies, are ones that have been established over time and tested, they tend to be more systematic, credible, and reliable methods of military operation. However, their much-institutionalized character also makes them predictable and recognizable by the enemy. Thus, relying on *Cheng* involves the risk of falling into the enemy's trap or encountering well-prepared counterattack.

Chi strategies, or abnormal strategies, reduce such predictability and allow one to take the enemy by surprise. Thus, successful use of *Chi* allows one to snatch decisive victory in a swift manner. For example, the US decision to use atomic weapons brought a dramatic end to World War II and prevented further loss of lives and resources. If the United States had continued with its conventional warfare against Japan, the war might have been much longer and bloodier, benefitting no one. However, *Chi* strategies come with their own risks due to their unpredictability and the abnormal characteristics. Therefore, one should not simply over-rely on *Chi* alone, but combine it with *Cheng* in order to reduce the risks and enhance the probability of the victory.

Liddell Hart's (1954) idea of "indirect approach" is congruent with Sun Tzu's *Chi* strategy. In his book titled *Strategy*, Hart said, "I began to realize that the indirect approach had a much wider application ... the direct assault ... provokes a stubborn resistance, thus intensifying the difficulty of producing a change of outlook. Conversion is achieved more easily and rapidly by unsuspected infiltration of a different idea." Here indirect approach refers to any move that imposes the psychological or physical shock due to surprise (Danchev, 1998). Sun Tzu's concept of *Chi* predominantly concerns the tactical disposition of troops, because during Sun Tzu's time, technology was mostly homogenous and did not play a large role in determining military capacity.

5.1.2 *Relationship between* Cheng *and* Chi

According to Sun Tzu, "Generally in a battle, one engages with the normal (*Cheng*) and gains victory through the abnormal (*Chi*)."[2] However, this statement does not necessarily imply that either one is superior to the other. Instead, it signifies the interdependency of *Cheng* and *Chi*. Sun Tzu said that *Cheng* should be paired with *Chi*, and *Chi* should be based on *Cheng*. If *Cheng* is weak, the effects of *Chi* will also be weakened, and the entire situation will become difficult to control. In contrast, if *Chi* is misused, it will also negatively affect *Cheng* maneuvers.

Moreover, according to Sun Tzu, *Cheng* and *Chi* are mutually interchangeable. *Cheng* maneuvers can be *Chi*, and *Chi* maneuvers can be *Cheng* as well. The emperor of the Tang dynasty, Tang Tai Tsung gave a good explanation for the transition between the two maneuvers: "A *Chi* strategy may become *Cheng*, if we make the enemy look upon it as *Cheng*, and vice versa. The whole secret lies in confusing the enemy, so that they cannot know our real intention" (Minford, 2008). For example, during the period of the Three Kingdoms, Zhu Geliang utilized the "empty fort strategy" (*Chi*) as a

---

[2]   The Chinese characters are: 凡戰者, 以正合, 以奇勝.

Cheng maneuver to save a town. The enemy, which was several times larger than Zhu Geliang's, approached the town where Zhu Geliang's army resided. Instead of fleeing or fighting directly with the enemy, Zhu Geliang ordered the gate opened as he sat in a conspicuous position and played the *guqin*, a traditional Chinese musical instrument. When the enemy observed the situation, they believed there was an ambush waiting for them and thus retreated instead of attacking. Zhu Geliang's deception was a *Chi* strategy, but as the enemy perceived it to be *Cheng*, it became so.

Although Sun Tzu categorized all strategies into two types – *Cheng* and *Chi* – he asserted one can create countless variations by combining *Cheng* and *Chi*. This implies that in a military campaign, there is no fixed principle to follow. The general should first examine the situation of the battlefield and flexibly apply military principles according to changes in the situation. In other words, the theoretical principles can turn into an infinite number of variations in reality. Sun Tzu compared the limitless combinative possibilities of *Cheng* and *Chi* to the following examples: "The musical notes do not exceed five, but the changes of the five musical notes can never be fully heard. The colors do not exceed five, but the changes of the five colors can never be completely seen. The flavors do not exceed five, but the changes of the five can never be completely tasted."[3]

5.2 PORTER: DISTINGUISHING OPERATIONAL EFFECTIVENESS (OE) AND STRATEGIC POSITIONING (SP)

In his 1996 article "What is Strategy?" Porter introduced two concepts called Operational Effectiveness (OE) and Strategic Positioning (SP). OE refers to conducting activities similar to those of the rival firms, but more efficiently than the rivals. In addition to "efficiency," which

---

[3] The Chinese characters are: 聲不過五, 五聲之變, 不可勝聽也; 色不過五, 五色之變, 不可勝觀也; 味不過五, 五味之變, 不可勝嘗也. Five musical notes refer to Gong (宮), Shang (商), Jue (角), Zhi (徵), and Yu (羽) for the equivalent of do, re, mi, sol, and la; five colors are blue, yellow, red, white, and black; and five flavors include sourness, spiciness, saltiness, sweetness, and bitterness.

involves avoiding the waste of materials and energy, OE also requires better utilization of materials, reducing defects in products, and developing better products faster (Porter, 1996). An example of OE is Toyota's just-in-time (JIT) production system for achieving higher productivity and a lower rate of defective products. The JIT system had immense significance, as it helped Toyota gain an advantage over US carmakers. SP, on the other hand, involves performing different activities from rivals or performing similar activities in different ways. An example of SP is Tesla Motors, a producer of cars distinguished by its use of electricity unlike other existing automobiles using conventional fuels. Therefore, SP emphasizes being different and delivering a unique value to the consumers. Both OE and SP can help firms achieve superior profitability.

Porter argued that OE is a necessary means for a company to outperform rivals, but not a sufficient means. Although the individual firm adopting OE techniques may increase profits in the short run, it will become more difficult to maintain competitive advantages in the long run. This is because rivals in the industry can easily imitate the best practices of each other and such best practices quickly disperse throughout the industry. Therefore, the imitation of activities will make firms increasingly similar to each other, leading the companies to the path of mutually destructive price competition. In this regard, Porter stressed that the ultimate beneficiaries of using OE are customers and equipment suppliers. Take Ford's introduction of the assembly line for example. In the early twentieth century, Henry Ford introduced the standardized production processes. From then on, this new method quickly spread to other firms in the industry and served as a foundation for mass production and industrial growth, thereby negating any relative advantages among the firms of adopting such production system.

Accordingly, in order to outperform rivals while creating a win-win environment, it is essential for firms to have SP. Porter further claimed that SP, not OE, should be the central strategy of a firm. OE techniques will lead to zero-sum competition, which drags everybody

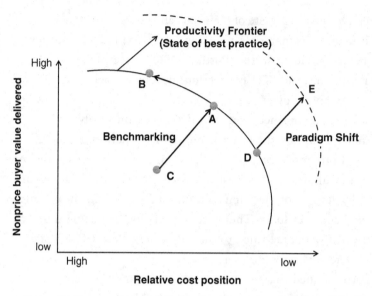

FIGURE 5.1 Operational effectiveness versus strategic positioning
Note: This figure is adapted from Porter (1996) and Moon (2010).

down. However, SP results in positive-sum competition, where firms can compete for different product attributes, customer targets, or product segments. Therefore, SP provides more choices for firms than OE. Since OE is a necessity and SP is a strategy, the difference between OE and SP is between what one must do, leaving no choice, and what one should do, providing room for choice (Prasad, 2010).

The distinction between OE and SP can be better understood by using the productivity frontier (see Figure 5.1). The productivity frontier represents the sum of the existing best practices. Porter said the strategies for cost and differentiation advantages involve a trade-off, where more of one thing necessitates less of the other. However, such trade-offs occur only when firms are located on the same productivity frontier line (Porter, 1996; Moon, 2010). In other words, if a firm at point A tries to shift its positioning to point B, it has to reduce its resources for cost advantage and increase those for differentiation advantage. These firms are usually from developed countries, while firms from developing countries are usually located under the

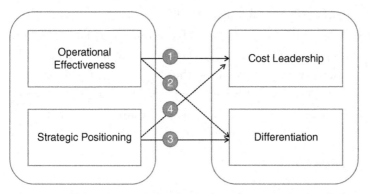

FIGURE 5.2 The relationship between OE-SP and cost-differentiation advantage
Note: This figure is adapted from Moon (2010).

productivity frontier (e.g., point C). There will be no trade-off between cost and differentiation, when the latecomers under the productivity frontier move from the lower to upper level (e.g., from C to A), or the first movers take off from the current state of the best practice (i.e., productivity frontier) to an even higher level (e.g., from D to E) (Porter, 1996; Moon, 2010). The act of moving from C to A can be classified as *benchmarking* (i.e., OE), while the act of moving from D to E can be called a *paradigm shift*. On the other hand, any point on the frontier can be a unique positioning (i.e., SP).

According to Porter (1996), cost advantage is derived more from OE, and differentiation is generated more from SP. However, a more comprehensive explanation on the relationship can be provided between OE-SP and cost-differentiation (Moon, 2010). Porter's view can be illustrated as the solid straight arrows (1 and 3) in Figure 5.2. The dotted arrows (2 and 4) show other possibilities, which Porter did not mention. In fact, SP can also lead to cost advantage. In fact, Porter's (1996) examples for three strategic positionings (i.e., variety, needs, and access-based) all result in cost advantages. Therefore, OE and SP are the processes to achieve competitive advantage of either cost or differentiation.

Similarly, OE can also lead to differentiation advantage. For example, Apple achieved the competitive advantage of differentiation in the smartphone business partly through benchmarking (i.e., OE) existing product technologies such as the phone, camera, Internet, and music player. Therefore, although the process (or part of the entire process) relies on imitation or learning, the result can be an entirely new invention (i.e., differentiation) (Moon, 2016b).

5.3   THE INTEGRATION OF SUN TZU AND PORTER

In battles, all methods of defense or offense can be sorted into two categories, *Cheng* and *Chi*, and these two in combination give rise to an infinite series of enhanced advantages (i.e., *Shih*). Hence, they can be regarded as the strategic tools of *Shih*, which lead to victory in battle. Similarly, in business, the competitive advantage of cost and differentiation is generated from two fundamental methods, OE and SP. *Cheng* can be related to OE, and *Chi* to SP. In the following section, I will explain their comparability in greater extent.

5.3.1   *The Characteristics of* Cheng-Chi *and OE-SP*

As noted earlier, the normal and regular military methods of *Cheng*, mostly used for direct confrontation, easily expose one's plans and moves to one's enemy. In business, OE involves engaging in similar activities better than rivals, which will definitely lead to direct competition with existing competitors. In this regard, *Cheng* is similar to OE, as it is a direct attack or attack through normal means. In addition, as Sun Tzu argued that *Cheng* is the necessary maneuver for engaging with the enemy but cannot secure the victory, Porter also claimed that OE is necessary for securing short-term advantages, but not sufficient for long-term ones.

Unlike *Cheng*, *Chi* strategies adopt irregular or abnormal techniques for attack. Although *Chi* is based on general military principles, it often changes in accordance with the environment. *Chi* is particularly important in surprise attacks. In other words, engaging *Chi* often means to attack the place where the enemy does not expect to be attacked. Therefore, through *Chi*, one can achieve easy victory by avoiding bloody, direct confrontation. In business, SP involves engaging in different activities or similar activities in different ways. Similar to how *Chi* strategies reduce direct confrontation in comparison to using *Cheng*, firms using SP are less likely to be competing directly in the same area.

5.3.2 *The Dynamic Relationships between* Cheng-Chi *and* OE-SP

Sun Tzu's theory states that *Cheng* and *Chi* are not fixed concepts, but *Cheng* can become *Chi* depending on a circumstance, and vice versa. For example, what would be *Chi* could actually be *Cheng* if the enemy sees through one's *Chi* strategy. Similarly, in business, if SP strategy is imitated by competitors and spread throughout the industry, the existing distinctive positioning will disappear and become OE. In addition, *Cheng* and *Chi* are interdependent. They can be combined together to create an unending series of strategic advantages, and weakness in either *Cheng* or *Chi* will affect the effectiveness of the other.

In contrast, Porter argued that firms should secure SP for long-term competitive advantage because using OE will only benefit consumers and equipment suppliers, as firms engage in destructive competition. Thus, Porter preferred SP, while understating the importance of OE. However, while SP is appropriate for first-comers or leading industry incumbents, it will be risky and costly for followers. In general, as it is difficult for both leaders and followers to be specialists in all competences required for their business, it is more effective to acquire the necessary technologies and other resources from the outside if possible, instead of developing everything by themselves. Therefore, firms, particularly followers, should first adopt OE techniques to efficiently acquire the needed competences and secure SP later to build their competitive advantage.

On the other hand, due to the popularity of multi-function products (see the business case in Chapter 3 for more details of this concept), a firm, either first-mover or late-comer, can pursue OE and SP simultaneously, much like with *Cheng* and *Chi*. China's emerging smartphone maker Xiaomi is a good example. Unlike other smartphone producers, Xiaomi has its distinctive positioning in distributing its products (i.e., online distribution only) and it also has its own unique business model.[4] However, for the hardware of its smartphones, Xiaomi adopts OE techniques by benchmarking Apple's iPhone at a much lower production cost.

5.4   MILITARY CASE: THE US FAILURE IN THE VIETNAM WAR

The Vietnam War is a military conflict that occurred throughout the territories of Vietnam, Laos, and Cambodia from 1955 to 1975.[5] This war followed the first Indochina War and was fought between North Vietnam, supported by communist allies, and South Vietnam, supported by the United States and other anticommunist nations. The United States and the South Vietnamese forces relied on air superiority and overwhelming firepower to conduct operations, involving ground forces, artillery, and airstrikes. Despite its military superiority, the United States lost the war after years of exhaustive fighting and eventually was forced to withdraw from the region. The South consequently lost the war and was integrated when the communist North seized control of the entire Vietnam.

The communist troops of the National Liberation Front (NLF) of South Vietnam (also called the Viet Cong) initiated hundreds of small-scale guerilla attacks per month. The Viet Cong conducted ambushes, set up traps, and escaped the US siege through a complex network of underground tunnels. For the US forces, even finding their enemy

[4]   Xiaomi's unique business model comes from benchmarking plus alpha. It is a smartphone maker, but majority of its profits come from the Internet service, which benchmarked Amazon while adding some elements of Google (Moon, 2016b).

[5]   Information for this case study is abstracted and modified from www.slideshare.net/ MBAFuturis/sun-tzu-strategies, www.encyclopedia.com/history/asia-and-africa/sout heast-asia-history/vietnam-war, history1900s.about.com/od/vietnamwar/a/vietnam war.htm, and www.u-s-history.com/pages/h1862.html.

proved difficult. Since the Viet Cong hid in dense brushes, the US forces dropped bombs that cleared large areas of vegetation. In each village they arrived, the US troops faced difficulty determining which villagers were the enemy, since even women and children helped build traps and shelter guerrilla members. Moreover, the Vietnamese were ordered by Viet Cong to stay as close to the US soldiers as possible to prevent air strikes by proximity. All of these circumstances weakened the US battle plans and allowed the Viet Cong to conserve their energy and resources. The Americans naturally became frustrated with the fighting conditions in Vietnam.

North Vietnamese leaders believed they could not indefinitely sustain the heavy losses inflicted by the Americans and had to win the war with an all-out military effort. The two forces of the Viet Cong and the North Vietnamese Army (NVA), about 85,000 soldiers, launched a major charge throughout South Vietnam, the famous Tet Offensive. On January 30, 1968, the North Vietnamese surprised both the US and South Vietnamese forces by orchestrating a coordinated assault with the Viet Cong on many cities and towns. However, the US forces and South Vietnamese army were able to repel the assault. The Tet Offensive was the turning point of the war as President Johnson, faced with an unhappy American public and pessimistic military generals, decided to de-escalate the war. In 1969, Richard Nixon became the new president and initiated his own Vietnamization plan to end the US involvement in Vietnam.

According to Sun Tzu, the United States with its strong *Cheng* could not easily defeat North Vietnam's *Chi*. The Viet Cong picked the time and place where they wished to engage by remaining hidden in the foliage. The Vietnam War serves as a lesson against relying simply on the superiority of power and size to win a war. On the other hand, relying only on *Chi* like the Viet Cong, will also make it difficult to control the course of war. For example, even though the Viet Cong and North Vietnamese army successfully caught the US and South Vietnamese forces off guard with the Tet Offensive, the US and the South Vietnamese forces were eventually able to retake their lost regions. The actual weakness exposed by the Tet Offensive was not the US military force but the will of its people. The Tet Offensive set the wheels in motion for the US withdrawal by turning the public against the war.

One difference between Porter's SP and Sun Tzu's *Chi* can be found from this case. Communist Vietnam's *Chi* strategy of guerrilla warfare was not new and had been used throughout the history. The major aim of *Chi* strategy is to make it difficult and confusing for enemies to predict one's activities and thus catch them off guard and unprepared. On the other hand, SP aims to block imitation from competitors. In order to achieve this objective, SP stresses uniqueness, being different from competitors, and creating new values. Porter (1996) also introduced two other conditions – trade-offs and fit – in order to make it costly for the rivals to emulate the firm's success strategy. (More details about the two conditions are explained in Chapter 6.) While the *Chi* strategy in military does not need to be new, the SP strategy in business should not only be distinctive (or new), but it should also satisfy the conditions of trade-offs and fit, which thus cannot be easily emulated by the rivals. The *Chi* strategy of the Viet Cong – the use of underground tunnels, the guerrilla strategy, and so on – was not just abnormal but very unique and could not be easily expected and emulated by the United States. In this regard, Porter's concept of SP strategy is helpful to better explain this military case.

5.5 BUSINESS CASE: WALMART'S COST LEADERSHIP STRATEGY

Walmart is a US multinational retailer corporation that runs chains of large discount stores. The company successfully runs a low-price chain of warehouse stores in several countries and established itself as an industry leader. How did Walmart maintain its cost advantage? This section classifies the progress of Walmart's business into three stages of development and investigates the corresponding strategy for each stage.

Stage 1 (1962–1992)

Walmart was established in 1962 with the goal of "offering consumers a wide selection of goods at a discounted price." In order to achieve this goal, Walmart located its stores in small towns where residents had few options for retail shopping (Li, 2011). Most of Walmart's early merchandise did not include brand-name goods. Moreover, by operating in small towns, Walmart avoided direct competition with other existing retailers while also taking advantage of low land prices. Hence, Walmart could enjoy its own economies of scale. Although the company later incorporated brand-name goods to maintain customer satisfaction, the prices of these goods were lower than those offered by other retail stores. Although Walmart began opening stores in large cities and metropolitan markets during this stage, the majority of its operations still took part in small and medium-sized cities.

Stage 2 (1993–2006)

Although Walmart's motto during this period was "Always low price," there were many instances where prices were higher than its competitors. In fact, only 15 to 20 percent of Walmart's items were priced lower than competing retailers (Zenith Management Consulting, 2005). However, Walmart masterfully manipulated public perception to maintain its low-price image and continued to succeed in business (Zenith Management Consulting, 2005). This marketing success was possible because Walmart was able to satisfy the core needs of its customers. Consumers often have certain core needs, and if a firm exceeds the expectations of consumers in these areas, it will often be excused for falling short in others. In Walmart's case, the prices of key goods were so low that consumers accepted Walmart's relatively poor service. Moreover, even though some items were priced relatively high, consumers were still willing to buy these items at Walmart while shopping for other goods. With the large inventories of Walmart, shoppers often spent less time comparing prices and consolidated their shopping into one trip (Zenith Management Consulting, 2005).

Stage 3 (2007–)

In the later stage, due to the pressures from environmental changes and imitation by other competitors, Walmart continuously improved its competitive strategy to maintain its cost leadership position. On September 12, 2007, Walmart introduced its new advertising slogan, "Save Money, Live Better." In addition to its past low-price-store image, Walmart added the image of helping its consumers "Live Better." In 2011, Walmart launched a major initiative to provide healthier food at economical prices. This concept was designed to help reduce the consumption of sodium, sugar, and trans fats, which are major contributors to the US epidemic of obesity, heart disease, and other chronic diseases.

Moreover, Walmart set a new goal of packaging scorecards to reduce its waste and costs further. In 2013, Walmart announced that it would reduce its packaging by 5 percent globally in comparison to its 2008 baseline. It set up the packaging scorecard in 2008 to help measure supplies in the process. Reduced packaging not only contributed to environmental protection by decreasing material consumption, greenhouse gasses, and waste, but also helped lower business costs related to purchasing, transportation, waste management, and inventory.

This business case of Walmart exemplifies how a low-cost retailer, started with OE strategies, gradually shifted to SP. In the first stage, Walmart started with OE due to its lack of managerial skills and capital endowments, and benchmarked its competitors while offering a wide variety of cheap goods. Walmart carefully selected its operating locations to avoid direct competition with other rivals. Although these methods may appear as SP, they do not fulfill the entire definition of SP. According to Porter, firms should target particular customer groups, product segments, or customer access points. However, Walmart's main targets were not much different from its rivals that target low-income, price-conscious consumers who buy in bulk. Therefore, in the first and second stages, Walmart mainly pursued OE for achieving cost advantage.

However, since 2007, the company changed its slogan to respond to the changing business environment. Bill Simon, president and CEO of Walmart USA said, "With more than 140 million customer visits each week, Walmart is uniquely positioned to make a difference by making food healthier and more affordable to everyone." Therefore, the company changed its previous position from being mainly the provider of low-cost goods, to being the provider of wellness with healthier foods at a reasonable price. Accordingly, its target group gradually shifted to those demanding healthier and better-quality goods, which is consistent with Porter's needs-based SP. However, while pursuing SP, Walmart did not give up its OE endeavors. For example, the initiative to reduce packaging costs, an example of OE, is still effective.

While maintaining OE techniques, Walmart has been slowly making changes in its product offerings (SP strategy), which allows it to further strengthen its cost leadership position for the long term. The success of Walmart's case shows that OE and SP are complementary, rather than conflicting. By combining OE with SP, rather than just focusing on SP, one can overcome the disadvantage of OE, which is the increased risk of direct competition and lower profitability. In this regard, this case can be better explained by borrowing Sun Tzu's claim that enhanced advantages can be achieved by jointly employing two strategies of *Cheng* (or OE) and *Chi* (or SP).

However, while Walmart has been very successful with its strategy in many countries due to the cost advantage, the company has failed in several foreign markets, such as South Korea, Japan, and Germany, because it failed to offer customers any compelling value proposition compared to local competitors. Therefore, in some foreign markets, Walmart should have competed with differentiated advantage to meet the needs of local business environment (Moon, 2010), which requires different combinations of OE and SP.

5.6 CONCLUSION AND IMPLICATIONS

The core message of Sun Tzu's military strategy in this chapter is to create enhanced advantage by combining *Cheng* (normal) and *Chi* (abnormal) strategies. After a thorough review of many existing studies, I defined *Cheng* as straightforward tactics characterized by direct confrontation and expected methods of fighting the enemy, and *Chi* as extraordinary tactics employing abnormal and unexpected maneuvers. Sun Tzu said *Cheng* is used to engage the enemy, while *Chi* is needed in order to achieve a victory. However, this statement does not mean that *Chi* is superior to *Cheng*, but that the combination of both tactics can create an enhanced advantage.

I went on to link Sun Tzu's *Cheng* and *Chi* to Porter's OE and SP. *Cheng* is similar to OE in the sense that both involve direct competition. On the other hand, *Chi* is similar to SP, as both involve performing different activities or doing similar activities in different ways, so they are less likely to involve direct competition. Taking a step further, I also noted their subsequent differences. *Chi* strategy aims to catch the enemy off guard and unprepared. In contrast, SP aims to distinguish one's position from the competitors and make it difficult to imitate, although the strategy itself might be well known. Another difference is that Sun Tzu stressed a combination of *Cheng* and *Chi*, for enhanced energies, while Porter preferred SP to OE, and regarded only SP as strategy.

To demonstrate the relevance of the theory presented in this chapter, I analyzed a military case of the Vietnam War and a business case of Walmart Inc. The military forces of the Viet Cong were far inferior to their US counterpart, but the Viet Cong's *Chi* strategy made it difficult for the US forces to defeat them effectively. It is interesting to note that the *Chi* strategy of Viet Cong is closer to Porter's SP strategy in that it is very unique and cannot be easily emulated by the United States. More importantly, the Viet Cong targeted the major weakness of the United States, the public opinion of the American people, and finally made the US military forces retreat from Vietnam. The detailed analysis of Sun Tzu's strategy on "strengths and weaknesses" will be provided in Chapter 6. In the business case, although Walmart started with OE strategy as a late-comer in the retailing business, it did not continue to rely on OE only, but adopted SP as well. Walmart was thus able to appropriately respond to the changing competitive environment and maintain its strengthened cost leadership position. Therefore, Sun Tzu's claim of converged use of *Cheng* and *Chi* is helpful to better explain the reasons behind Walmart's success.

6   Unique Positioning

Sun Tzu: Avoiding enemy's strengths and attacking their weaknesses
Porter: Trade-offs and strategic fit

The characters *Xu* and *Shi* appear in the sixth chapter title of Sun Tzu's *The Art of War*, and signify two opposite concepts: weakness and strength, respectively. Weaknesses involve the conditions of being fearful, disorderly, hungry, exhausted, few, unprepared, and other qualities that make one's army vulnerable. On the other hand, strengths include the conditions of being brave, organized, well nourished, relaxed, plenty, prepared, and other qualities that fortify an army.

The chapter "Weaknesses and Strengths" not only instructs how to avoid the enemy's strengths and attack their weaknesses, but also shows how to *create* weaknesses of the enemy, so that one can direct one's strengths to the enemy's weaknesses. To explain *Xu* and *Shi*, Sun Tzu gave a metaphor of the flow of water. He compared the "flow of strengths and weaknesses" to the way water flows from a high position to the ground. This metaphor purports to tell the significance of positioning oneself to extract the most benefits from the manipulation of weaknesses and strengths. This concept of utilizing the strengths and weaknesses is one of the central ideas of Sun Tzu's philosophy (McNeilly, 1996). In fact, Emperor Tang Tai Zong of the Tang Dynasty claimed that the entire thirteen chapters of Sun Tzu's treatise were no more than a discussion of strengths and weaknesses.

Sun Tzu's strategy of dealing with strengths and weaknesses can be compared to Porter's strategy of achieving sustainable advantage. Like Sun Tzu, Porter argued that attacking the competitor's strengths is not advisable as the end result would be destructive competition. Thus, he suggested firms pursue a strategy in order to occupy a unique positioning in the industry by serving a selected customer segment or satisfying previously neglected needs of a broad base of consumers. Both Sun Tzu's (avoiding strengths and attacking weaknesses) and Porter's (unique positioning) strategies are critical to achieve victory in war and gain competitive advantage in business. However, these advantages will be degraded if one's military activity is exposed to the enemy or if a firm's competitive advantage is imitated by rivals. Hence, Sun Tzu and Porter offered several conditions for sustaining one's advantageous positioning.

In the following sections, I will first conduct an in-depth analysis of Sun Tzu's three strategies that guide how to avoid the enemy's strengths and to attack their weaknesses: seizing the initiative, concentrating one's forces, and concealing one's disposition. Then, I will introduce Porter's three conditions for sustaining the advantageous position: strategic positioning, trade-offs, and fit. The third section will compare and contrast Sun Tzu's and Porter's strategies. At the same time, I will also show how some of Sun Tzu's strategies can be incorporated to enrich Porter's strategy for sustaining competitive advantage. Lastly, the military case of Hannibal's victory at Cannae and the business case of Southwest Airlines' unique positioning will be provided to help readers understand and utilize the strategic linkages between war and business.

6.1 SUN TZU: AVOIDING THE ENEMY'S STRENGTHS AND ATTACKING THEIR WEAKNESSES

Attacking the enemy's weak points allows troops to leverage limited resources and expedite victory, while challenging the enemy's strongholds leads to wasted resources including time, money, and lives. This seemingly commonsense knowledge leads to another simple, but extremely important conclusion that is sometimes easier said than done. To maximize the gain from the war at the lowest cost, one must not challenge the enemy on what they do the best, but challenge them on what they do the poorest. Numerous military strategists emphasized the importance of avoiding the enemy's strengths and attacking their weaknesses. "Besiege Wei to Rescue Zhao" is a well-known

Chinese historical military case that applied this strategy in actual war. In 354 B.C., the country of Wei attacked Zhao and laid siege to its capital Handan. Zhao turned to the country of Qi for help, and Qi general Sun Bin realized it was unwise to engage Wei directly.[1] Instead, he decided to attack Wei's capital of Daliang. When Wei General Pang Juan heard that the capital was under siege, he promptly rushed his army back home to defend the capital. The army of Wei retreated in haste, and the tired troops were eventually ambushed and defeated by Qi forces. Qi was able to rescue Zhao despite the strength of the Wei army by attacking their weak point, while the Wei general barely made his escape back to home. Strategically, Sun Tzu introduced the following three principles for the strategy of avoiding the enemy's strengths and attacking their weaknesses.

6.1.1   Seizing the Initiative

Sun Tzu stated, "Whoever is the first in the battlefield and awaits the coming of the enemy will be fresh for the fight; whoever is the second in the battlefield and has to hasten to fight will arrive exhausted." This statement highlights the importance of seizing the initiative in order to gain control of the situation instead of letting the enemy have it. Sun Tzu stated, "Therefore, the clever combatant imposes his will on the enemy, but does not allow the enemy's will to be imposed on him." Montgomery, a famous British general during World War II, stressed the importance of seizing the initiative by saying, "[Make] the enemy dance to our tune throughout . . . Never react to the enemy's moves or thrusts" (Kiszely, 2000). Mao Zedong, a founder of Chinese Communist Party, similarly stressed the importance of initiative when he said, "The initiative will determine the army's degree of freedom. If the army loses initiative, it will be in a passive position, and the whole army will not be free, and thus will have the risk of being defeated" (Chen and Lu, 2006: 326).

---

[1]   Sun Bin is a descendant of Sun Tzu.

Seizing the initiative is a critical factor leading to victory. If the enemy captures the initiative, one will have to hasten to defend against the enemy. This will easily expose one's weaknesses to the enemy and significantly reduce the likelihood of defeating them. On the other hand, by seizing the initiative, one will successfully have time to set up a critical precondition to evading the enemy's strengths and to striking their weaknesses.

In order to seize the initiative, Sun Tzu said one should control the enemy's movements with calculated baits and bluffs. To be more precise, one can entice the enemy toward a carefully planned area by luring them with potential benefits, and prevent them from approaching by bluffing with potential harm. Therefore, a general should be skilled at creating an illusion of benefits and harms as necessary in order to take the initiative.

6.1.2 Concentrating One's Forces and Dividing the Enemy's Forces

While the first principle, "seizing the initiative," concerns manipulation of one's own and the enemy's strengths and weaknesses in general, the second principle pertains to creating the conditions for selectively strengthening one's forces and selectively weakening the enemy's. This strategy is particularly important for an army at numerical disadvantage. Sun Tzu stressed the importance of this second principle by stating, "If one sends reinforcements everywhere, one will be weak everywhere." For example, if the two sides are neck and neck on numbers, and one's forces are distributed in ten places while the other concentrates all of its forces in one place, naturally the latter will have ten times the strength of the former.

Moreover, if one overstretches one's forces trying to defend every place under attack, every place will be weak and no single point will be well defended. Being aware of this problem can help one avoid rendering oneself vulnerable due to overstretching. On the other hand, if one can also render the enemy vulnerable by inducing the enemy to overstretch themselves, one can easily take advantage of the enemy by attacking where the enemy's force is most thinly stretched, or the weakest in any regard. In this respect, even if one has a relatively smaller number of forces, one can surprise the enemy at their weakest point and make it difficult for the enemy to concentrate their forces in an effective manner. Therefore, even the weaker armies can prevail against stronger ones. History records the cases of smaller armies triumphing over the superior forces by correctly identifying the enemy's strengths and weaknesses, dividing the enemy's forces, and concentrating their own strengths against the weaknesses of the enemy.

6.1.3   Concealing One's Disposition

Sun Tzu's third principle consists of concealing one's disposition for successful concentration of one's forces and effective division of the enemy's. Sun Tzu said, "In making tactical dispositions, the highest pitch one has to keep is concealing them. One will then be safe from the prying of the subtlest spies and from the machinations of the wisest brains." The principle of concealing one's disposition has meanings beyond the literal definition of hiding and making the enemy unaware of one's movements; this third principle involves the idea of confusing the enemy through dispersal of false information, thereby hiding one's strategic intentions. If the enemy does not possess precise information and is unaware of the direction of your attack, they will tend to disperse their forces in all directions for possible attack from all sides. This act will put the enemy at a both psychological and physical disadvantage and dramatically decrease the availability of their soldiers at the point of one's attack (Sleevi, 1998).

The act of concealing one's disposition can be attained with the help of two other strategies. One is to detect the movement of the enemy and predict their plans. By knowing the enemy's movement and plans, one can establish an appropriate response to the enemy's actions, defend against the enemy's attack, and even attack the enemy's weaknesses. Hence, Sun Tzu said if one knows the time and location of the battle beforehand, one can still fight the enemy even after traversing

1,000 li.[2] For the second strategy, Sun Tzu recommended, "Do not repeat the tactics which have gained you a victory, but let your methods be changeable in the infinite variety of circumstances." The frequent changes of tactics will make it difficult for the enemy to predict one's movements. For example, North Korea has conducted a wide range of provocations in recent history. They are not limited to military skirmishes along the border, but also engagements in various types of conflicts, such as terrorism, military espionage, cyber-attacks, assassinations, missile launches, and nuclear tests (CSIS, 2010). The variety of these tactics makes it difficult for the international community to formulate an effective defense and response.

6.2 PORTER: TRADE-OFFS AND STRATEGIC FIT

A company can outperform its rivals only if it can establish differentiations that can be preserved. Porter introduced two concepts of achieving superior performance against the rivals: operational effectiveness (OE) and strategic positioning (SP) (see Chapter 5 for details). However, as Porter (1996) argued, companies that limit themselves to OE only will soon be caught up by the followers, which will lead to destructive hyper-competition and diminishing returns. The consistent source of long-term competitive advantage comes from occupying a unique position from which firms can deliver a unique mix of value to consumers. In addition, Porter added two other concepts for consolidating firms' strategic positioning, trade-offs and fit. These two are the conditions designed to increase the barriers and costs of imitation by other firms. Trade-offs arise from the incompatibility of activities, whereas fit relies on the complementarity of activities. The following explains how these conditions contribute to firms' sustainable competitive advantage.

6.2.1 Three Types of Strategic Positioning

Strategic positioning is to choose a different set of activities or to perform activities in a different way. Porter claimed that strategic

---

[2]   One li equals to 500 meters.

positioning does not necessarily mean occupying a niche market (i.e., the needs of a specific customer segment); it can also take place by finding the common needs of a broad customer segments (i.e., a particular need from a broad range of customers). Porter introduced three types of strategic positioning: variety-based, needs-based, and access-based positioning.

The first, *variety-based positioning*, is to provide a subset of the industry's products or services. Jiffy Lube is a good example. The company serves a variety of customers, by specializing in only the service of automotive lubricants without offering other car repair or maintenance services. The second is *needs-based positioning*, which targets a specific customer segment. Companies with the second strategy will serve most or all needs of a particular group of customers. IKEA, for instance, tries to meet the entire home furnishing needs of young customers, who demand stylish but low-cost furnishing. Finally, *access-based positioning* targets a particular product variety and customer segment. Companies selecting this strategy will then provide a limited range of customers with a narrow set of products or services. Porter said companies employing this strategy always have access to customers through different ways. Carmike Cinemas, for example, operates movie theaters only in cities with populations under 200,000. The small-town customers are less diverse compared to urban inhabitants, preferring genres like comedies, Westerns, and family entertainment. Therefore, Carmike Cinemas correctly determined that a smaller number of screens and less sophisticated projection technology would meet the demand in small towns.

6.2.2   Trade-Offs

Engaging in a unique position, however, is not sufficient to assure sustainable profitability because a profitable positioning will always attract imitation from competitors. In order to sustain one's competitive positioning, there should be trade-offs, which occur because of the incompatibility of activities stemming from limited resources. A trade-off means that more inputs placed into one activity result in less available resources for another. Trade-offs can prevent rivals by increasing the costs of engaging in similar activities, because companies that reposition or straddle two positions simultaneously will undermine their existing strategic positioning and degrade their overall competitive advantage.

Accordingly, once a company has found a unique position, it has to refrain from over-expansion of business activities and concentrate on developing core capabilities. As one company cannot do all things for all customers, trade-offs will inhibit other companies from imitating or intruding on one's own position. Firms are thus pressured to decide what to do and, more importantly, what not to do. Porter incorporated the terminology, "productivity frontier," to explain the occurrence of trade-offs.[3] According to Porter, there will be no trade-offs below or above the frontier; whereas there will be significant trade-offs along the line of the frontier.[4] Therefore, Porter's stuck-in-the-middle concept is valid only along the productivity frontier, not below or above the frontier.

6.2.3 Fit

Porter said that competitive advantage does not result from a particular activity, but from the entire system. The fit among activities refers to the synergistic integration of an organization's resources. The fit substantially reduces cost or increases differentiation, and as a result, it enables the firm to sustain its advantages, as it is harder for competitors to copy the entire system. Even though competitors may be able to identify the interconnectivity, they will still have difficulty in replicating it, because it requires the integration of decision and activities among different departments of a company. The competitive fit requires a high level of complementarity among activities. If a firm

---

3   Porter (1996) defined productivity frontier as the sum of all existing best practices (i.e., strategic positioning). It is explained by two dimensions – relative cost position and nonprice buyer value delivered. The point on the frontier represents the maximum value delivered through a product or service at a given cost (Porter, 1996).

4   Refer to Figure 5.1 and the related explanation in Chapter 5 for the conditions of trade-offs.

only imitates some parts of its competitor's whole activity system, it will at best gain little, but at worst degrade the whole of its own performance.

Therefore, it is essential to create a fit among the company's numerous activities. If there is no fit among activities, there can be no distinctive strategy and little sustainability. There are three types of fit: (1) consistency between each activity and the overall strategy, (2) re-enforcement of activities, and (3) optimization of effort.[5] Porter claimed that if a company's positioning relies more on the second and third types of fit, it will be more difficult for rivals to copy the company's positioning, and thus the company's competitive advantage will be more sustainable.

6.3 THE INTEGRATION OF SUN TZU AND PORTER

The strategy of "avoiding strengths and attacking weaknesses" aims to create or aggravate the weaknesses of the enemy, build one's own strengths, and attack the enemy by concentrating one's strengths at the enemy's weak point. On the other hand, Porter's strategy of sustaining competitive advantage lies in the establishment of a unique positioning, while decreasing the likelihood of competitors' imitation by improving trade-offs and fit. Therefore, both strategies deal with the question of how to build and maintain the superior position over the rivals. In the following section, I will compare and contrast Sun Tzu's three key principles with Porter's three conditions for sustaining competitive positioning.

6.3.1 Seizing the Initiative versus Strategic Positioning

Seizing the initiative is important because it can secure the favorable position of maneuvering the enemy instead of being maneuvered by the enemy. When discussing this strategy, Sun Tzu particularly stressed the

---

[5] As an example of the second type of fit, Neutrogena's marketing activities in a luxury hotel provided positive influences on the sale of its other products, and thereby reducing its total marketing costs. The third type of fit, optimization of effort, is achieved through efficient coordination and exchange with external parties (e.g., suppliers and buyers), thereby reducing redundancy and wasted resources.

importance of acting on the right timing in order to rob the enemy of any opportunity for counteraction. On the other hand, the concept of strategic initiative in business refers to "the ability of a company or a strategic business unit to capture control of strategic behavior in an industry" (MacMillan, 1982). Therefore, firms with strategic initiative can ensure their favorable positions in competition, while forcing competitors to take less favorable position.

Firms occupying a unique positioning are often viewed as the first mover in serving a specific consumer segment or finding specific needs that are neglected by established firms.[6] However, not many firms can successfully find a unique position and secure above-average profits. For example, nine out of ten start-ups end up failing in the long run (Griffith, 2014). These firms fail because they make things people do not actually want. In other words, their products fail to deliver a substantial value to the consumers, even if they manage to appear unique.

6.3.2   Concentration of Resources versus Trade-Offs

Sun Tzu warned that if one tries to cover everywhere, every place will be weak. Therefore, Sun Tzu suggested concentration of resources (i. e., one's strengths) at the decisive point (i.e., the enemy's weak point) in a most effective way to attack the enemy and achieve victory in war. This principle of Sun Tzu is analogous to the concept of Porter's trade-offs, because both of them emphasize the importance of selection and concentration of resources on a certain area. Firms should select which customer group should be targeted and which products or services should be served, instead of providing all things to all customers.

---

[6]   SP can be linked to Sun Tzu's military strategy in both Chapter 5 and the current chapter, based on the two characteristics of SP. First, the unique positioning enables a firm to avoid direct competition with other rivals. The advantage of "indirect competition" is related to Sun Tzu' Chi strategy in Chapter 5. Second, SP emphasizes the first-mover strategy, in contrast to "me-too" strategy of OE, and thus the "first-mover advantage" can be well compared to Sun Tzu's military principle of "seizing the initiative" in this chapter.

If one has to ascertain a core competitive advantage, then all activities should support this core advantage. Therefore, one has to make a choice among various activities, placing greater resources and efforts into activities that are related to the core competence and less on noncore areas. By using Sun Tzu's concentration strategy, one can generate maximum power in fighting against the enemy; similarly, tailoring activities to the core competences can create maximum synergy effect among related activities with limited resources. On the other hand, Sun Tzu also suggested that for the effective attack on the enemy's weaknesses, the enemy's forces should be dispersed in many directions, thereby degrading their strengths at key points. In business, the profitable strategic positioning will always attract imitative competitors. However, if one can successfully create trade-offs among the activities, the rivals may have to reposition or straddle two or more incompatible activities, thereby weakening their existing competitive advantage.

6.3.3   Concealing One's Disposition versus Fit

To impose a surprise attack on the enemy's weakness with one's strengths, the third precondition is to carefully detect the enemy's movement and plans while simultaneously concealing one's own disposition and plans. In order to do this, one can deliberately leak false information to the enemy and misdirect the enemy to make wrong decisions. Another method Sun Tzu suggested is to frequently change the direction of attack or tactical disposition, in order to confuse the enemy.

Sun Tzu's principle of concealing one's disposition can be compared to Porter's concept of fit, which does not involve concealment but serves the same purpose. Concealing one's disposition is to prevent the enemy from knowing one's real intention, while fit is to prevent rivals from imitating one's strategy, thereby maintaining competitive advantage. However, the tools or the means of achieving this goal are different. The central idea of concealing one's disposition in military warfare is to make one's real intention unknown to the enemy. In contrast, in business, the overall fit is very much open to other competitors, far from being concealed. What really prevents other competitors from imitating it is the complication of fit, which is the synergistic convergence of activities rather than the mere combination of independent activities.

6.4 MILITARY CASE: HANNIBAL'S VICTORY AT CANNAE

The Battle of Cannae occurred in 216 B.C. near the town of Cannae in Apulia, southeast Italy.[7] Led by Hannibal, the Carthaginian army devastated a numerically superior army of the Roman Republic. The Battle of Cannae is considered as one of the most brilliant tactical victories in military history. Hannibal's successful strategy can be systematically analyzed using Sun Tzu's three principles of "avoiding strengths and attacking weaknesses."

The battle started with Hannibal's capturing of the Roman supply depot in Cannae, a crucial location for the Roman supply chain. In response, the Romans assembled a massive army, led by the two commanders, Paullus and Varro, and advanced to face Hannibal's army. Varro ordered the legions to change the normal army formation for this particular engagement. Instead of aligning the legions in a wider line as he usually did, he deployed his army in a narrow and deep line. He placed 75,000 infantrymen in three lines at the center and 5,000 cavalrymen in the wings, in hopes to pierce through the Carthaginian line and overpower them. However, the formation left little room for flexible movement and positional change in response to the changing circumstance.

On the other hand, Hannibal's force only amounted to 35,000 infantrymen and 10,000 cavalrymen. Hannibal needed to create an advantage that could overcome the difference in numbers. He showed his strategic brilliance by placing his strong cavalry and best infantry groups on the flanks and the relatively inferior infantry in the center,

---

[7]   Information of this case study is abstracted and modified from www.thefinertimes.co m/Ancient-Wars/battle-of-cannae.html, and www.greatmilitarybattles.com/html/ battle_of_cannae.

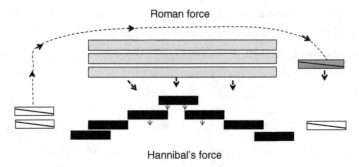

FIGURE 6.1 The disposition of the Roman and Carthaginian armies
before the battle

where the fighting would be the fiercest. Once Hannibal's entire army
was in place, he ordered the center to move forward to create a convex
curve toward the Romans (see Figure 6.1). Hannibal's strategy was
designed to let his cavalry defeat the weaker Roman cavalry deployed
on its right flank and swing around to attack the rear of the Romans.

Once the battle commenced, the Roman and Carthaginian caval-
ries were engaged on the flanks. Eventually the strong Carthaginian left
flank overpowered and slaughtered the Romans, while the right flank
simply kept the Roman cavalry occupied. Having defeated the Roman
cavalry on the left flank, the Carthaginian cavalry moved around and
assaulted the allied cavalry on the right. The attack from two directions
caused the allied Roman cavalry to flee. Meanwhile in the center,
Hannibal called his forces to slowly retreat backward. Led to think that
they were winning the initiative, the Romans took the bait and continued to move forward. With the center forces retreating and the flanks
holding their positions, the Carthaginian army formed a deep crescent
shape with the Roman infantry trapped inside (see Figure 6.2). The
Romans were eventually packed into a narrow confinement where they
could not move or use their weapons efficiently. Hannibal then had his
flanks turn inward on the Roman infantry and the Carthage cavalry rode
around to assault the Romans' rear. Trapped on all sides of the semicircle,
the Romans were ultimately slaughtered by Hannibal's forces.

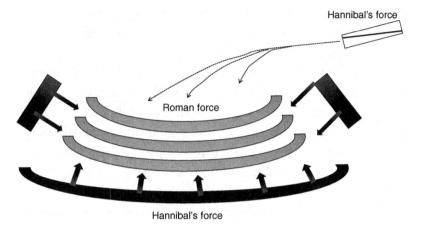

FIGURE 6.2 Hannibal's tactical disposition for defeating the Roman armies

With these strategies Hannibal overcame the numerical disadvantage and defeated the Romans. Sun Tzu's three principles from the chapter "Weaknesses and Strengths" can show exactly why Hannibal's strategy was bound to bring him success in Cannae. The first principle is to seize the initiative in the battlefield by strategically unveiling potential advantages or disadvantages to the enemy. After the experience of the two consecutive defeats in two major battles against the Carthaginians, the Romans employed a strategy of attrition, reluctant to engage in direct and large-scale confrontation. Therefore, Hannibal's capture of Cannae was a move calculated to drive the Romans to the battlefield by cutting off the Roman supply chain, thereby taking the initiative in battle.

The second principle is to strategically align one's forces according to the distribution of strengths and weaknesses in enemy force's disposition. The Romans were stronger in the center with weaker flanks. Hannibal thus deployed his numerically and qualitatively stronger cavalry on the flanks to assault the weaker Roman counterparts. In addition, the convex curve formations earned enough time for the Carthaginian cavalry on the flanks to overwhelm the Roman counterparts and move toward the rear, while drawing the Romans toward the center. Having defeated the Roman flanks on both sides, the Carthaginian cavalry then stealthily approached the Romans from the rear, who were caught in a condensed space and unable to maneuver or defend themselves effectively.

The third principle is to thoroughly comprehend the enemy's disposition while keeping one's own strategy incomprehensible by the enemy. Hannibal knew that the Romans would concentrate their forces in the center to tear through the intentionally thin Carthaginian line. On the other hand, the Romans completely failed to decipher Hannibal's intention or disposition. As a result, Hannibal caught the Romans completely by surprise.

In Porter's theory, maintaining uniqueness is the key to successfully competing against rivals. Although the circumstance is a warfare instead of a business competition, Hannibal's reverse-Roman tactical disposition fits as the brilliant exhibition of uniqueness that brought victory in the fierce battlefield. Porter's theory also involves an important concept of trade-offs, where investing in certain core competences necessitates the withdrawal of investment in other areas. Hannibal's troops were inferior to the Romans in terms of overall number and strength of force. However, Hannibal had both numerically and qualitatively stronger cavalry. He placed his strong cavalry on the two flanks to attack the weak counterpart, instead of distributing them in all directions. Porter argued for the importance of strategic fit in the organization for sustaining one's profitable position in a competitive market. The effective coordination between Hannibal's infantry and cavalry enabled his forces to slaughter the Romans and seize victory.

Sun Tzu's and Porter's theories are undoubtedly compatible with each other in many aspects as shown in this case study. Nevertheless, as I have been frequently emphasizing, one should bear in mind that they have different perspectives on *the opponent*: Sun Tzu called it the enemy and Porter the consumer (in addition to business competitors). The enemy's weaknesses are to be exploited and crushed with one's unique strengths, but the consumer's needs are to be served and catered to with unique values one has to offer.

However, even if a firm holds a unique position with its products or services, the uniqueness will not translate into competitive advantage if it fails to deliver meaningful value (as demonstrated by many start-ups' failure cases).

6.5 BUSINESS CASE: SOUTHWEST AIRLINES' UNIQUE POSITIONING

In 1971, Southwest Airlines, a US-based low-fare airline headquartered in Dallas, began operations with three planes shuttling between three cities – Houston, Dallas, and San Antonio.[8] Today, it ranks number one in the nation for the numbers of passengers served. Southwest now employs more than 53,000 employees and serves 101 destinations across the United States and eight foreign countries. More than 100 million customers board Southwest flights annually (Southwest Airlines website, 2017). More importantly, it has remained profitable and achieved continuous growth for the past decades, whereas other major US airlines experienced financial difficulties in the 2000s. It has earned an above-average rate of annual returns in the US airline industry, and in 2014 the company was crowned as the top-performing stock in the S&P 500 (Tully, 2015). Visible elements of Southwest's business model have been emulated by almost all major US airlines, but few achieved the same level of success. What is different about Southwest? The following analyzes Southwest's success strategy by applying Porter's concept of SP and two additional conditions for sustaining competitive advantage.

Southwest Airlines did not follow the strategies of established competitors in the airline industry, but instead targeted the industry segment that was overlooked by extant airlines. In the past, most airlines were full-service airlines that used a hub-and-spoke system. However, Southwest, uniquely, decided to target the low-cost sector with short haul, point-to-point, and nonstop travel. It specifically targeted small and medium-sized cities that take no more than two

---

[8] Information of this case study is abstracted and modified from case studies on Southwest Airlines by Porter (1996) and Moon (2014a).

hours of travel. As a result, Southwest regarded automobile makers as its real competitors over other airline companies. In order to fully establish its strategic positioning, Southwest Airlines simplified its operations as much as possible, tailoring all of its activities to one specific target. Through these efforts, Southwest realized Porter's concept of trade-offs as follows.

First, unlike other carriers with their collection of different aircraft models, Southwest used only the Boeing 737. This standardization saved Southwest millions of dollars in maintenance and operating costs. Mechanics were trained only for one airplane model and crews became easily transferable, because they were all familiar with the same plane. Second, Southwest provided minimal customer service. It did not offer meals, assigned seats, interline baggage checking, or other premium services. This seemingly unaccommodating service policy allowed Southwest to maintain a twenty-minute turnaround time, while other airlines usually had to spend ninety minutes for similar processes. With the increased efficiency, Southwest reduced the idle time that airplanes spend on ground. This is important, because a big part of Southwest's profitability came from its ability to maintain a high frequency of flights. Despite the standardization and simplification of services, Southwest provided additional services and benefits that its competitors did not. For example, it was one of the few airlines that provided free baggage checking with some limitation and no fees for changing tickets. The simplified but effective services and low fares allowed Southwest to achieve some of the highest levels of customer satisfaction.

However, it is important to note that trade-offs by themselves are not the sole answer to a company's strategy. Southwest's success should also be attributed to the result of the fit in the company's activities. Southwest selected specific activities that complement and reinforce each other to create a self-reinforcing system. Southwest was able to offer low-cost services not only because of its high productivity of the well-paid gate and ground crews, but also because of its omission of seat assignments, interline baggage checking, and premium classes. Since the aforementioned activities were usually the major causes of delay, Southwest's unique strategy helped facilitate rapid gate turnaround.

Southwest maintained its unique positioning and sustained its activity system through achieving a good fit. Southwest's success was enough to tempt Continental Airlines to copy Southwest's strategic positioning and divide its resources. Continental Airlines created a new subsidiary called Continental Lite, which tried to emulate some of Southwest's activities. However, Continental failed to make the right trade-offs and to create a good fit. Continental divided its resources, while Southwest focused all of its resources on one point (i.e., core competence). Continental Airlines paid an enormous penalty for its inefficient allocation of resources. The airline lost hundreds of millions of dollars, and its CEO was eventually ousted.

Because of domestic market saturation, slow growth, and rising costs, Southwest recently began to expand its activities to international operations and long-haul segments to establish a new growth engine. As a domestic-oriented airline, international flights currently account for only 1 percent of Southwest's network. However, it also shows a large potential for future growth. Many analysts are doubtful of Southwest's successful expansion due to the incompatibility of the services required for international flights with the existing point-to-point services. However, the CEO and President Gary Kelly stressed that Southwest has successfully adapted in the past and must continue to do so in response to the changes in the airline industry (Nicas and Carey, 2014).

For example, high fuel prices, which deeply affected Southwest's operation costs, compelled it to shift from short-haul flights to more fuel-efficient long flights between larger cities. In order to expand its portion of long-haul travel, Southwest wished to accelerate its entry into the international market and avoid fierce domestic competition with other major airlines. Because of its lack of experience in international operations, Southwest acquired AirTran Airways in 2011, and by 2014 it had completed full integration, including worker training, airplane standardization, and carrier network linkage. This is consistent with Porter's strategy for strengthening fit while expanding the scope of business. The synergy with AirTran has played an important role in Southwest's growing profits, from $178 million in 2011 to $754 million in 2013 (Forbes, 2014).

On the other hand, Sun Tzu's strategy introduced in this chapter can be incorporated in business to enrich Porter's strategy for sustaining competitive advantage. Sun Tzu emphasized the importance of knowing the enemy's disposition, and this is the core condition for concentrating one's resources, dividing the enemy's forces, and hiding one's disposition from the enemy. Southwest clearly understood its competitors' strategy – broad differentiation with full services – and concentrated its resources on cost strategy focusing on limited services and regions. This cost focus strategy thus divided its competitors' resources when they attempted to emulate Southwest's strategy. Unlike in war, Southwest did not have to hide its disposition from its competitors. Sun Tzu's strategies, nevertheless, provide valuable insights for conducting systematic analysis of the success of Southwest.

6.6   CONCLUSION AND IMPLICATIONS

The key theme of the chapter "Weaknesses and Strengths" in *The Art of War* is to avoid the enemy's strengths and exploit their weaknesses. Sun Tzu listed three main principles to achieve this goal. First, by seizing initiative, one can control the overall battle situation according to strategic needs. Second, by concentrating one's forces and resources and dividing the enemy's, one can convert the enemy's strengths into weaknesses. Third, in order to transform one's weaknesses into strengths, it is essential to make one's plans unpredictable to the enemy.

Sun Tzu's three principles can be connected to Porter's business strategies related to strategic positioning, trade-offs, and fit. The specific coupling comprises: the concept of strategic positioning with Sun Tzu's strategy of seizing the initiative, because both of them aim at pursuing the first-mover advantage, thereby establishing a favorable position while avoiding direct and costly competition; the concept of trade-offs with Sun Tzu's strategy of concentration of one's forces, because both involve placing resources in a core area; and the concept of fit with Sun Tzu's concept of concealing one's disposition, as both aim to maintain one's current favorable status by preventing the imitation by competitors or detection by the enemy.

In war, an advantageous position is one that is favorable for attacking the enemy. However, in the Battle of Cannae, with the deceptive tactic which bestowed victory to Carthaginians, the weaker forces in the center had to be sacrificed. The results (i.e., victory) override the means in priority for Sun Tzu. This means using deception is not only plausible but desirable if it increases the chance to gain victory. The military strategy, however, when it is very deceptive, is risky and does not come without a price. On the other hand, in business Porter stressed unique positioning which can lead to a superior advantage. However, although a firm may provide a unique product, it will fail if it does not deliver a meaningful value to the end users as many start-ups fail. Therefore, we can derive an important implication for business that not being unique by heavily focusing on SP, but creating values to the consumers is important. We can then reduce the fruitless innovative efforts and failed entrepreneurship.

7 Overcoming Disadvantages

Sun Tzu: Turning the devious (disadvantage) into the straight (advantage)
Porter: Turning Corporate Social Responsibility (CSR) to Creating
          Shared Value (CSV)

The Chinese title of *The Art of War*'s seventh chapter, located in the middle of Sun Tzu's book, is "*Jun Zheng*," translated as "maneuvering" in this book. While the first character, *Jun*, in the title is relatively straightforward to interpret, meaning "military," the second character, *Zheng*, has generated a stream of debate regarding its exact meaning. The most authoritative interpretations involve two slightly different meanings. Cao Cao, a renowned strategist and a major lord of the Three Kingdoms period in China, interpreted *Zheng* as fighting for victory. On the other hand, Wang Xi and Li Quan argued Sun Tzu meant fighting to gain advantages or benefits rather than just nominal victory. Finally, Guo Hua-ruo took an intermediary position where he asserted the word *Zheng* conveys both meanings, because gaining advantages and achieving victory are closely related. After considering all of these interpretations, I concluded that the modern English term that can capture the meanings of *Jun Zheng* is maneuvering, which refers to the skillful and deliberate movement of troops to gain advantages for victory. In war, maneuvering is especially important for seizing the initiative to occupy a favorable position, from which it will then be easier to achieve victory.

The first six chapters of *The Art of War* outline the general strategy and principles of warfare. Beginning with the chapter *Jung Zheng*, the second half of *The Art of War* is devoted to more specific military tactics for practical situations than the first half, which is mostly spent on laying out the general principles of managing a war. However, the tactics shown in the second half are not detached from the first half of Sun Tzu's book. Instead, each tactic presented is firmly rooted in the principles raised in the first six chapters of *The Art of War*. For example, the principle of securing a favorable time and place for a battle introduced in the chapter "Maneuvering" is consistent with easy victory, the key theme of "Tactical Disposition" (chapter 4 of Sun Tzu's book). In addition, many tactics suggested in the chapter "Maneuvering" are related to the *Chi* operations introduced in "Enhanced Energy" (chapter 5 of Sun Tzu's book).

In Sun Tzu's military philosophy, exerting maximum force is not the best way to win a military struggle. Instead, the most esteemed method of obtaining a victory is a maneuver that skillfully minimizes cost for maximum gains. The key theme central to Sun Tzu's definition of efficient maneuvering is, "turning the devious into the straight and turning adversity into advantage."[1] To further explain, Sun Tzu's proposal is that an efficient maneuver involves moving in an unexpected and seemingly disadvantageous way that leads to success in the end.

In this respect, Sun Tzu's strategy of turning the devious into the straight can be compared to Porter and Kramer's (2011) concept of creating shared value (CSV); in both cases, the primary objective is to turn disadvantages into advantages. Porter and Kramer developed three strategies for CSV: reconceiving products and markets, redefining productivity in the value chain, and enabling local cluster development. I found that some of Sun Tzu's maneuvering tactics, related to communication skills and tools for unifying the army while maneuvering, can be a guideline to further improving Porter and Kramer's CSV strategy. On the other hand, Porter and Kramer's win-win or shared value perspective of CSV can help explain the success behind military maneuvering such as the Long March of the Chinese Red Army.

This chapter is organized as follows. It first conducts an in-depth analysis of advantages and disadvantages of maneuvering, and its three principles to turn the devious into the straight. Following the

---

[1] The Chinese characters are: 以迂為直, 以患為利.

analyses, this chapter examines the points of similarity and difference between Sun Tzu's maneuvering strategy and Porter and Kramer's CSV strategy. For the case studies, this chapter analyzes the military case of the Long March of the Chinese Red Army and the business case of Nestlé's operation in India to demonstrate the utilization of the strategic linkages between war and business.

7.1 SUN TZU: TURNING THE DEVIOUS (DISADVANTAGE) INTO THE STRAIGHT (ADVANTAGE)

7.1.1 *Advantages and Disadvantages of Maneuvering*

The claim of Sun Tzu that one must maneuver by "turning the devious route into the straight" is referring to the strategy for securing a favorable position. A devious route would take longer than a straightforward one, all other conditions being the same. However, in war, the time required to arrive at a destination is not only affected by the physical distance but also by other factors such as road conditions, troop size, and the strength of the enemy force encamped along the road (Wu and Yu, 1993). For example, there could be a strong enemy presence in the shorter route and relatively few enemy troops along the devious route. In this case, it will be safer and time-efficient to take the devious route rather than the straight. Hart (1954) also emphasized the importance of indirect strategy when he said, "In strategy, the longest way around is often the shortest way home."

Nevertheless, there are also dangers inherent in taking the devious route. Sun Tzu said if the entire army (including supplies and provisions) is required to travel a longer distance to gain advantages, the army will be at the risk of arriving at the destination past the desired schedule. For successful maneuvering, speed is an important factor. McNeilly (1996) gave four reasons why speed is essential in maneuvering. First, speed is a substitute for resources. Second, speed is critical to exploit weaknesses and opportunities. Third, speed can produce surprises and shocks. Fourth, speed allows for the buildup of momentum.

However, Sun Tzu also warned against a blind worship of speed in maneuvering. For example, if one reduces the size of one's army to gain an advantage of speed, there could be critical limitation in carrying needed resources or supplies. Sun Tzu warned that, "If the army does not have heavy equipment, it will be lost; if it does not have food provisions, it will be lost; if it does not have material reserves, it will be lost." Therefore, what matters is not the absolute speed, but the speed of oneself relative to the enemy's. One can be slow as long as the enemy is slower, and one can gain an advantage either by improving one's own speed or by slowing the enemy down (Schmitt, 1990).

7.1.2 Principles of Turning the Devious into the Straight

Sun Tzu recommended three principles in order to successfully turn a disadvantage into an advantage. The first principle is in fact introduced in his chapter "Laying Plans" when Sun Tzu said that all warfare is based on the art of deception. To successfully deceive the enemy, one must be able to successfully command a shock or surprise factor which can be achieved in three ways: deceiving the enemy, confusing the enemy, or keeping the enemy ignorant (Schmitt, 1990). Of the three, the first is the most effective but also the most difficult to do because the enemy has to be convinced of the deception, which is more challenging than simply hiding the truth from the enemy (Schmitt, 1990). To safely arrive at the desired location, therefore, one has to be able to lead the enemy's attention to the wrong direction.

Second, an army should be mobilized only when a gain is foreseen. The objective of a war is always to secure the nation's interests through military victories. The winner gets to secure his interests while the loser must make concessions. Therefore, Sun Tzu said, one should only go to war in the interest of the nation. The same is true for maneuvering. In order to obtain an advantageous position over the enemy, one can distract the enemy or entice them toward the wrong direction. However, one should always keep in mind that the enemy can attempt the same strategy. Therefore, one needs to be vigilant to avoid being deceived by the enemy.

Third, an army should be responsive to changing conditions. This means an army should be flexible and well coordinated to either disperse or concentrate its forces according to the enemy's movement and terrain conditions. The flexible changes of one's disposition can not only contribute to effective movement, but also help conceal one's movement or even confuse the enemy. Du Mu, a poet of the Tang Dynasty, commented that one can disperse and re-concentrate one's forces to confuse the enemy and observe how they react to the changes (Cleary, 1988). Chapter 8 of this book will discuss more about Sun Tzu's tactics for variation in detail.

In addition to the three general principles noted, Sun Tzu also pointed out the potential assistance of neighboring countries or local guides for successful maneuvering. As such, he advocated the importance of forming alliances in accordance with one's interests. One should also employ reliable local guides to maneuver in the foreign terrain more effectively. In addition to coordination with neighbors and other external parties, Sun Tzu stressed the importance of fast, precise, and cost-effective internal communication. In Sun Tzu's time, this could be accomplished by using gongs, drums, and flags, as it was difficult to relay verbal commands within large armies. These tools not only allowed for effective communication but also unified the army; according to Sun Tzu, a seamless command communication prevents brave soldiers from advancing alone and timid ones from fleeing the battleground. Sun Tzu's discussion of maneuvering involves not just the physical movement of the army but also the communication system of how the general must master the art of effective communication in order to lead the army and obtain assistance from a third party.

7.2   PORTER: TURNING CORPORATE SOCIAL RESPONSIBILITY (CSR) TO CREATING SHARED VALUE (CSV)

In recent times, firms have faced common problems of distrust by consumers and the society. It was common in the past to ignore the environmental and social concerns, and as a result, business practices have gained a negative reputation despite their large contribution to increasing the wealth of the society. In response, companies have attempted to improve their unethical and selfish images through corporate social responsibility (CSR) activities. However, CSR has proven to be inadequate, as these corporate responses have been neither effective nor sustainable.

Porter and Kramer (2011) pointed out that value creation must be seen from a broader perspective by reconceiving the essence of opportunities in the social agendas for business. A way of doing so is to pursue a strategy of creating shared value (CSV). CSV refers to corporate practices that enhance the competitiveness of a company, while simultaneously advancing social and economic conditions of the communities in which it operates (Porter and Kramer, 2011). The central premise behind CSV is that the competitiveness of a company and the health of the communities are mutually dependent. The key to the next wave of growth and redefining capitalism is capitalizing on these connections between societal progress and economic growth.

Porter and Kramer argued that CSV, a method of value creation, is different from CSR, a method of redistribution between the firm and the society. In other words, firms conducting CSR often use a portion of their profits to deal with some social issues. However, through CSV firms create new business opportunities, and society can also obtain related benefits by engaging in activities with firms. This is why Porter and Kramer suggested that CSV could facilitate the transformation of the relationship between business and society from a trade-off to a win-win or coevolutionary situation.

The following introduces Porter and Kramer's (2011) method for distinguishing the two concepts of CSR and CSV. The concept of fair trade is a good example of CSR. Firms engaging in fair trade offer higher prices to poor farmers, and thus the benefits to these farmers come at the expense of firm profits rather than increased values. On the other hand, CSV occurs when firms support farmers in improving farming techniques and efficiency to enhance productivity. The increase in the farmers' productivity, along with the corresponding increase in product quality, eventually would improve their income levels. As shown in this example, CSV is the result of sharing production processes rather than the outputs (e.g., profit). How, then, can one create shared value? Porter and Kramer introduced the following distinctive strategies.

Reconceiving Products and Markets In order to meet neglected social needs, firms have to reconceive their products. The neglected social needs represent the needs of low-income communities of less developed countries. This is consistent with the concept of "bottom of the pyramid" expressed by Prahalad (2004a). For example, the Swiss company Nestlé introduced iodized salt in its products to less developed countries when the company found that children in these regions were receiving less than healthy amounts of iodine. Porter and Kramer also claimed that new methods of product development can be applied to serve existing markets. For example, companies may switch the focus of their food product development from taste and quantity optimization to nutrition and quality maximization.

Redefining Productivity in the Value Chain Firms will unavoidably face various social problems when dealing with value chain activities. These social problems often are the cause for the cost increase. Thus tackling these problems will help reduce production costs or increase the degree of differentiation. On the other hand, the society as a whole can obtain substantial benefits. Consider the case of Nestlé again. In order to secure a sustainable coffee supply from all around the world, Nestlé helped the local farmers with improving production technology and methods as well as with acquiring loans from the bank by providing them assurance services. Accordingly, Nestlé obtained a sustainable supply of good-quality coffee from the farmers.

Enabling Local Cluster Development Companies do not operate in isolation from their surroundings. To compete and thrive, for example, they need reliable local suppliers, good infrastructure such as roads and telecommunication connections, access to talent, and an effective and predictable legal system. Therefore, firms must establish and utilize clusters in order to maximize the synergistic effects that contribute to increasing business and social benefits. The cluster partners can be firms, universities, governments, and other social communities. By cooperating with various related parties, firms can focus on their area of specialization – what they are good at – and increase overall productivity and value creation.

Many approaches to CSR consider businesses as rivals to social well-being. They interpret the nature of firms as cost-reduction minded entities that try to exploit the external society and the environment. Therefore, firms' CSR strategy is more concerned with short-term campaigns (e.g., donations). This might work for temporarily appeasing the public and enhancing their corporate reputation or recovering from the damaged image (e.g., Nike's use of child labor), but these activities will not enhance firms' internal competitiveness. The worst part of CSR is that it becomes less effective as it is not sustainable over time. This is why Porter and Kramer (2011) said the legitimacy of business has fallen to its lowest level in history. Firms should look beyond the one-time promotional effect and incorporate social issues into their value chain and corporate strategy to increase profitability. They should seek to gain real competitiveness in the long run rather than offering short-run, one-time solutions to the social problems.

7.3 THE INTEGRATION OF SUN TZU AND PORTER

7.3.1 *Fundamental Principle (Similarity) and Effect (Difference)*

Common sense dictates that a straight route is shorter than a devious one. However, this is not always the case, as many factors other than distance itself may come into play. It might be more advantageous to take the devious route if, for example, enemy forces have prepared an ambush or the terrain is difficult to traverse in the straight route.

Therefore, Sun Tzu's message in this chapter is that the seemingly long and difficult alternative might provide a better solution for certain problems.

As for CSV – or aiming to make money by solving social problems – although it looks more complicated, time-consuming, and costly compared to the conventional ways of doing business without regard to social influences, firms ultimately obtain more benefits, particularly from the perspective of sustainability. CSV may negatively affect financial performance in the short run, but in the long run it can provide greater social satisfaction and further market opportunities, which are vital for the firm's sustainable development. Although they share the same fundamental principle – turning a disadvantage into an advantage – the effects of these strategies are different. Proper military maneuvering only benefits one's own force, at the expense of the enemy. However, the CSV strategy can benefit both the firm and society.

7.3.2   Objective (Similarity) and Means (Difference)

Sun Tzu said that military maneuvering should only be conducted when there is an advantage. The bottom line is that the gains from taking the devious route should be greater than the costs. For CSV, Porter and Kramer claimed that the guiding principle is not philanthropy, but the self-interested act of creating economic value by addressing social issues. Therefore, firms are motivated to conduct CSV only when the benefits are greater than the costs in dealing with social activities.

However, there is a difference between the two in terms of the means of achieving advantages. In military maneuvering, deception is necessary to achieve this goal. The successful use of deception can misguide the enemy and force them away from the true reality. With the enemy's combat power diverted, one can strike a surprise attack on the enemy's weak points, thereby achieving strategic advantage (Wee et al., 1991). In business, however, CSV is a more sustainable way of achieving competitive advantage in the long run. Therefore, unlike maneuvering in war, firms should not deceive the society but they need to find the connection between corporate and social benefits to meet neglected social needs while ultimately gaining strategic advantages for their businesses.

7.3.3 *Relationship with Other Alliances*

In maneuvering, Sun Tzu emphasized making alliances with neighbors and consulting with local guides to take advantage of local terrain. Similarly, for CSV, Porter and Kramer highlighted the importance of developing a local cluster. Porter and Kramer said that no company is self-contained and the success of a company requires the support from other companies, organizations, and institutions. In addition, Sun Tzu said one should know the real intention of one's neighbors before making alliances with them. Similarly, Porter and Kramer said the formation of open and transparent markets is important for building an efficient cluster because the transparent market allows companies to secure reliable partners by making information equally accessible for all players.

Porter and Kramer's three strategies for CSV are very helpful for scholars and practitioners, but some of Sun Tzu's ideas on maneuvering strategy can be used to further enrich the theoretical development of CSV. For example, we saw Sun Tzu articulate how to organize and unify the movement of soldiers while maneuvering them. He mentioned the use of gongs, drums, and other tools to communicate effectively. At the first glance, these examples may seem primitive and irrelevant to today's business world. But if one can look beyond the superficiality of methods, applying Sun Tzu's idea to CSV will be very helpful for firms in business. Unlike traditional business practices, CSV involves various social communities with an emphasis on long-term growth and profitability, and effective communication among related firms, organizations, and institutions. Porter and Kramer have articulated many benefits of building local clusters; however, the benefits associated with clusters cannot be achieved without effective interorganizational communication. In the field of CSV, further studies are needed particularly on *how* to obtain the relational advantages through effective communication.

7.4   MILITARY CASE: THE LONG MARCH OF THE CHINESE RED ARMY

The Long March was a military retreat by the Red Army of the Communist Party of China in order to escape the chase by the *Kuomintang* (Chinese Nationalist Party) army.[2] Throughout the conflict, there were a series of marches as Communist armies in the south escaped to the north and west of China. Among them, the march from Jiangxi province, which began in October 1934, was the most well known. The Long March is regarded as one of the most impressive physical feats of the twentieth century. Although the Red Army lost most of its men during the Long March, the event was a turning point for the success of the Communist Revolution.

In the autumn of 1933, the *Kuomintang* led by Chiang Kai-shek launched a huge attack against the Communists based in Jiangxi and Fujian provinces in Southeast China. Against the advice of Mao Zedong, the Communists went ahead with the strategy advocated by Russian agents led by Otto Braun and initiated full-scale attacks against the *Kuomintang*. Mao was expelled from the Chinese Communist Party's Central Committee as he opposed the plan. The strategy of Braun, however, proved to be extremely costly for the Communists. They lost men and equipment, and moreover they could not get supplies from another Communist base at Hunan because Jiangxi base was besieged by the *Kuomintang*.

The Red Army decided to abandon their Jiangxi Soviet base and accepted Braun's idea of a full-scale retreat from Jiangxi to another Communist base in Hunan. The retreat, termed the Long March, started in October 1934, with 87,000 soldiers, and it took the Red Army forty days to get through the blockhouses surrounding

---

[2]   The case is abstracted and modified from www.historylearningsite.co.uk/long_march_1934_to_1935.htm, and www.history.com/topics/long-march.

Jiangxi. However, they were then immediately attacked by the *Kuomintang* at the Xiang River, where they lost over half of their men. After failing to break through the *Kuomintang*'s Fifth Encirclement Campaign, the Red Army planned to move to another safe place. However, the *Kuomintang* had already prepared several traps and monitored their movements closely. At this critical moment, the Red Army held a meeting in Zunyi, where leadership was transferred back to Mao.

Mao, with the support of Zhu De, immediately adopted new tactics. He wanted the Red Army to move in a completely unpredictable way. When moving away from Xiang River, the Red Army took winding routes that made it extremely difficult for the *Kuomintang* to anticipate their move. Mao also split up the Red Army into smaller units and planned an escape toward a new destination – Shanxi province in northern China. The Long March was physically demanding as it involved traversing extremely treacherous terrain.

Officially, the march lasted over 370 days across 8,000 miles – consisting of twenty-four rivers, eighteen mountain ranges (five covered with snow), and eleven provinces – until the army finally arrived at the caves of Yan'an of Shanxi province on the edge of the Gobi desert in northern China. The army fought an average of one battle a day and spent a total of fifteen days in major battles. By October 1935, fewer than 10,000 men, about only one-tenth of the force that left Jiangxi, had survived the march. However, the survivors combined forces with other Communist troops in Yan'an to build a formidable military force of 80,000.

This Long March shows a case of the devious route for achieving the desired goal more effectively. Sun Tzu suggested three principles to turn the devious into the straight. The first principle is that warfare is a game of deception. In the beginning, the Communist Party of China led by Braun engaged in direct head-to-head fighting with the *Kuomintang*, which resulted in failure. When the Communist Party decided to retreat from Jiangxi, Braun still insisted on taking a straight path, which resulted in additional losses. In contrast, Mao's strategy utilized twisted patterns to disguise their movement. Thus, the *Kuomintang* was unable to predict the Red Army's movement, and Mao's troops safely escaped. Mao's devious route turned out to be more effective than Braun's straightforward retreat, consistent with the teaching of Sun Tzu.

The second principle is that military forces should be mobilized only when there is a foreseeable gain. Due to the failure in breaking the Fifth Encirclement Campaign launched by the *Kuomintang*, the Red Army, led by Mao, had no option but to retreat to another safe place for long-run development. In this case, the gain that motivated the army was survival itself. During the Long March, the Red Army suffered great losses in terms of the number of soldiers, equipment, and other resources. Despite the enormous costs, the Red Army successfully traversed very long distance and overcame numerous difficulties to arrive at the new base in Shanxi province. Otherwise, the whole army would have been annihilated by the enemy.

The third principle is that an army should operate by appropriately dividing and concentrating forces. In the beginning of the march, the Red Army moved both combat and support forces simultaneously. However, this strategy slowed down their movement substantially. In order to overcome the disadvantageous position, the Red Army eventually restructured the entire army and reduced support forces to bolster the strength of combat forces. In addition, in order to flexibly organize movement during the march without being discovered by the enemy, the Red Army divided their forces into several small units and later combined them into a single force in Yan'an. Their performance was much enhanced when their strategy became consistent with this third principle.

Sun Tzu emphasized caution and continuous calculation of advantages and disadvantages, but there is no explicit explanation of what the advantages are. The military case of the Long March illustrates some specific examples of these advantages. Although the Red Army suffered heavy losses, they gained substantial boosts to their psychological and social consolidation. Psychologically, the victorious march strengthened the trust in Mao's leadership and the idea that a strong will can overcome any difficulty. Socially, along the routes of the Long March, the Red Army not only obtained help from local peasants, but gained many new recruits. These activities actually contributed to the strong ties between the Communist party and the public.

These advantages were critical for the Red Army to successfully complete the march. Without the help of local people, the result would have been quite different. However, what is also important is the contribution of the Red Army to the social and economic development of rural areas, by leading them to class struggle, stimulating the armed peasants for uprisings, and redistributing the wealth among the rich and the poor (Zhang, 2016). Sun Tzu emphasized the importance of assistance from local people for guides, yet in the Long March, there was a clear case of mutual assistance between the Red Army and the public. This cooperative relationship is particularly important for building sustainable and long-term relations, as is the case of CSV in business.

7.5 BUSINESS CASE: NESTLÉ'S CSV ACTIVITIES IN INDIA

Nestlé's relationship with India started in 1912, when it began trading as the Nestlé Anglo-Swiss Condensed Milk Company Limited, importing and selling finished products in the Indian market.[3] Nestlé, a Swiss company, sold food and health products, such as baby food, bottled water, coffee, dairy products, pet food, and snacks. After India's independence in 1947, the Indian government required foreign firms to establish local production in some industries. In response to this policy, Nestlé set up its first factory in 1961 in Moga, where the government wanted Nestlé to help develop the dairy industry in India .

In 1962, the Northern district of Moga was very poor. People lived without electricity, proper transportation, telephones, or medical care. A farmer typically owned less than five acres of poorly irrigated and

---

[3] The case is abstracted and modified from Porter and Kramer (2006), Moon (2014b), and Harvard Business Review (2011).

infertile soil. Many households kept a single cow that produced just enough milk for their own consumption, and more than half of the calves died as newborns. At the same time, the farmers did not have access to good methods for refrigeration, transportation, and quality control; thus, the milk they produced was often of poor quality, frequently contaminated, and could not be moved very far.

In order to improve the poor conditions in Moga, Nestlé built refrigerated dairy collection centers in each town and sent trucks to collect milk. Nestlé also sent veterinarians, nutritionists, agronomists, and other quality control experts to monitor the milk production. Medicines and nutritional supplements were provided for sick animals, and monthly training sessions were held for local farmers. Nestlé also educated farmers on basic farming and animal husbandry practices and helped increase milk yields through improved dairy farming, irrigation, and crop management practices. In addition, the company provided assistance with cattle feed, quality fodder seeds, veterinary medicines and mineral mixture, and procurement of bank loans.

With financing and technical assistance from Nestlé, farmers began to dig previously unaffordable deep wells. The improved irrigation not only fed cows but increased crop yields, producing surplus wheat and rice and raising the standard of living. Support from Nestlé went beyond the dairy farmers. The company helped construct drinking water facilities, lavatories, and village schools in the area. This was a joint effort with local schools, parent associations, and village administrations. Another project involved the funding of tuberculosis clinics to treat residents in Moga and other nearby villages.

When Nestlé first opened its milk factory, it was only able to collect milk from 180 local farmers. Today, Nestlé buys milk from more than 75,000 farmers in the region, collecting twice a day from more than 650 village dairies. The death rate of calves decreased by 75 percent, while milk production increased by fifty times. As the quality of milk improved, Nestlé was able to pay higher prices to farmers than those initially set by the government, and the steady biweekly payments enabled farmers to obtain credit from the bank. Competing dairies and milk factories opened, and an industry cluster began to develop.

By working very closely with farmers and administrators in the Moga Milk District, Nestlé helped raise the quality of milk, while improving the health and living standards of farmers and other residents. Today, Moga has significantly higher standards of living than any other neighboring regions. The majority of homes have access to electricity, and most have installed telephones. Primary education is available for all villages, and secondary education for many villages. Moga has also more doctors than neighboring regions. Meanwhile, the increased purchasing power of local farmers has in turn greatly expanded the market for Nestlé's products, further supporting the firm's business activities.

Companies can improve the competitive context in which they operate, by investing in their communities. Nestlé's activities are consistent with Porter and Kramer's CSV strategy, since Nestlé pursued its business development together with social development. Nestlé's activities reflect Porter and Kramer's second and third CSV strategies particularly well. Local farmers were directly involved in Nestlé's value chain activities, including inbound and outbound logistics, and operations. Nestlé worked closely with the farmers of the Moga Milk District, investing in local infrastructure and transferring world-class technology to build a competitive milk supply chain. It simultaneously generated social benefits through improved health care, better education, and economic development. This in turn contributed to enhancing the purchasing power of local people, and benefitted Nestlé as well through the increase of sales. Moreover, the efforts and constant communication with local authorities and agencies played a crucial role in building trust and understanding the real needs of local communities.

Nestlé's strategy can also be explained by Sun Tzu's military strategy of this chapter. The requirement by the Indian government for local production in the region of Moga was initially a huge disadvantage for Nestlé as it would increase production costs raising from the region's poor infrastructure. At that time, it seemed more practical for Nestlé to outsource or import the necessary raw inputs from other countries. However, Nestlé invested a large amount of money in the region in various ways. These investments and other strategies meant it took longer for the company to get its business running and making profits, but the results have been far more successful than expected. Moreover, the improvement of local living standards further promoted the consumer demand for milk and other products. This is in agreement with Sun Tzu's idea of "turning the devious into the straight." Nestlé's CSV strategy turned the disadvantageous position into an advantageous one for its business in India.

However, the recommendation of Sun Tzu, to utilize deception, is never allowed in the business world. Some companies may wish to improve their image through CSR or CSV activities, and they assume that the social benefits they generate will compensate for their mistakes in business to some extent. However, in reality, consumers shy away from companies with negative reputations, regardless of their significant contributions to the society. An incident of Nestlé serves as a good example. Nestlé's Maggi line of instant noodles sold in India was found to contain a high level of lead and monosodium glutamate in early 2015 by local safety regulators. Nestlé underestimated the problem and remained quiet for the first few weeks following the first recall order, declaring its products safe to eat. Unfortunately for Nestlé, however, the consumers were not convinced easily. The situation turned into a full-blown crisis aggravated by the slow response; stock prices dropped around 15 percent before the company finally decided to recall all Maggi noodles from store shelves (Chhabara, 2015).[4] This incident shows how firms need to address critical issues with greater authenticity compared to the military situation of Sun Tzu.

---

[4]   Nestlé Maggi noodles have been the brand products for more than three decades in India, and in 2014 its sales revenues accounted for more than 20 percent of India's total revenue (Chhabara, 2015).

7.6 CONCLUSION AND IMPLICATIONS

In this chapter, I discussed the strategy of turning the devious route into the straight, in which a seemingly inefficient or hazardous devious route can be more effective in gaining a positional advantage in war. Although Sun Tzu emphasized the importance of speed, it should not be sought in an absolute term but in a term relative to the enemy. While Sun Tzu's advice on maneuvering can definitely be applied to strong armies in minimizing losses, it can also be a valuable teaching for the armies that find themselves at a disadvantage in battles. At the same time, however, the corresponding dangers in adopting this strategy must be recognized. For successful maneuvering, Sun Tzu suggested three principles: use deception; be motivated only when a gain is foreseen; and be responsive to the changes in the environment.

For business, this chapter examined the concept of CSV proposed by Porter and Kramer. The key theme of CSV is to change both managerial and societal attitudes toward the coevolutionary relationship between the business and society. In fact, the two dimensions are in an interdependent rather than a trade-off relationship. According to this new perspective, firms can generate a greater economic value by addressing social needs and challenges, and by finding a mutually beneficial area between the two. Porter and Kramer have made great contributions to the academic world and beyond. Not only does their work show a path to further growth for economies and societies, but it also suggests how firms can gain back trust and legitimacy from the society in which they operate.

Both Sun Tzu and Porter can improve their strategies by incorporating useful concepts from each other. For military strategy, Sun Tzu emphasized the help from neighboring countries and local people to achieve success when maneuvering. However, as shown in the military case of this chapter, the Red Army did not just unilaterally obtain assistance from local people, but it also made significant contributions to local economic and social development. This coevolutionary (i.e., win-win) relationship with the public further strengthened the Red Army. In this respect, Porter's CSV concept can provide some meaningful implications for Sun Tzu. On the other hand, CSV strategies can also be further developed by incorporating Sun Tzu's strategies in establishing effective communication for firms when developing a cluster with external parties. If Nestlé had pursued more active and effective communication with local governments, media, and the public in India, the incident might have been less serious.

8 Strategic Flexibility

Sun Tzu: Variation of tactics
Porter: Consistency and changes in business strategy and operations

Charles Darwin argued 150 years ago in his book, *On the Origin of Species*, "It is not the strongest of the species that survives, nor the most intelligent that survives. It is the one that is most adaptable to change." Sun Tzu 2,500 years ago also attributed immense significance to varying tactics according to environmental changes, which is the main topic of his eighth chapter, *"Jiu Bian"* or "Variation of Tactics." The title means nine changes, with *Jiu* meaning nine. However, *Jiu* in the chapter "Variation of Tactics" does not literally mean the number nine. Instead, it indicates an indefinitely large number. Therefore, I have chosen to translate the title as "Variation of Tactics." Although some strategists (e.g., Cao Cao) interpreted it as nine types of changes and tried to find out nine specific military tactics, many other scholars view it as representing an infinite number, as Sun Tzu did not exactly enumerate nine types of tactical variations in his chapter *"Jiu Bian."*

The keyword of the chapter "Variation of Tactics" is flexibility: flexible interpretation and application of the principles that can fit the changing situation as opposed to letting the principles bind one's movements. Strategy is the concept at the higher level and tactic is at the lower level of operation. Strategy is the thought that directs one's behavior and tactic is the means of implementing the thought; strategy tells *what* the right thing is and tactic tells *how* to do the right thing (Michaelson and Michaelson, 2003). A war tends to course through numerous turns and twists, often in a fashion outrunning the observers' expectations. That is why Sun Tzu emphasized in this chapter that the tactics to realize the strategic goals should be flexible enough to adapt to the environmental changes. A good general, or a strategist, should seek to actively engage in steering the situations to his own advantage and shaping the war's course in the desired direction.

I will compare Sun Tzu's variation of tactics with that of Porter's at the strategic and operational levels. Porter (1996) argued that frequent changes in competitive strategy will be costly and less efficient, and moreover confuse the customers and other stakeholders. According to Porter, this is because the strategic change requires both internal fit (among internal organizations) and external fit (with external parties such as suppliers and buyers), and such fit as a routine is difficult to achieve in a timely fashion. On the other hand, Porter said that firms should continuously change their operations depending on the changing competitive forces (i.e., industry structure). This idea of preserving a consistent strategy while varying the operations or the methods for carrying out the strategy is essentially the same as the core argument of Sun Tzu in "Variation of Tactics."

On the other hand, Porter was more concerned about the necessity of adaptation to the environmental changes and benefits that bring for firms than their disadvantages. This insufficiency in Porter's review on adaptation to environmental changes can be complemented by borrowing ideas from the military principles of Sun Tzu, who argued varying tactics should be based on comprehensive contemplation of both favorable and unfavorable factors in a particular situation. The focus of the current chapter is at comparing Sun Tzu's and Porter's theories on using variation of tactics to match situational changes. For the case studies, I will introduce the military case of the Trojan War and the business case of Haier Group to help readers understand and utilize these strategic linkages between war and business.

8.1　SUN TZU: VARIATION OF TACTICS

According to Sun Tzu, a general who does not have a complete understanding of the variation of tactics will not be able to take advantage of them and make full use of his troops. This principle requires the general to have an ability to control the situation, rather than being bound to established procedures (Griffith, 1963). Clausewitz (1968 [1832]) also made indirect references to the importance of the variation of tactics. He argued that military genius is a very important factor in war, and he particularly emphasized the capacity of making an appropriate decision and transforming it into practice for different situations, given the four elements comprising the situation of war – danger, exertion, uncertainty, and chance.

8.1.1 Variation of Tactics for Five Exceptional Situations

In the beginning of the chapter "Variation of Tactics" of *The Art of War*, Sun Tzu introduced five specific situations of varying the tactics, where it is not appropriate to apply the general principles.[1] In these situations, it is particularly important for generals to recognize the appropriate time and place to attack the enemy.

First, there are roads not to-follow. Even if a road may seem easy to pass in normal situations, there are times when one should not follow it, but choose the devious and difficult one, because there could be traps and dangers prepared by the enemy.

Second, there are armies not to attack. Even when it seems like a perfect opportunity to attack the enemy, one should refrain from attacking, because there is a possibility that the enemy will fight to the death or because the enemy troops may have been sent as bait.

Third, there are fortified castles not to attack. Even if a castle is isolated and seemingly easy to attack, it should not be attacked if it is well stocked with provisions and defended by strong troops under the command of a wise general and loyal soldiers.

Fourth, there are terrains not to contest. Some lands are relatively easy to obtain, but difficult to maintain. Thus, even if one is able to contest over and win the land, such terrain may have little value or one will probably be counterattacked and suffer casualties.

Fifth, there are commands of sovereigns not to accept. Although the order of sovereigns should be normally followed, it is not to be

---

[1]   Refer to Griffith (1963) and Shi (2000) for more explanation of the five exceptional situations.

followed when the general realizes that there would be disadvantages and consequent harm. Cao Cao said, "In military operations, the general does not need to be restricted by the commands of the sovereign."

In addition to the listed five things to avoid for effective variation of tactics, Sun Tzu also listed five dangers to avoid for a military leader: one who is determined to die can be killed; one who is determined to survive can be captured; one who is easily angered can be insulted; one who is sensitive to moral integrity can be obstructed by a sense of shame; and one who loves his people can be indecisive.[2] These five dangers are warnings against the five virtues (i.e., intelligence, trustworthiness, benevolence, courage, and sternness)[3] of a general explained in Sun Tzu's first chapter "Laying Plans."

However, there is a controversy over what Sun Tzu meant by the variation of tactics. One argument is that the variation of tactics refers to the five things to avoid. However, as Sun Tzu said, "A general who does not know the art of varying tactics will not be able to make full use of his army," even if a general knows about the five things to avoid, the variation of tactics is not just about those five, but includes a more fundamental concept that encompasses far more numerous situations.

8.1.2 Principles of the Variation of Tactics

Sun Tzu proposed two major principles for the variation of tactics: one is considering both the favorable and unfavorable factors, and the other is making a complete preparation for every possible situation. Like two sides of the same coin, any situation is bound to have both favorable and unfavorable factors. If a general sees only the favorable perspectives of the situations but ignores unfavorable ones, he is doomed to fail because he cannot make fair judgment when misfortunes are ahead. Alternatively, if a general understands the

---

2   The Chinese characters are: 將有五危: 必死可殺, 必生可虜, 忿速可侮, 廉潔可辱, 愛民可煩.

3   The Chinese characters are: 智信仁勇嚴.

unfavorable but cannot see the favorable factors, he will not be able to turn around the unfavorable situation. Therefore, for appropriately varying the tactics, wise generals should consider both favorable and unfavorable factors simultaneously. Sun Tzu said, "By considering the favorable factors (when faced with difficulties), one will be able to accomplish tasks. By considering the unfavorable factors (when everything proceeds smoothly), one will be able to avoid possible disasters."[4]

The favorable and unfavorable factors are not fixed. One can move the enemy and turn their advantages into disadvantages, while turning one's disadvantages into advantages through appropriate manipulation of the benefits and harms (e.g., Sun Tzu's maneuvering strategy introduced in Chapter 7). However, the transition does not happen automatically, but requires extra effort. Sun Tzu gave some useful examples to better understand this concept. For example, one intimidates the enemy by inflicting injury upon them, so that the enemy can no longer be a threat; one keeps the enemy constantly occupied, so that the enemy has no time to pay attention to one's army; one entices the enemy by offering advantages, thereby making the enemy follow one's orders.

More importantly, in order to simultaneously consider both the favorable and unfavorable factors, Sun Tzu emphasized the necessity of thorough preparation for the uncertain future. He said, "Do not assume the enemy will not come, but always be ready for them. Do not presume that they will not attack, but make oneself so strong that one's forces are invincible."[5] The former part of this advice means that one should make oneself fully prepared to be able to respond whenever the enemy attacks, rather than merely relying on the expectation that the enemy will always comply with one's plans or anticipations. For the latter, he highlighted the way of preparation – that one should enhance one's absolute military competence – so that strengths can be

---

[4]   The Chinese characters are: 雜於利, 而務可信也; 雜於害, 而患可解也.
[5]   The Chinese characters are: 無恃其不來, 恃吾有以待也; 無恃其不攻, 恃吾有所不可攻也.

even more reinforced and weaknesses can be supplemented, leaving no opportunity for the enemy to take advantage of. This thought also warns people against engaging in groundless opportunism relying on the external chance event and advocates the strengthening of internal capacity for winning the victory.

8.2   PORTER: CONSISTENCY AND CHANGES IN BUSINESS STRATEGY AND OPERATIONS

8.2.1   Porter's Definition on Strategy

In the field of strategic management, scholars try to search for the sources of firms' competitive advantage. Although there are different views for explaining the sources of firms' superior performance, Porter's (1980) frameworks (e.g., five forces model and generic strategy) are particularly important. As previously explained, the main argument of the five forces model is that the industry structure determines the firm's profitability; and the essence of strategy formulation is to cope with competition. Firms need to match their strengths and weaknesses to the given industrial structure; thus a strategy can be regarded as finding a position in the industry where the forces are the weakest. Porter then clearly defined competitive strategy as the search for a favorable competitive position in an industry.

In addition, Porter (1980, 1985) introduced generic strategies in terms of the source and scope of competitive advantage, and argued that firms have to choose one of these four generic strategies.[6] Otherwise, they will be "stuck in the middle," which will result in the poor performance of the business. Porter (1996) then changed his definition of strategy, saying that strategy is the creation of a unique and sustainable position by serving different types of products or services and delivering a core value. However, despite changing definitions of strategy, the central idea of Porter's strategy has not changed. It is about keeping away from the competition. Although "me-too" strategy may help a company improve efficiency in the

---

[6]   Cost leadership, broad differentiation, cost focus, and differentiation focus.

short run, it will ultimately lead to destructive competition through price discount, thereby decreasing the margins along with the competition in the long run.

Then what is a good strategy? Porter (1996) suggested two preconditions for maintaining sustainable competitive advantage: trade-offs and fit. Trade-offs are important to strategy because they create the need for making a choice and deliberately limit what a company can offer. Fit is important because it requires consistency and harmony among the various activities for strategic positions and combines them into a "strong network," thereby locking out imitation by rivals. Porter (1996) warned growth imperative is hazardous to strategy, because efforts to grow in size blur uniqueness, create compromises, reduce fit, and ultimately undermine the current competitive advantage. Therefore, *strategic continuity* is important to reinforce and extend company's position.

8.2.2 Changes in Strategy and Operations

Once a firm has occupied a favorable position in an industry, then when should it change its current strategic position? According to Porter (1980), a firm may have to change its strategy if the industrial structure changes. For example, the industry structure may change when consumers look for a change, when entry barriers become lower with the introduction of new technology, and so on. However, before a firm changes its position, it has to make sure that the choice of new position is driven by the ability to find new trade-offs and then create a new system of activities with a good fit among them. This is because a sound strategy and implementation of the strategic goals require a strong support of the organizational structure. Some scholars, such as Chandler (1962) and Bartlett and Ghoshal (1989), also stressed that the establishment of a corporate strategy should be in accordance with the organizational structure.

On the other hand, Porter (1996) claimed that one should distinguish between the continuity of strategy and the change in operations. While maintaining a unique positioning, firms should pay attention to keeping up with constant change in specific operations of value chain activities (e.g., production and service), compared to the best practices at the current time.[7] Therefore, a strategy should be kept consistent over time, but the process of implementing the strategy should continuously improve (Porter, 1997).

For a broader understanding of the strategic scope, Porter (1987) made a distinction between a competitive strategy and a corporate strategy, for a diversified firm. Competitive strategy concerns how to create a competitive advantage in the business where a firm competes. In contrast, corporate strategy concerns two major questions: (1) which business fields the firm should be engaged in, and (2) how it should manage the array of business units. The importance of corporate strategy is that a firm can benefit more from business diversification than from a single business because there can be synergy effects which make the firms gain additional benefits. Therefore, competitive strategy is analyzed at the single business (unit) level, but corporate strategy at the company (or companywide) level, comprising multiple business units.

8.3   THE INTEGRATION OF SUN TZU AND PORTER

8.3.1   Comparison of Changes in Military and Business Strategies

A military strategist must consider the ultimate objective of warfare as well as the general principles that should be applied when heading into war. In Clausewitz's (1968[1832]) view, warfare is the extension of politics, so a strategy weighs the benefits of warfare as it would contribute to the attainment of political goals. Once it is agreed that

---

[7]   Dynamic capability theory (Teece, Pisano, and Shuen, 1997) has a similar view to this. Dynamic capability theory was developed to complement the limitation of resource-based view of the firm, which is static to fully explain the volatile business environment. The term "dynamic" is defined as "the capacity to renew competences so as to achieve congruence with the changing business environment" (Teece et al., 1997: 515). The authors argued that the successful firms in the current global market are often characterized as follows: (1) timely adaptation, (2) fast and flexible production innovation, and (3) management capability by redeploying and combining internal and external competences.

warfare is necessary to achieve the political goals, leaders then turn to tactics, which dictate the specific ways in which military resources can be allotted and positioned in order to obtain advantages in warfare.

Sun Tzu argued in this chapter that a military leader should master the general military principles and also flexibly apply them in practice. The general principle refers to the universal strategic guideline and it is applicable in multiple situations. For example, many of Sun Tzu's basic military guidelines (e.g., winning without fighting, swift victory, and *Cheng* and *Chi*) are valuable even in modern wars and also for countries outside the Chinese cultural realm. On the other hand, although the general principles are theoretically correct, they are not meant to be taken literally, word by word in a fixed matter in actual practice. Every war takes on a different form and situation due to infinite combinations of different reasons. Even when strategies may seem to be similar to one another, if one looks at them in detail, one may find different factors that are difficult to generalize and apply to other wars.

In business, change is an ever-present feature for firms both at the strategic and operational levels (Burnes, 2004). It is not only because of different situations among different firms, but even within the same firm, both corporate and competitive strategies would change in different periods in order to achieve continuous growth. For example, General Electric's business position has changed over time (Ocasio and Joseph, 2008). When it acquired Thomas Edison's company in 1890, it focused on lighting business. However, currently its business is composed of capital, energy, technology infrastructure, and home & business solutions (i.e., the change of *corporate strategy*).

Another example is Hyundai Motors, which started as a cheap, compact car producer, but has changed its strategic position to produce more luxury cars (e.g., Genesis) and technologically advanced cars (e.g., hybrids) (Moon, 2016b). As firms are growing, they are willing to or even required to change and adjust their strategy in accordance with the change in their positions in the industry. According to my concept of dynamic evolution of firm's strategy, one has two types of strategic evolution (Moon, 1993). The first type of strategic evolution follows a route that begins with a cost focus, then cost leadership, and finally broad differentiation. The second route is from cost focus to differentiation focus, and then to broad differentiation.[8]

Unlike Sun Tzu who mainly advocated for the variation of tactics, Porter emphasized more the continuity of strategy, although Porter also mentioned the importance of change at the operational level in business. This may be because of the distinctive nature between war and business. War is a one-time transaction, while business is a multi-time transaction. Thus, the long-term (i.e., sustainability) aspect of strategic consistency in business is more important. In this respect, it is advised that business strategies not be frequently changed at a strategic level. Porter (1985) said a firm should stick to its (competitive) strategy (i.e., one of the four generic strategies) because otherwise it will allocate resources inefficiently and customers will get confused about what the firm represents (i.e., stuck in the middle). This statement implies that frequently changing strategy is not preferable, as strategic continuity is important to reinforce and extend the firm's position. However, despite the need for a consistent direction in the overall strategic goal, the specific implementation of strategies (like the variations of military tactics) should not be fixed, but be flexible with environmental changes in order to effectively take advantage of the situation.

8.3.2   The Essence of Strategies

Sun Tzu suggested variation of tactics that should be flexibly applied according to the conditions in the actual battlefields. It is important for the generals to make a right decision. If not, the decision will lead to a disaster in war. The essence of right decision making is to know what to do and what not do to, as Sun Tzu explained do's and don'ts for several cases. In business, it is also important for firms to know what to do and what not to do. The core message of Porter's strategy is

---

[8]   For more information, see Chapter 4 and Moon (1993).

making choices of what to do and what not to do. Strategy is a matter of "choice" (Prasad, 2010). As in the five forces model, choosing the favorable position in an industry to minimize the threats from various industrial competitive forces is the essence of strategy. Regarding the generic strategy, choosing the appropriate set of activities to match with the one of the generic strategies, thereby avoiding the problem of being stuck in the middle, is the essence of strategy. From this perspective, Porter's (1996) operational effectiveness does not count as a strategy, because it is what a firm should do and has nothing to do with choice.

8.4 MILITARY CASE: THE VICTORY OF THE GREEKS IN THE TROJAN WAR

The Trojan War is a military conflict that occurred between Greeks, often referred to as Argives or Achaeans in classical literature, and Trojans that appears in Homer's epic poem, *The Iliad*.[9] While the very existence of Troy itself was doubted for a long time, a recent archeological discovery ascertained the city's historical existence, which in turn greatly enhanced the credibility of accounts of a great war that brought on the end of this city.

According to the Homeric tradition, the conflict occurred because of the scandalous love affair between Prince Paris of Troy and Queen Helen of Sparta. The legends claim that Paris, who was a guest at the palace of Menelaus, the king of Sparta, stole away with his wife, Helen, and the outraged Menelaus appealed to other Argive lords, who instantly responded to the call to punish Troy for its treacherous behavior and to restore the damaged honor and pride of Achaea. After the first battle between the two armies, the Trojans fled to their city. Troy was a part of a city-state alliance system on the Anatolian peninsula, and it was supplied by neighboring city kingdoms. Therefore, the

[9] Information of this case study is abstracted and modified from www.greekmyths-greek mythology.com/trojan-war-myth/, www.ancient.eu/Trojan_War/, and www.wattpad .com/13106893-the-greek-mythology-the-trojan-war.

Greeks continued to raise numerous campaigns across the area to keep Troy's allies from supplying and reinforcing it.

The Greeks won many important battles and gathered a large amount of resources and other spoils of war from these battles. However, the Greeks could not break down the walls of Troy, because of the steep terrain and strong fortification which was difficult to attack. It took the Greeks ten years to maintain all these operations, and the Greeks suffered great losses, because of the long supply lines and long years of maintaining these operations. The situation led the Greek leaders to come to the conclusion that it was not good to continue on with the same old strategy.

According to Homer's *Iliad*, one of the Greek lords, Odysseus – whose name always appears with modifiers such as clever, wise, or cunning – came up with the idea of building a giant wooden horse, which later came to be known as the Trojan Horse. Its insides were hollow so that soldiers could hide there. Once the statue was finished by the artist Epeius, a small group of Greek warriors along with Odysseus himself climbed inside. The remaining troops sailed away from Troy, pretending to have tired of the long, fruitless campaign. Sinon was the only man left behind. When the Trojans marveled at the huge creation, Sinon put on a show of anger against the Greeks, who he claimed to have deserted him. He assured the Trojans that the wooden horse was safe and would bring luck to the Trojans. Only two people, Laocoon and Cassandra, in Troy, insisted on burning the horse, while other Trojans remained reluctant.

Despite some suspicions and suggestions to burn it, the Trojans decided to dedicate the horse to goddess Athena and joyfully placed it in front of her temple inside the city's walls to celebrate the victory. That night, after most of the Trojans were asleep or drunken, Sinon let the Greek warriors out of the horse. Those warriors opened the gate for the Greek army that had sailed back under cover of night. They flooded in like a tide and slaughtered the Trojans. The Greek army decisively ended the war by destroying the city of Troy. The Greeks basically achieved what they struggled with for ten years over a single night.

While many scholars agree that the Trojan War did take place in one form or another, whether *The Illiad*'s account of the details of the war is faithful to actual history is up to heated debate and doubts. Regardless of the fact, however, the famous plot line of this mythic war is interesting in terms of how it embodies Sun Tzu's key concepts regarding the variation of tactics. Sun Tzu suggested the variation of tactics according to different situations. Before they slaughtered the city of Troy, the Greeks had utilized different ways such as attacking the ally cities of Troy in order to deplete their resources but still could not break down the walls of Troy. The steep terrain placed the Greeks on an almost decisively disadvantageous position defying all kinds of traditional methods of attack. This is what Sun Tzu meant by fortified castles not to attack.[10]

On the other hand, Sun Tzu stated that a general should consider the favorable and unfavorable factors simultaneously. If one takes into account of the favorable factors within the unfavorable situations, one can resolve the difficulties. Given the obstacles of fortified walls, Odysseus, supposedly the best tactician, came up with the brilliant tactic of bringing the wooden horse inside the walls. At the same time, he played with the psychology of the Trojans by making them loosen their guards and indulge in moods of festivities and relaxation through the pretend-retreat of the Greek fleet. By utilizing a combination of *Chi* strategies, the Greeks obtained a victory in the war.

The Greeks turned their disadvantages into advantages by using the idea of a wooden horse. This allowed them to make an effective attack from the inside, which would not have been possible from the outside of the city walls. In this respect, the Greeks' strategy is consistent with Sun Tzu's idea of turning the devious into the straight introduced in Chapter 7. The direct route proved to be more difficult than the devious one due to multiple factors affecting the route such

---

[10] As a matter of fact, the sequel of *The Iliad*, *The Odyssey*, notes that except for a very few, such as Nestor and Menelaus, many Greek lords and warriors ended up losing everything due to the war despite their victory, as the long-time absence due to the campaign brewed treason back home and accidents happened on the return way.

as the city walls, the strength of the enemy, and the enemy's alliances. By utilizing the nontraditional wooden horse (*Chi*), the Greek army did not have to directly face the powerful and advantageously positioned troops of Troy, but were able to offer the enemy a bait to entice them.

According to Porter's strategy, the essence of strategy is to know what to do and what not to do. After realizing that the traditional way of long siege of the city was costly and inefficient, the Greeks employed the nonconventional way of using the wooden horse, which yielded much faster and successful results. However, Porter said that a good strategy has trade-offs. Although this *Chi* strategy might bring victory easily, it could have a high risk. (A similar argument has also been illustrated when explaining the risks of maneuvering strategy in Chapter 7.) In order to make the Trojans believe that the war was effectively over, they divided the armies into two groups by hiding the small force in the wooden horse, while the majority pretended to sail away. If the army hidden in the wooden horse were discovered or burned by the enemy, the result would have been totally different. Therefore, strategists must know that an extreme *Chi* strategy may be the least safe.

8.5 BUSINESS CASE: HAIER'S SUCCESSFUL TRANSITION THROUGH CHANGES IN ITS BUSINESS STRATEGY

Haier Group was founded in 1984 with its headquarters in Qingdao, China.[11] It has grown from a small plant on the verge of bankruptcy into a global leader of home appliances. According to Global Major Appliances Brand ranking presented by Euromonitor International, Haier has been honored as the world's number one home appliance brand for the eight consecutive years since 2009 (Hindu Business Line, 2017). Haier also has the world's largest sales volume in four types of home appliances: refrigerators, washing machines, freezers, and wine chillers (Business Wire India, 2017). Its overall strategy of development

[11] The information of this case study is abstracted and reorganized from Haier Group homepage (www.haier.net/en/about_haier) and Liu and Li (2002).

can be divided into five growth stages – brand building strategy, diversification strategy, internationalization strategy, global brand strategy, and networking strategy. Haier has passed the first four stages and is now on the fifth stage. The five stages explain the firm's changing strategies for different periods. The explanation below provides details of how it has successfully implemented and achieved its strategic goals.

Stage 1 (1984–1991): Brand Building Strategy
Haier began by producing one product, refrigerators. During this period, the demand was larger than the supply in Chinese domestic appliance market. In order to gain the economies of scale, at that time, most Chinese domestic firms pursued mass production strategy, while neglecting product quality. However, Haier recognized that the increasing supply will ultimately exceed consumers' demand, and there would be fierce competition among companies, which would decrease profits. In order to avoid such a situation, Haier pursued comprehensive quality control and differentiation strategy from the beginning. For example, in order to reduce the defective product rate and strengthen the employees' quality awareness, the company set a rule that the salaries of all employees would be adjusted according to their performance (Liu and Li, 2002). Haier also actively imported production technology and equipment from abroad to meet the international standards. These efforts to differentiate quality helped Haier occupy the leading position in the domestic market.

Stage 2 (1991–1998): Diversification Strategy
With more competitors entering the white goods market, the competition became more severe. Although the competitors had cut down the prices, Haier could avoid the price war and maintain its leading position by making more innovative changes as well as maintaining strict quality control. On the other hand, during this period, the Chinese government encouraged mergers and acquisitions among

firms. However, most of other Chinese firms maintained their existing specialization strategy and did not expand into producing other products. Furthermore, high quality became the basic requirement of consumers and Haier expected – given the quality advantage of its refrigerator – consumers would buy some other related products. Thus, Haier shifted to a diversification strategy, which broadened its product portfolio to cover almost all kinds of household electrical appliances and electronic consumer goods, thereby creating high synergy effects (Lin, 2005). It actively merged and acquired other firms to enlarge its business and product lines. Haier's strategy was to acquire firms which produced quality products but had inefficient management. This expansion strategy helped Haier easily and rapidly acquire the firms which had a good potential for further growth at a lower cost. Haier then improved the performance of acquired firms by adopting Haier's management system to these firms.

Stage 3 (1998–2005): Internationalization Strategy
In the late 1990s, domestic market became highly saturated and with China's entry into WTO, many multinational firms entered the Chinese market, further intensifying the domestic competition. On the other hand, at this stage many Chinese firms went abroad, driven by the Chinese government's "go abroad policy." However, they found that it was difficult to conduct business in the foreign markets, so many returned to the Chinese market, while continuing international operations mostly through obtaining licensing from foreign firms. Haier, however, tried to create its own brand in the international market. After accumulating international experiences in some developing markets of Asia, Haier decided to penetrate into the advanced countries. Unlike other Chinese firms, Haier put forward the thought of "difficult first, easy later" and established a brand name in developed countries. This strategy proved to be effective, because after the brand was established in the United States, Haier could enter the markets of other developed and developing countries with greater ease.

Stage 4 (2006–2012): Global Brand Strategy

The Internet era brought the customization of the market, and the traditional "production, storing, selling" model no longer satisfied the changing needs of global consumers. Therefore, Haier needed to change its existing producer-centered product-selling mode to user-driven "on-demand manufacturing and delivery" mode. In order to adapt to the environmental changes and better serve local needs in the global market, Haier shifted from an internationalization strategy (i.e., creating international brands with its own resources) to a global brand strategy (i.e., making use of global resources to create localized mainstream brands in the foreign markets). Haier thus consolidated the global resources in R&D, manufacturing, and marketing to create a global brand.

Stage 5 (2013–): Networking Strategy

Along with the expansion of the online networking system, the development of advanced technology, and easier accessibility for users to diverse information, Haier realized that there should be a dramatic change in consumers' lifestyle and needs (e.g., smart devices). As its traditional business model could not satisfactorily meet this changing trend of demand, Haier shifted to a networking strategy. For this strategy, Haier created a platform and promoted consumers to show their demands using various available channels. Haier also utilized multiple resources through the world networks to quickly meet the consumer demands.

The evolution of Haier's business strategy over the last thirty years shows its efforts to adapt to the environmental changes and to maintain its leading position in the world. Most importantly, Haier pursued its own unique positioning from the beginning, rather than blindly following the strategy of other domestic companies. For example, in the beginning, rather than pursuing the low-cost strategy by blindly enlarging the volume of products, Haier strictly controlled each product and pursued superior quality, thereby creating a unique competitive advantage in the Chinese market. Therefore, even when domestic market was saturated, Haier could avoid fierce and destructive price wars while commanding high premium price. The firm could pursue its own competitive strategy, by deliberately choosing a set of activities different from its rivals. This case shows that competitive strategy is about how to avoid competition through creating and sustaining unique positioning rather than how to compete on a head-to-head basis.

Haier's strategy of pursuing differentiation with continued updates of its operational effectiveness is consistent with Porter's strategic guidelines. Selection of quality control strategy from the beginning might be costly, but such differentiation strategy is the core of the viable competitive strategy in the long run. Haier could then become a world-class company with its continued innovations, meeting the changing needs of global consumers.

As for Haier's strategy in international expansion, the firm chose the developed countries for a manufacturing base for further development rather than the developing market that was relatively easy for penetration. First of all, building the manufacturing base in the advanced countries deprived Haier of its greatest advantage – China's vast pool of low-cost labor. Mr. Zhang, Haier's CEO, said, "Every multinational set up in China. Margins are low here. If we do not go outside, we cannot survive" (Economist, 2004). Therefore, instead of choosing the low-cost location such as other Asian developing countries, Haier chose the opposite way, because Haier regarded its biggest competitors as the ones located in these advanced markets, and believed that if it succeeded in difficult markets, it would then be able to easily enter other ones (Hunt, 2005). In addition, Haier's establishment of its production base in the developed countries allows it to seek higher technology and learn local consumption preferences and other sophisticated management knowledge and skills. This is exactly what Sun Tzu was talking about when he said there are roads not to follow. Sometimes the road that seems to be more difficult or more likely to fail can lead to success (i.e., Sun Tzu's military concept of turning the devious to the straight in Chapter 7).

Haier's investment in more advanced countries than China is in fact hard to be explained by conventional theories which assume that investment should flow from more to less advanced countries. This is an unconventional investment which can be explained by Moon and Roehl's (2001) imbalance theory. Haier's investment in advanced countries was not to exploit its existing ownership advantages, but to explore new advantages that are necessary for its competition in the global market. Due to advantages from benchmarking and learning the experiences of the leading multinational firms, the latecomers do not have to consume the same length of time and amount of effort to acquire the knowledge and skills that have been developed by the first movers.

In Sun Tzu's words, Haier succeeded because it considered both the favorable and unfavorable factors and consistently changed its strategy to meet new challenges, leaving its overall differentiation strategy unchanged. The effect was evident even during the 2008 global recession. While the export of Chinese air conditioners to the United States fell by 10 percent in January 2009, Haier actually increased its exports to the United States by 20 percent during the same time period (Appliance Magazine, 2009). It could do so by making a timely introduction of energy-efficient models, following Haier's recognition that the American market would increasingly demand energy efficient models as the energy price was increasing at that time and this justified Haier's extra effort of developing new products for this purpose. In this regard, Haier's success can be explained by an appropriate decision-making of *what not to do* (i.e., focusing on Chinese domestic market) and *what to do* (i.e., investing in the advanced countries to learn what their consumers need and developing new products).

8.6 CONCLUSION AND IMPLICATIONS

Although Sun Tzu's chapter "Variation of Tactics" is the shortest among his thirteen chapters, it contains a very important lesson: both political and business leaders should not be obsessed by the general strategic guidelines, but should flexibly apply the guidelines according to the particular situations. Sun Tzu introduced five exceptional situations (i.e., roads not to follow, armies not to attack, fortified castles not to besiege, terrains not to contest, and orders from sovereign not to follow). Sun Tzu said the variation of tactics should be based on the consideration of both favorable and unfavorable factors. Only considering either advantages or disadvantages will cause one to easily make the wrong decision.

This chapter then linked Sun Tzu's concept of variation in tactics with Porter's principles of changes in strategy, because both are related to the choice between what to do and what not to do. In war, in order to pursue the variation of tactics, one should clearly know what to do and what not to do after giving equal weight to assessing both the favorable and unfavorable factors. In business, executives should also choose which activities to focus on because strategy is about making a decision with the trade-offs in mind and creating a good fit among activities. If there is no consistency among activities in line with the firm's overall image and objective, immense costs will be incurred. Therefore, Porter (1996) said the essence of strategy is choosing *what not to do*.

Many business strategists tend to consider more advantages than disadvantages when proposing a project, particularly in start-up firms and entrepreneurial businesses. Porter is thus very insightful to say that strategy is to choose not just what to do but also what not to do. Nevertheless, even Porter seems to be a little more in favor of "what to do," particularly unique things, as he emphasizes unique strategic positioning. In contrast, Sun Tzu put equal or even more emphasis on "what not to do" or potential disadvantages because defeat (or failure) should be prevented first of all, as the result of failure is much more disastrous in war than in business. On the other hand, Sun Tzu's variation of tactics is often too radical and risky, although the success story is always attractive. These extended analyses can better understand the success strategies employed in the military case of the Trojan War and the business case of Haier Group.

9 Extended Strategies

Sun Tzu: Troop deployment and enemy investigation
Porter: Extended generic strategies

Literally, *Xing Jun* in Chinese, the title of the chapter "Marching" in *The Art of War*, means troops moving from one place to another; it does not include any other activities besides the march in its literal meaning. However, *Xing Jun* in Sun Tzu's chapter has a broader spectrum of meaning. Zhang Wenmu explained that *Xing Jun* refers to the march of the army and other related activities during the march. Indeed, "marching of the army" encompasses broad military activities, including fighting, encamping, investigating the terrains, observing the enemy's situation, and managing the army.

As for the army on the march, it is very important for generals to know the principles of encamping in advantageous locations, away from disadvantageous terrains, and investigating the enemy. They affect whether one can obtain initiatives and victory in battle. For encamping, Sun Tzu suggested specific methods of deploying the army in four situations, including mountains, rivers, marshes, and plains. For investigating the enemy, Sun Tzu summarized thirty-two principles to identify the enemy's situation and intention by observing their activities and surrounding environment. With respect to knowing the enemy, there are three relevant chapters out of the thirteen chapters of *The Art of War*: "Strategic Attack," "Marching," and "The Use of Spies." The chapter "Strategic Attack" discusses the importance of knowing the enemy at the strategic level, while the other two chapters deal with the tactics of figuring out the enemy's movement and obtaining critical information of the enemy. The difference is that the chapter "Marching" introduces the practical methods of obtaining the enemy's information through investigating their activities from the outside. Hence, the information is simpler and more primitive. On the other hand, the chapter "The Use of Spies" focuses on the importance and effective ways of employing spies, which can help one obtain more critical and secretive information.

For comparison, I selected Porter's extended generic strategies, namely, Moon et al.'s (2014) eight generic strategies, which added another pillar, competitive target, to Porter's original generic strategies. As the extended model distinguishes products and customers for competitive target, it can better explain the complex practices pursued by the firms in the real world (such as Toyota's mid-sized car). These models can be well applied to the Western developed market, but they need other considerations when entering underdeveloped markets of developing countries, in particular. For serving the low-income consumers in less developed countries, a complete understanding of the environmental issues should also be incorporated in the strategic designs, in addition to understanding the consumer behaviors. This is because the environmental factors may increase the firms' cost and risk of doing business. In this respect, Sun Tzu's method of interpreting enemy's signals and intentions by understanding both their behaviors and their surrounding environment can provide meaningful implications to the business strategy and practices.

This chapter begins by explaining Sun Tzu's principles in his chapter "Marching" for moving and deploying troops in different terrains and investigating enemy's situation. After the analyses, I will examine the linkage between Sun Tzu's military thought and the extended model of Porter's generic strategies (i.e., eight generic strategies). For case studies, I will analyze the military case of Han Xin's battle and the business case of Tata Motors to help readers understand and utilize these strategic linkages between war and business.

9.1 SUN TZU: TROOP DEPLOYMENT AND ENEMY INVESTIGATION

Sun Tzu in his chapter "Marching" introduced specific principles of how to move and encamp and how to fight against the enemy in four types of terrains: mountains, rivers, marshes, and plains. Although the specific ways of dealing with each type of terrain are different, there are some general principles of moving and deploying the troops. The army should be positioned in the higher altitude, so that one can easily investigate the enemy's movement, while one's own movements are kept away from enemy's sight. The army should also be placed on dry ground; the camping ground must be the sunny side and shades must be avoided, so that men and horses may rest, restore their strength, and stay free of diseases. Therefore, obtaining advantageous battleground in war helps one successfully defend against the enemy's attack, maintain the good condition of soldiers, and effectively attack the enemy. The following section will explain in more detail Sun Tzu's various principles for investigating the enemy's activities.

9.1.1 Principles of Investigating the Enemy

Sun Tzu introduced thirty-two ways of estimating and predicting the enemy's capacity and movements. These experiences can be categorized into two types. The first is to identify the enemy's situation through observing the characteristics and changes of natural phenomena (Type I). Nine of the thirty-two principles belong to this category, including the movement of trees, obstacles in the heavy grass, flight of birds, fear of animals, and four situations of dust. The second type, consisting of the other twenty-three principles, is to identify the enemy's situation through investigating their behaviors (Type II) (see Table 9.1).

Sun Tzu repeatedly said warfare is a game of deception, which has two implications – one should be able to deceive the enemy to win, and one should be aware of the enemy's use of deception. Therefore, knowing the enemy's intentions and their strategic movements is a precondition for victory. Sun Tzu repeatedly emphasized the significance of collecting and interpreting information in war. Using spies would be an effective method, but it takes a relatively long time and also involves a high risk of being detected by the enemy. Therefore, Sun Tzu in the chapter "Marching"

Table 9.1 *Types of observing the enemy*[1]

Type I (observing the natural phenomenon and its changes)	1. If a large number of trees move, they are approaching.
	2. If there are many visible obstacles in the heavy grass, it is to make us suspicious.
	3. If birds take flight, there is an ambush.
	4. If animals are afraid, enemy forces are mounting a sudden attack.
	5. If dust rises high up in a sharply defined column, chariots are coming.
	6. If dust is low and broad, the infantry is advancing.
	7. If dust disperses into thin shafts, the enemy is gathering firewood.
	8. If dust is sparse, coming and going, the enemy is encamping.
	9. If birds congregate, the place is empty.
Type II (investigating the enemy's behavior)	1. If the enemy in proximity remains quiet, they are relying on their position of natural stronghold.
	2. If the enemy challenges one to battle while far off, they want one's forces to advance.
	3. If the enemy's campground is easy to access, they occupy terrain to their advantage.
	4. If the enemy speaks humbly but increases their preparations, they will advance.
	5. If the enemy speaks belligerently and advances hastily, they will retreat.
	6. If the enemy's light chariots move out first and take position on the flanks, they are deploying disposition.
	7. If the enemy seeks peace without setting any prior conditions, they are executing a stratagem.
	8. If the enemy moves rapidly and deploys their chariots into formation, they are anticipating a decisive battle.
	9. If the enemy troops half advance and half retreat, they are enticing.
	10. If the enemy soldiers stand leaning on their weapons, they are hungry.

[1] See Sawyer (1994) for more explanation for each of these tactics.

Table 9.1 (*cont.*)

11. If the enemy soldiers go out to draw water and drink for themselves first, they are thirsty.
12. If the enemy sees potential gain but does not advance to secure it, they are tired.
13. If the enemy cries out to each other at night, they are afraid.
14. If the enemy is turbulent, their general lacks severity.
15. If the enemy's flags and pennants move around, they are in chaos.
16. If the enemy's officers are angry, they are exhausted.
17. If the enemy feeds their horses with grain and kills their livestock to eat, and if the enemy does not hang their cooking-pots over the camp-fires, showing no intention to return to their camp, they are determined to fight to the death.
18. If the enemy troops repeatedly congregate in small groups here and there, whispering together, they have lost confidence in their generals.
19. If the enemy frequently grants rewards, they are in deep distress.
20. If the enemy frequently imposes punishments, they are in great difficulty.
21. If the enemy general is at first excessively brutal and then fears his subordinates, he is at the pinnacle of stupidity.
22. If the enemy sends emissaries with offerings, they want to rest.
23. If the enemy is angry and confronts one's army for a long time without engaging in battle or breaking off the confrontation, one must watch them carefully.

introduced alternative methods of obtaining the necessary information on the enemy. Even though the thirty-two methods of investigating the enemy may look simple and primitive, they are very useful and effective.

Moreover, the battlefield situation changes moment by moment, which requires the general to pay a close attention to the changes. In this respect, the thirty-two tactics are very important to secure timely information, based on which one can flexibly modify the plans and launch an attack or counterattack on the enemy. Another important implication is that Sun Tzu incorporated the targets of investigation from a broader scope, not only the enemy's behavior itself but also the detailed changes of the enemy's surrounding situations, such as the movement of the dust, birds, and trees. This calls for a caution against overlooking seemingly insignificant details, as they could contain valuable information about the enemy. Through utilizing such comprehensive sources of investigation, one can obtain more useful information about the enemy.

More importantly, Sun Tzu connected these witnessed behaviors to the capacity to see through the enemy's intention. For example, Sun Tzu said, "If the enemy seeks peace without setting any prior conditions, they are executing a stratagem." To make this kind of an observation, a general must possess extraordinary analytical skills. Thus, Sun Tzu re-emphasized in this chapter "Marching" that one should not simply rely on the number of the army while advancing. A capable general should be able to keep an eye on the enemy, formulate the right strategy, and maximize the strength of his army. More details will be discussed in the following section.

9.1.2 Principles of Building an Army

People might think that the army with a larger number of soldiers would be stronger than the army with a smaller number. However, history documents quite a few famous cases of a smaller army defeating a larger one. Therefore, the size of the army does not equal the strength of the army, and the large size of an army does not guarantee a victory in war. There are many other factors, such as communication costs and organizational inertia, which negatively affect the competitiveness of a large-sized army. Hence, Sun Tzu warned not to advance while simply relying on the number of troops in his chapter "Marching"; he plainly stated, "In war, large numbers alone confer no advantage."[2]

However, we should carefully understand the real meaning of this verse, which does not mean that the number of soldiers is not important. The strength of a force is influenced by both the size and skill of the army. Sun Tzu acknowledged the advantage of owning a large size of forces. As discussed in Chapter 3, Sun Tzu said, a small army that acts inflexibly will become the captives of a large army. However, the advantages of large size of forces are not absolute unless the forces are well trained. This is why Sun Tzu emphasized the importance of training soldiers rather than just relying on the number of soldiers in the very beginning of the book (i.e., the first chapter in *The Art of War*). If a general lacks competence, merely relies on the size of the army, and underestimates the enemy, he will be easily captured by the enemy. In contrast, if he knows the enemy and masters the military tactics, he can defeat the enemy even if his troop size is smaller.

9.2 PORTER: EXTENDED GENERIC STRATEGIES

9.2.1 *A New Integrated Framework by Adding the Third Pillar of Competitive Target*

Porter's (1980, 1985) analytical tool of generic strategies aims for a firm to better serve a specific or broader industry segment than the rivals do.[3] However, Porter's generic strategies do not distinguish the differences between the target types: customers and products. Thus, Porter's original generic strategies may not fully explain the differences in some specific strategies of firms in the real world. For example, according to Porter's (1985) four generic strategies, both IKEA and Jiffy Lube's strategies are categorized as cost focus, but in reality, their focus strategies differ. According to Porter (1996), IKEA

---

[2] The Chinese characters are: 兵非益多也.

[3] According to Porter (1985), market segment is different from industry segment. Market segment aims to identify differences in the needs of buyers and their purchasing behavior; hence it relates more to the marketing activities in the value chain. However, industry segment encompasses the entire value chain, broader than the notion of market segment.

focused on a specific group of customers (i.e., young buyers) by serving a variety of products, while Jiffy Lube focused on a particular service for a wide array of customers.

Porter implicitly acknowledged the need to distinguish these two cases, so in his 1996 article he introduced three additional strategies for securing distinctive positioning: variety-based, needs-based, and access-based. However, this categorization is a little confusing and not complete because Porter did not incorporate the distinction between the two competitive targets of product and customer. To solve this problem, Moon et al. (2014) introduced a new integrated framework, by adding one more pillar, competitive target. Competitive target is categorized into two types: product and customer. Competitive target for product is to provide a specific type of product or service to a broad variety of customers. Competitive target for customer caters to a particular group of customers with a variety of products or services. Combining competitive target (i.e., product or customer) and competitive scope (i.e., broad or narrow) generates four types of strategies to serve: broad customer, broad product, narrow customer, and narrow product. Each type is further divided into two, based on two sources of competitive advantage – cost and differentiation. Thus, there will be a total of eight strategies as shown in Figure 9.1.[4]

Broad strategy aims to meet the broad needs of products and services for a broad array of customers. *Product-based strategy* aims to meet the particular needs of products and services for a broad array of customers. *Customer-based strategy* aims to meet the broad needs of products and services for a narrow group of customers. *Narrow strategy* aims to meet the needs of a limited range of products and services for a particular group of customers. This new model is more comprehensive than the original Porter (1980, 1985, and 1996) models and helpful for distinguishing the subtle differences between the great variety of strategies of firms in the real world.

---

[4]   See Moon et al. (2014) for details of this model.

CUSTOMER-BASED STRATEGY

		Broad	Narrow
PRODUCT-BASED STRATEGY	Broad	**Broad** Differentiation *(Differentiation)*	**Customer-based** Differentiation *(Needs-based Positioning)*
		Broad Cost Leadership *(Cost Leadership)*	**Customer-based** Cost Leadership
	Narrow	**Product-based** Differentiation *(Variety-based Positioning)*	**Narrow** Differentiation *(Access-based Positioning)*
		Product-based Cost Leadership	**Narrow** Cost Leadership

FIGURE 9.1 Eight generic strategies
Source: Moon et al. (2014).
Note: The strategies in the parentheses correspond to those of Porter (1980, 1985, and 1996).

9.2.2 Two New Concepts

In addition to extending Porter's generic strategies, Moon et al. (2014) introduced two concepts of "capturing the core" and "broadening without diluting." Porter warned against the danger of pursuing two strategies of cost and differentiation simultaneously, which he called "stuck in the middle." However, there are many academic debates on this issue among the scholars in existing studies, and some companies pursue this mixed strategy successfully. Moon et al. (2014) argued that the real question is not whether companies can or cannot mix the two strategies, but whether they can broaden their strategies without losing their core competitive advantages. In other words, as long as a company does not lose its core competitive advantage, it can expand its competitive scope and target.

In many cases, the seemingly "stuck in the middle" strategy is in fact a strategy for broadening while maintaining the core competitive advantage. Moon et al. (2014) took a successful example of the Japanese mid-sized car manufacturer's success (e.g., Toyota) in the US automobile industry. According to Porter's definition, this firm must have fallen into the trap of "stuck in the middle." However,

Moon et al. (2014) argued that this firm was not stuck in the middle, but maintained the customer focus strategy, which was designed to meet the needs of customers for mid-sized cars, as they became increasingly quality- and price-conscious.

Porter (1996) said acquiescing compromises and inconsistencies in pursuit of growth will erode the firm's competitive advantage obtained from its original business portfolio or target customers. However, broadening the firm's competitive scope may not always result in the dilution of competitive advantage. If the firm's competitive advantage is sufficiently well established, and as long as the broadening still "captures the core" (either cost or differentiation), it can be powerful enough to be effective and applicable beyond its original scope of business. This perspective is particularly helpful for explaining firms' path of evolution from a lower to a higher developed stage, as well as the changes in firms' strategy in response to changes in the business environment. For example, Hyundai's introduction of hybrid cars expanded its product lines, but still maintained its existing source of competitive advantage (i.e., cost leadership), since it offered a lower price than its competitors in the same market segments. Therefore, the expansion in competitive scope of customers and products should be distinguished from the change of competitive advantage (i.e., cost or differentiation).

9.2.3   Extending Porter's Generic Strategies

Porter's framework of generic strategies is useful for understanding the competitive environment and finding a firm's unique positioning. However, although it satisfactorily explains the competitive strategy of developed firms in the well-developed markets, it shows limits when applied to other situations, such as the underdeveloped markets, particularly the ones belonging to the bottom of pyramid (BOP) market.[5] About two-thirds of the global population lives in the BOP market,

---

[5]   C. K. Prahalad (2004a) first conceptualized BOP in his book *The Fortune at the Bottom of the Pyramid: Eradicating Poverty through Profits*. He suggested that firms doing business in the wealthy areas can also be profitable in the low-income markets. Then, this kind of firms' activity will ultimately bring prosperity to these poor regions.

where the annual income is less than $2,000 (Prahalad, 2001). Some studies (e.g., Margolis and Walsh, 2003; Prahalad, 2004b; Porter and Kramer, 2011) suggested targeting the needs of these neglected people. In practice, an increasing number of firms are searching for business opportunities in these areas.

However, because of circumstantial differences in comparison to the developed market, many firms have faced substantial challenges when doing business in the BOP market. Hence, some scholars such as Karnani (2007) emphasized that many firms could not fully exploit the benefits of serving the BOP market and criticized that firms were too optimistic about the potential opportunities, while underestimating the challenges and difficulties in entering these new markets. The main problems can be summarized as follows. First, people in the BOP market have limited purchasing power; they spend about 60 percent of their income on the basic needs for survival (Braun, 2008), and thus their disposable income for other products and services is very small. Therefore, firms have to redesign their business model by creating products or services with fewer resources and less cost (Prahalad and Mashelkar, 2010).

The second problem is the poor condition of physical infrastructure, such as transportation, finance, education, and health, which increases the costs and risks of doing business. For example, Tata Motors of India introduced the world's cheapest car (i.e., Tata Nano) but failed, partly due to the poor transportation infrastructure and traffic conditions of India. In fact, there have been many developed multinational firms that invested in the developing countries, simply to exploit their cheap labor or fast-growing market, but failed in the end because of the unexpected costs arising from the underdeveloped institutional conditions and poor infrastructure. For example, Google left China in 2010 because of the Chinese government's censorship of search results, which severely restricted Google's business and degraded its competitive advantage in China.

Therefore, in addition to thoroughly understanding the BOP market needs and consumer behavior, firms entering the BOP market need to pay a close attention to the environmental issues that may incur additional costs and risks. However, Porter's original and the extended generic strategies focused primarily on the consumer needs and largely neglected the importance of environmental factors when entering new markets, because the environmental conditions in the developed countries are less likely to be critical problems for firms. Therefore, in order to achieve profits, instead of asking "given our cost structure, which segments can we serve?" firms should ask "given that we need to cater to the unserved, what should our cost structure be?" (Prahalad and Mashelkar, 2010). Serving the traditionally underserved customers requires the firms to place greater weight on environmental factors.

9.3 THE INTEGRATION OF SUN TZU AND PORTER

9.3.1 Observing the Enemy's Situation versus Competitive Target

Sun Tzu emphasized the importance of knowing the enemy throughout his entire book, but he proposed the specific methods of estimating and predicting the enemy's capacity and behavior for the first time in the chapter "Marching." Sun Tzu emphasized not only the importance of information itself, but also the skills of analyzing and discerning the information. He introduced thirty-two ways to analyze commonly witnessed behavioral and natural phenomena. Sun Tzu advocated knowing the enemy's real intentions by observing the behavior and surroundings of the enemy, in order to take initiatives and favorable positions in a battle. In particular, Sun Tzu emphasized the significance of targeting in devising a military strategy in war. Once the enemy's intentions and capacity are well understood, one can discretely concentrate one's military force to attack the critically weak points of the enemy. In contrast, without knowing the enemy, one has to prepare for every possible attack from the enemy and may end up having to stretch oneself too thin.

In business, Porter (1985) emphasized the consideration of industry segmentation for devising business strategy. The industry is segmented by distinctive product varieties, different types of customers, or multiple distribution channels; hence, serving different segments requires different strategies and capabilities. Porter (1985, 1996) then suggested to choose a unique positioning and concentrate the firm's resources, rather than to serve all markets, which is similar to Sun Tzu's advocacy of concentration of forces. By extending Porter's generic strategy, Moon et al. (2014) provided a 2×2×2 model (i.e., eight strategic choices), designed to be more comprehensive than Porter's (1980, 1985) original generic strategy for choosing a unique positioning and concentrating the firm's resources.

On the other hand, Sun Tzu's principles of observing natural phenomenon and its changes can provide important insights for understanding the business environment. In war, it might be difficult to observe the enemy's movement directly from a far distance. Thus, one can obtain information of the enemy, by interpreting the environmental signals, such as the movement of trees, birds, animals, and even the dust on the ground. Similarly, in business, the environment, particularly the social conditions and industrial infrastructure, should be incorporated when designing a business strategy for serving unfamiliar markets such as low-income regions. Firms can then better respond to the challenges and get prepared beforehand.

9.3.2 *Principle of Building an Army versus Broadening without Diluting*

Sun Tzu said both the size and skill of the army are important for building up one's military forces. If the size of an army is too small, it would be difficult to control the battle. However, Sun Tzu also said that size alone cannot constitute an important advantage; the quality of soldiers is more important than the sheer number of forces. The size of the army can become a competitive advantage only when it is accompanied by well-trained and highly motivated soldiers, the condition of knowing the enemy, and the well-designed disposition.

This military thought of Sun Tzu is similar to the extended Porter model, Moon et al.'s (2014) concept of broadening without diluting. Building the size of the army can be analogized to the broadening strategy (i.e., expanding the scope of business), and enhancing the quality of the army can be analogized with the deepening strategy (i.e., strengthening the competitive advantage). Just as advancement that merely relies on size will allow the army to be easily captured by the enemy, in business if a firm broadens but dilutes its uniqueness, it will lose its competitive advantage. For example, Tata Group, founded in 1868, has expanded into a wide array of industries over the past decades, including salt, IT, steel, watches, power plants, cars, and hotels. However, as these businesses had a low level of synergy among each other, most of its businesses showed poor performance (Economist, 2016).

In contrast, if a firm only deepens its strategy without broadening, its growth will be restricted to a certain level. In the era in which multi-competence becomes a growing source of competitive advantage, a firm can enjoy significant benefits of synergy creation by practicing a broad scope of diversification (Moon, 2016b), and even avoid a disaster that could be incurred due to a deadly failure in one business area. For example, despite the heavy hit from the recall of Galaxy Note 7, Samsung Electronics could still survive because of the large amount of profits earned from the business of parts and components. Therefore, both deepening and broadening are needed for a firm to grow as well as sustain its competitive advantage. However, in warfare, they are more likely to become simultaneous processes; whereas in business, deepening should come first and then the next step would be broadening without diluting the deepened competitive advantages.

9.4 MILITARY CASE: HAN XIN'S VICTORY IN THE BATTLE OF JINGXING

The battle of Jingxing was a very famous battle in Chinese history, in which Han Xin defeated a larger army of the country of

Zhao.[6] In 204 B.C., Han Xin, the general of the country of Han, with his army of 10,000 men marched a long way to attack Zhao. Chen Yu, Zhao's commander, deployed a force of 200,000 to Jingxing, a narrow and dangerous pass that Han Xin's army must take over in order to subdue Zhao. Li Zuojun, another general of Zhao, suggested to Chen Yu that he could easily win by blocking the routes of Jingxing and cutting down the food supply of Han Xin's army. However, Chen Yu declined this suggestion, and thought that since he had a much larger force, he did not have to fear Han Xin's small army. He also thought that because Han Xin's army came from thousands of miles away, they must be exhausted. Based on these considerations, Chen Yu insisted on fighting face to face, instead of using other *Chi* strategy.

Upon learning that Li Zuojun's suggestion was not adopted, Han Xin was very pleased. He carefully studied the geographic situation of Jingxing as well as the personal weakness of Chen Yu. He then ordered his army to camp near the pass. In the evening, he selected 2,000 agile cavalrymen, each with the flag of the Han army, to secretly creep into the areas behind Chen Yu's army base. The next day, Han Xin sent his forces to engage in the battle across the river intentionally to lure the enemy. Zhao's army laughed at Han Xin for this supposedly foolish tactical mistake of camping near the river.

The two troops fought for a while until Han Xin's army suddenly abandoned their flags and drums and made a feigned retreat to the bank of the river. The Zhao troops fell for Han Xin's trick and Zhao ordered the whole army to attack the Han army, leaving the camp empty. On the other hand, Han's 2,000 cavalry took the chance by occupying the camp and replacing Zhao flags with Han flags. Meanwhile, the remainder of Han's army by the river had no choice but to fight desperately, until the Zhao commanders gave up and decided to retreat to their camps (see Figure 9.2). However, when

---

[6]   The information of this case is abstracted and modified from english.cri.cn/1702/2005-4-29/121@232806.htm, www.historyofwar.org/articles/battles_jingzing.html, and en.wikipedia.org/wiki/Battle_of_Jingxing.

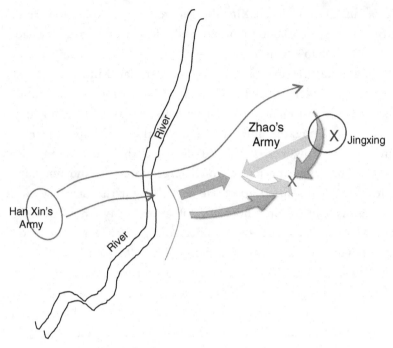

FIGURE 9.2 Battle of Jingxing

they saw Han flags flying over the camp, they assumed the king of
Zhao was captured and began to flee. Then Han's army attacked from
the front and rear, inflicting a heavy defeat on the disorganized Zhao
army. As a result, the Zhao troops were crushed; the general was
killed; and the king of Zhao was captured.

After the battle, Han Xin's subordinates inquired about the
reason for the astounding deployments. Han Xin explained, "In such
a situation, men will fight because it is impossible for them to flee.
Our soldiers are mostly from other armies that surrendered. If they
were put in a place with no way to retreat, they will automatically
fight desperately. If they were put in a place with rooms for retreat,
they will take the chance." Sun Tzu advised, "After crossing rivers,
one must distance oneself from them." From this perspective, Han
Xin chose an opposite tactic, because he had his army camping near

the river. In addition, Han Xin's army size was much smaller than Zhao's. If the size of the army were the absolute measure of competitiveness, Han Xin would definitely have been defeated, but the result was the opposite. Han Xin had a complete and correct knowledge of the enemy's strategy and skills in flexibly manipulating the operations.

In addition, Zhao's tactical mistakes also contributed to Han's victory in this battle. First, Sun Tzu said that warfare is a game of deception, and one should combine both *Cheng* and *Chi* strategies to achieve the victory. However, the general of Zhao refused to utilize any *Chi* strategy. He tried to confront with the adversary directly by using only *Cheng* strategy. Therefore, he failed to exploit the chance to send his troops to cut off the route of Han's provision. Second, Sun Tzu advocated the strategic movement after a thorough investigation of the enemy's situations. Furthermore, Sun Tzu claimed, "If the enemy challenges one to battle from a distance, they are enticing one to advance." Merely relying on the large size of the army, the general of Zhao failed to read the enemy's real intention and just blindly sent all of his troops to chase after Han troops who pretended to escape. The battle of Jingxing shows the importance of Sun Tzu's military thoughts that the large size of the army does not guarantee a victory in war and one needs to have a thorough understanding of the enemy's intention.

On the other hand, similar to the case of Trojan War in Chapter 8, this kind of *Chi* strategy, while exciting and fancy, is also very risky if read by the enemy. Moreover, repeating this deception strategy is not advisable, as the enemy would not be deceived again. Military strategists can take an important lesson from business strategy: deepen the internal capabilities first before relying on fancy *Chi* strategies, as Moon et al. (2014) stressed. If a general overuses *Chi* strategy, even his army and the sovereign may not trust him. Despite his tremendous contribution to the victories of many battles and the foundation of new unified China in 202 B.C., the miserable execution of Han Xin by his sovereign in the end might have been related to this.

9.5   BUSINESS CASE: TATA MOTORS' FAILURE IN
TATA NANO

Tata Motors, a subsidiary of the Tata Group, is an automotive manufacturing company headquartered in Mumbai, India. The company produces passenger cars, trucks, vans, and buses. It is the world's seventeenth largest motor vehicle manufacturing company, the fourth largest truck, and the second largest bus manufacturer (Tata Motors, 2015). Tata Motors has greater competitiveness in commercial vehicles than passenger cars, which are dominated by foreign automakers in India. Therefore, strengthening its position in the passenger car market had been critical for Tata Motors' sustainable development in the long run.

In 2009, Tata Motors launched Tata Nano, the least expensive car in the world at about $3,000, attracting the world's attention. This car did not target already existing car drivers, but millions of Indian motorbike and motor scooter drivers. It aimed to convert these motorbikers into car drivers and exploit the huge market potential. Therefore, Tata Nano was also named as the "People's Car" or "One-Lakh-Car." Tata Nano was first conceived of by the Chairman of Tata Group, Ratan Tata. He got the idea of Nano when he was once waiting in the traffic. He noticed a single, small scooter carrying overcrowded family members. After this experience, he envisioned making an affordable car for these poor people.

The low price of Tata Nano was only around half of the second cheapest car, Suzuki Maruti 800 in India. In this respect, the introduction of such cheap car to the auto industry can be regarded as a disruptive innovation. In order to radically reduce the costs, Tata Motors consciously sacrificed some functions by including just the basic items: no air conditioner, no airbags, no automatic windows, no adjustable passenger seats, and no fancy functions such as central locking. There was not much space for luggage in this car and the volume for the fuel tank was also small. Overall, Tata Motors gave the lion's share of their attention to reducing the cost of almost everything, from design to production. However, despite its revolutionary cheap price, the sales performance was disappointing.

Because of the poor market performance, Tata Motors later introduced a new model (i.e., Nano LX) in 2013 with the updates on design, such as refurbished exterior, improved interiors, a sound system with four speakers, and dual glove boxes. The price increased to around $3,500 accordingly. The newly launched car changed its target from poor people to middle-class young urban buyers, under thirty-five years old. However, the sales were again disappointing. There were several reasons for Tata Nano's failure. Many doubted the possibility of producing such a cheap car that could meet the minimum of Indian safety and emission standards, not to mention the global standards. Some also pointed out the problems such as production delays and dealer network. Matthew Eyring, the president of Innosight, a global consulting firm, said the real problem with the car was the fact that Tata Motors relied on its initial hype. On this chaotic management and strategy, he remarked, "A cheap car that's not really cheap. A safe car whose safety has been questioned. A poor people's car that poor people aren't buying. That sounds like a failure, certainly" (Jagannathan, 2011).

For motorcycle drivers to buy a new car, the price was still high, since it was two times that of motorcycles. On the other hand, Tata Motors failed to consider other environmental factors, such as India's poor traffic conditions and road infrastructure. People in the street were normally reluctant to follow strict traffic rules. In addition, car maintenance fee is a burden to the auto buyers in India. For the motorcycle drivers, these realities actually increased the cost and inconvenience of becoming car owners. Therefore, given the road conditions and other problems, the potential market was much limited, and when the price and quality were not competitive enough to compensate for all of these environmental problems, Tata Nano did not have a chance to stand, falling below its original goal to serve the BOP market needs. This case thus reflects the importance of Sun Tzu's guide for investigating the environmental factors for a more comprehensive understanding of the enemy's (or consumers') situation and intentions. In addition, Sun Tzu advocated observing the enemy's behaviors before devising a strategy. However, Tata Motors blindly pursued the cost strategy, without knowing the real needs of the competitive target (i.e., customers). Tata Motors' failure is a good example that demonstrates how the failure in capturing the real needs of the competitive target can affect overall strategy.

Using Moon et al.'s (2014) framework and concept, one can understand that Tata failed in both capturing the core (i.e., cost advantage) and broadening its customer target (i.e., incorporating the potential consumers of motorcycles). First, for the strategy of capturing the core, Porter said although the cost strategy mainly pursues lower cost for higher profits, a successful execution of the cost strategy requires the maintenance of a certain level of quality. However, in the case of Tata Nano, it tried to lower the production costs at the expense of quality. Second, for the broadening strategy, Tata Motors failed to understand the real needs of the target customers. In order to exploit low-end customers, Tata Motors introduced the world's least expensive cars, but failed to meet the needs of its target customers, and also unintentionally excluded other potential buyers, due to its image of "poor man's car." By being unable to capture either the core competence or a broader base, Tata Nano essentially became "stuck in the middle." An important lesson can be learned from this case: by knowing precisely what kind of customers and products exist in a given industry, firms can formulate the most effective strategies without making the mistake of "stuck in the middle."

The recommended strategic direction for the future of Tata Motors would be to target both two-wheelers (e.g., motorcycles and scooters) and passenger cars but with distinctive competitive strategy, instead of trying to simply shift the two-wheeler drivers to the auto market. The strategic evolution can be designed as follows (see Figure 9.3). In the first stage, Tata Motors should benchmark the market leaders in both markets and then add some of its own attributes to outperform the rivals. Specifically, in the two-wheeler market, Tata

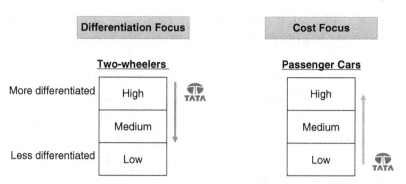

FIGURE 9.3 Strategic direction for the future of Tata Motors

Motors should pursue the differentiation strategy, by setting a similar price but higher quality than the closest competitor (e.g., Bajaj Auto[7]'s premium models). This is because Tata Motors already has established a strong position in the commercial vehicles, with which it might possess an advantage in producing the premium models compared to the domestic two-wheeler makers in terms of technology and distribution network.

On the other hand, as for the passenger car market, since Tata Motors has disadvantages in this segment compared to other foreign firms in India, it would be appropriate to start with a cost focus strategy, like Tata Nano. However, what Tata Motors should do is to sell at a lower price with quality similar to its major competitor (e.g., Suzuki Maruti 800). The original Tata Nano had lower price but at the same time lower quality, and the redesigned models had higher price but not so distinctive quality. Even after catching up with the similar level of quality of its competitors, consumers might still prefer the foreign models because of their long years of established brand name. For example, Suzuki's small-sized models have dominated the Indian market for the past three decades. In order to compete with such incumbents, Tata Motors might have to push additional marketing strategy, such as an aggressive mileage strategy, which is what Hyundai Motor

[7] An Indian two-wheeler maker.

Company did when it strengthened its quality and brand in the US market in the late 1990s, by providing a 10-year, 100,000-mile warranty plan.

The strategy of the second stage is to expand the market segment. As for the two-wheeler segment, Tata Motors can gradually expand to the medium and low-cost models; for passenger cars, it can then move from low-cost and small-sized cars to premium and large-sized cars. The logic of shift is that given its success in the previous segment and established brand name, consumers will be likely to try other models. This strategic evolution is consistent with the deepening and broadening strategy of Moon et al. (2014).

9.6 CONCLUSION AND IMPLICATIONS

Sun Tzu in this chapter dealt with two main issues: one is to move and deploy the troops by taking the advantages of terrain and avoid the dangerous geographical locations; the other is to collect and process the information obtained through observing easily witnessed natural phenomena and behaviors of the enemy. In addition, Sun Tzu suggested the core principle of engaging in war: "Large numbers alone confer no advantage." Sun Tzu warned about the danger of excessive reliance on the size of force and showed the possibility that a small army can win over a large army if they are well trained and organized under well-designed strategy and tactics.

For business, Porter's generic strategy and its extended model have been introduced. Sun Tzu's advice on how to investigate the enemy in order to understand their intentions can be linked to Moon et al.'s (2014) third pillar, competitive target, which was added to the two dimensions of Porter's four generic strategies and three types of strategic positioning. If a general observes his enemy accurately, he can use the information to strike at the enemy's weak points. Similarly, if a firm well understands how the market is segmented, it can use competitive targeting to concentrate its resources. Another linkage is that in war, the size of military force cannot work as an advantage unless the soldiers are well trained. Similarly, in business, broadening strategy should be pursed based on the strategy of capturing the core; otherwise the company will suffer the problem of being "stuck in the middle." Furthermore, there is yet another important lesson from Sun Tzu for application to business. As firms often do not pay much attention to the social environment of unfamiliar regions, such as the BOP market, Sun Tzu's tactics of investigating the enemy's situation and environment can give useful implications.

These linkages are well demonstrated in the military case of Han Xin's victory in the battle of Jingxing and the business case of Tata Motors' failure in Tata Nano. Sun Tzu's explanations of strategies reveal a critical difference between the two cases: Han Xin implemented his strategic movement after thoroughly investigating the enemy's situation and intentions, while Tata Motors blindly pursued a cost strategy without truly understanding the needs of the target customers and social environment. An important implication is then that weaknesses of an army are not critical problems as long as one is aware of them and able to make sure that they would not be detected or attacked by the enemy. However, in business, as the critical problems in products and services could bring fatal blows to the firm, they have to be fixed and improved before serving the market.

10 Location Advantage

Sun Tzu: Exploitation of terrain advantages
Porter: Cluster development for improving location advantage

The title of Sun Tzu's tenth chapter, *Di Xing* (Terrain, the English title), literally refers to the physical geography – the natural layout of the earth's surface. While Sun Tzu stressed the importance of terrain in war repeatedly throughout his entire book, only this chapter has terrain as its title and discusses the subject as the main topic. Sun Tzu was probably the first military strategist who systematically examined the types of various terrains and suggested useful guidelines for dealing with these terrains when engaging the enemy. Sun Tzu in his chapter "Terrain" proposed appropriate military tactics for six types of terrain, by articulating, "Terrain can help the army." This means that terrain is a supplementary factor for victory, but it cannot guarantee a victory in warfare. Sun Tzu then emphasized the capability of generals to fully exploit the advantages of terrain.

If a general is highly competitive, a disadvantageous position can be turned into an advantageous one, and even a small army can defeat a large army. In contrast, if a general does not have adequate capability, even if the army has a numerical advantage over the enemy, it will be doomed to failure. The generalship determines whether one can exploit the advantages or avoid the disadvantages of terrain. Therefore, while Sun Tzu spent one third of *Di Xing* on the discussion of terrain itself, he devoted two-thirds of the chapter to stressing the importance of the general's ability to comprehend and utilize the specific characteristics of the terrain. Specifically, Sun Tzu introduced six calamities[1] which do not arise from natural disasters but from the faults of a general. He also suggested some requirements of a good leadership of the general.

---

[1] The six calamities are: Flight (走兵), insubordination (馳兵), collapse (陷兵), ruin (崩兵), disorganization (亂兵), and rout (北兵).

For the current chapter, I connect Sun Tzu's ideas on terrain with Porter's cluster theory, which stresses the importance of location in building firms' competitive advantages. However, Porter's clusters focus on the linkage and synergy generation within a single cluster, while neglecting the importance of intercluster linkage, particularly with foreign clusters (Moon and Jung, 2010). Both geographic concentration and international linkage with other clusters are critical to the competitiveness of clusters and the firms in the current competitive landscape (Huggins, 2015). Moreover, Porter did not explicitly explain the different levels of performance of firms within a cluster. In this respect, this chapter suggests that Sun Tzu's military principles can provide meaningful implications for further development of Porter's cluster theory.

The rest of this chapter is structured as follows. For the overviews, I will first introduce Sun Tzu's operational tactics in different types of terrain and Porter's cluster theory. Then, I will examine the linkage between Sun Tzu's and Porter's strategies. For case studies, I will explain the military case of the Battle of Myeongnyang led by Admiral Yi Sun-shin, which is considered to be one of the most successful cases in the history of naval battle, and the business case of the development of Silicon Valley, which is regarded as the world's most successful high-tech and knowledge-based cluster.

IO.I SUN TZU: EXPLOITATION OF TERRAIN ADVANTAGES

Sun Tzu in his first chapter identified five (internal and external) elements to consider before going to war, and terrain is one of the external factors, which can significantly affect the fate of military campaign. In war, securing a geographical advantage is critical for one to gain the initiatives and achieve victory in the battle. On the other hand, locating in a disadvantageous terrain will not only weaken one's military strengths, but also incur the danger of being defeated. Sun Tzu categorized terrains into six types by their nature, namely accessible terrain, entangling terrain, temporizing terrain, narrow

Table 10.1 *Six types of terrain*

Type	Characteristic	Tactics
Accessible terrain	Freely traversed by both sides	Occupy the higher and sunny positions
Entangling terrain	Easy to get in, but difficult to get out	Do not engage in the war if the enemy is prepared
Temporizing terrain	Disadvantageous for both to enter	Do not go to war, even if the enemy entices
Narrow terrain	Narrow access route and tortuous retreat route	Be the first to occupy the strategic position and wait for the enemy
Precipitous terrain	Rugged and precipitous	Be the first to occupy the sunny heights and wait for the enemy
Distant terrain	Far away from each other and equally matched in military strength	Do not start a battle

terrain, precipitous terrain, and distant terrain.[2] The characteristics of these six types of terrain and tactics of dealing with them when one is engaged in war on these terrains (see Table 10.1) are as follows.

Accessible Terrain It refers to the terrain that is freely accessed by both sides. For this kind of terrain, one should first occupy the higher and sunny positions, because these grounds can keep supply routes unimpeded and thus gain advantage in battle.

Entangling Terrain It refers to the terrain that it is easy to enter, but difficult to exit. In such a terrain, the enemy can be easily defeated if they are unprepared. In contrast, if the enemy is prepared, one will be in a disadvantageous position once engaged in battle because one's army can be caught in a situation where it is difficult to retreat.

---

[2] Accessible terrain (通形), entangling terrain (挂形), temporizing terrain (支形), narrow terrain (隘形), precipitous terrain (險形), and distant terrain (遠形).

Temporizing Terrain It refers to the terrain that is disadvantageous for both one and the enemy to enter. In such terrain, one should not engage in a battle, even if the enemy entices one's army. Instead, one can entice the enemy by feigning retreat, and if the enemy comes half way forward, one will be in a more favorable situation to attack the enemy.

Narrow Terrain It refers to the terrain where the access route is narrow and the retreat route is tortuous. In such a situation, one should be the first to occupy the strategic point and wait for the enemy; never attack if it has been occupied by the enemy.

Precipitous Terrain It refers to the terrain that is rugged and precipitous. In this terrain, one should be the first to occupy the sunny ground on the higher altitude and wait for the enemy. If the enemy has already occupied the terrain, do not follow them, but try to trick them out of it.

Distant Terrain It refers to the terrain in which both sides are located far away from each other. In such a situation, and when both sides have equal level of military capacity, it is not easy to provoke a battle, and fighting will give little advantage to either side.

Based on this categorization, Sun Tzu advised the advantageous position for fighting, and also provided tactics for how to cope with the difficulties when one is at disadvantageous terrains or dangerous positions. Among the six types of terrains, the tactics for dealing with narrow terrain and precipitous terrain seem to be similar. In both situations, Sun Tzu emphasized being the first to occupy the terrain and then to wait for the enemy. Despite the similarity, however, there is a marked difference. For narrow terrain, if the enemy has already occupied, one should only engage in the war when the enemy is not prepared. However, for the precipitous height, which is very steep, one should never follow the enemy if they have already occupied the terrain, but one should lure them out of the terrain.

According to Sun Tzu, the six types of terrain must be observed carefully and understood well by the general. In his third chapter, Sun

Tzu said, "If one knows either the enemy or oneself only, the likelihood of victory is half." Yet in the chapter "Terrain," Sun Tzu emphasized the importance of completely understanding the terrain by saying, "If one knows that the enemy can be attacked and that one's troops are capable of attacking the enemy, but one does not realize that the nature of terrain is not appropriate for fighting, the chance of victory is again half." Therefore, he further claimed, "If one knows the enemy and oneself, one will never be endangered; if one knows the heaven and the terrain, one will then achieve a complete victory." This implies that an army's physical strengths cannot guarantee victory, and the environmental factors must be incorporated when designing a military strategy. Zhu Geliang, the premier and strategist of the country of Shu Han during the Three Kingdoms period, gave a similar statement saying, "Those who do not comprehend terrain can never be qualified as generals."

10.2　PORTER: CLUSTER DEVELOPMENT FOR IMPROVING LOCATION ADVANTAGE

Due to the increasing globalization and decreasing cost of transportation and communication, firms nowadays can easily outsource capital, information, and materials from abroad on the global scope. Hence, many argue that the locational advantage or the role of location in competition will necessarily diminish. However, Porter (1990, 1998) argued that ironically location will still matter despite the globalization of business. This is because the internationally competitive firms tend to colocate in a specific place or region, such as the financial companies in the US Wall Street, IT firms in the US Silicon Valley, automobile companies in southern Germany, and fashion shoe firms in northern Italy. Porter (1998) called such geographic agglomeration, *cluster*.

The concept of cluster, however, did not originate from Porter. The first cluster theory dates back to Alfred Marshall's work on concentration of specialized industries in a particular location, in his *Principles of Economies* (Marshall, 1890). After this work, there have been extensive studies to enrich the cluster literature, including agglomeration economies, economic geography, urban and regional economics, national innovation systems, industrial districts, and social networks (Porter, 1998). However, Porter's work on clusters is the most influential compared to other works by economic geographers, and his notion of cluster has since become the standard in the field (Martin and Sunley, 2003).

Then, which particular characteristics of Porter's work made it so attractive and impactful in both academia and practice? Preceding studies emphasize some specific aspects of clusters using models or theories, but Porter's framework is more comprehensive and focuses more on providing practical implications for policy makers. He tried to link the cluster to the competitiveness of firms, regions, and nations. His work is also easier to understand and more readily applicable in practice, effectively filling the gap between theory and practice (Martin and Sunley, 2003). Accordingly, his work has attracted broader attention from business managers, governments, and other cluster practitioners (Ketels, 2011).

Porter's cluster study was first informally introduced in his well-known book, *The Competitive Advantage of Nations* (Porter, 1990). He found that the competitiveness of a nation usually draws from some specific internationally competitive industries, rather than all the industries. These competitive industries are often concentrated in a particular region within a nation. Porter then formally and systematically organized the cluster theory in the seventh chapter of his 1998 book named *On Competition*, and later updated and expanded it in the 2008 edition.

Porter (1998: 199) defined a cluster as "a geographically proximate group of interconnected companies and associated institutions in a particular field, linked by commonalities and complementarities." Therefore, the two core elements of cluster can be identified: geographical proximity and interlinkage among the involved firms and organizations. The geographical scope of cluster can be a city (e.g.,

Bangaluru[3] IT cluster), a state (e.g., California wine cluster), a country (e.g., Italian fashion cluster), or a network of neighboring countries (e.g., Singapore/Johor in Malaysia/Riau in Indonesia or the SIJORI growth triangle). Porter categorized the players within the cluster into four types: (1) the end-product or service companies; (2) suppliers of specialized inputs, components, machinery, and services; (3) financial institutions, firms in related industries, and other institutions (e.g., universities, government); and (4) downstream industries (e.g., consumers). The linkage among these players is created through either competition or cooperation. On the other hand, although proximity is important, what is more critical is the interlinkage among firms and organizations.

Porter (1998) explained cluster's crucial role in enhancing firms' competitiveness from the following three perspectives. First, clusters increase the productivity of firms within the area. In a cluster, firms can get easier access to specialized and experienced employees and suppliers, specialized information, and institutions and public goods. Hence, firms can save the time and cost of seeking them in other locations. The linkage with the complementarities can also create potential synergy effects. The complementarities can rise from the related products or services and marketing effects (such as attracting more customers from related products). Firms within a cluster can also benefit from powerful psychological effects of becoming better motivated because of the intensified competition compared to outside firms. These favorable factors collectively contribute to the enhanced productivity of the firm.

Second, clusters drive the direction and pace of innovation. The sophisticated buyers within a cluster often play a vital role in providing the window or early signal of future market trends. There are other pressures, such as competitive pressure and peer pressure, which promote the introduction of more competitive products. Moreover, the easier access to various resources required

---

[3]   It was renamed from Bangalore in 2006.

for innovation could also make it possible for firms to expedite the plans or strategic designs in practice. Porter argued that firms' local outsourcing has competitive advantage in terms of reduced costs, more flexibility, and sustainability compared to distant outsourcing and development.

Third, clusters encourage the formation of new businesses. Barriers to entry are lower in the cluster than other places. The concentrated consumers also promote the creation of new businesses. Firms can easily get access to the needed staff, skills, capital, and other inputs, which are available from the external market or acquired from the established companies. Some empirical studies (e.g., Gilbert, McDougal, and Audretsch, 2008; McCann and Folta, 2011) have shown that the younger firms and new ventures benefited more than the incumbent and other established firms in clusters due to the easier accessibility to their needed resources.

Therefore, it is not advisable for firms to choose a location simply by considering particular input costs alone; rather, firms should choose their location based on the costs of the entire system, including both hard (e.g., labor cost and infrastructure) and soft factors (e.g., finance, education, and health system). Porter claimed that clusters are not born out of a vacuum, but that their formation is usually linked to some historical events, sophisticated and unusual local demand, existence of related supplier industries, or innovative companies' stimulation. After the establishment of a cluster, its evolution or decline depends on its self-reinforcing pattern and adaptation to the environmental changes. Sometimes the shift in buyers' needs or the technological discontinuity or other destructive innovation can make clusters lose their existing competitive advantage. Cluster works more than just promotes firms' competition: it is a vehicle that brings companies, governments, and other institutions together in a constructive manner to boost the regional and the national economy. The soundness and growth of clusters require these players' collective efforts. In particular, the role of the national and local governments is very important to create a globally competitive and efficient business environment of the cluster.

10.3 THE INTEGRATION OF SUN TZU AND PORTER

Both Sun Tzu and Porter articulated the importance of locational advantage for gaining a victory in war and enhancing firms' competitive advantage in business. However, such advantage is not automatically generated, but it requires the input of additional efforts. The successful exploitation of locational advantages is affected by a general's capability in war, and by the collective engagement of companies, governments, and other institutions in business. The following section will compare and contrast the two theories and find out which military principles of Sun Tzu could be usefully incorporated into Porter's cluster theory.

10.3.1 The Role of Location in Competitive Advantage

In war, in addition to comparing the internal strengths of one and the enemy, it is also critical to analyze whether one has an advantageous or disadvantageous position in the battleground. The advantages obtained from a terrain may outcompete the disadvantages from internal strengths, such as the size of an army force and military equipment. On the other hand, it is also possible that the disadvantageous situation promotes the fighting spirit of soldiers. Take the example of a military case from Chapter 9. Han Xin purposely deployed his army in front of the river, and thus completely cut the retreat route. The reverse way of exploiting the influences of terrain played a critical role for making the force fight to the death. Therefore, the advantages or disadvantages of terrain imposed on an army could be controllable factors depending on how the general skillfully exploits them, instead of being predetermined fixed factors.

In business, despite the diminishing role of location due to the greater availability of resources from abroad on the global scope, Porter argued that location surprisingly plays an increasingly important role. This nearly counterintuitive discovery is closely related to the concept of clusters and their roles. Although many traditional roles of location may have diminished along with the globalization, the new roles of clusters in competition have become more important than ever in the global economy. The previous section of this chapter introduced three roles of clusters: increasing firm productivity, promoting innovation, and encouraging new businesses. Clusters formulate a better business environment and innovation system, which is difficult to be reproduced in another location over a short period of time. Such a business environment serves as the base of productivity improvement, which determines the firms' competitive advantages and the prosperity of a nation's economy.

Therefore, Porter warned that firms should not locate their investments in foreign countries simply based on a superficial survey of merits, which may give distorted image of advantages. Good evidence is the return of many US firms with overseas production operations (i.e., reshoring) after the 2008 global financial crisis. Despite high costs of labor and other resources in the home country (i.e., the United States), the overall production cost could be lower compared to overseas production because of the improved domestic business environment and reduced logistics costs.

10.3.2   The Key Actors Influencing Location Advantages

The locational advantage in war and business cannot be obtained without proper strategies. For military, Sun Tzu stressed the role of a general who must be able to skillfully examine the environmental situation to exploit advantages of terrain or to avoid its disadvantages. Although the army has secured a favorable situation, if the general is incapable of exploiting the locational advantage, the entire army will fail. Therefore, Sun Tzu in the chapter "Terrain" summarized that there are six types of calamities caused by incapable generals, instead of natural disasters.

As the general's capability determines whether one can fully utilize the advantages of terrain, in business Porter similarly argued that locational advantages do not naturally arise, but are created with effort. The birth, evolution, and decline of clusters all rely on the efforts of companies, governments, and institutions. Inappropriate government policy would even negate locational advantages. Porter particularly distinguished cluster policy from industrial policy. Industrial policy tends to pick up winners or favor local companies. However, cluster policies aim to provide a favorable business environment, which is favorable to all firms; there is no distinction between local and foreign firms. The sustainability of clusters is the result of collective action of public and private sectors. In addition to the government contribution, the private sectors should also cooperate with the government in making the clusters competitive. This can explain the failure of some government-controlled clusters, such as the Kaesong Industrial Complex between North and South Korea, and the Greater Tumen Initiative controlled by China and its neighboring countries (Moon, 2016b).

10.3.3 Extension of Porter's Cluster Theory by Borrowing Sun Tzu's Concepts on Terrain

Porter in fact emphasized the general benefits of clusters to all firms located within the clusters indifferently. However, as Sun Tzu suggested, there is a distinction between advantageous and disadvantageous positioning within the same terrain. Hence, Sun Tzu advised in the case of accessible terrain, for example, one should first occupy the sunny and high place which is favorable for fighting against the enemy and securing the safe supply routes. On the other hand, if the enemy has first occupied the advantageous position, the army should flexibly respond to the enemy. In business, although all firms co-located in the same cluster can benefit from the environmental externalities, not all firms have the same performance. Although Porter acknowledged the higher performance of firms within the cluster than those outside the cluster, he did not explicitly explain the differences in performance among the firms within the cluster. Not only Porter, but existing studies on cluster are nearly silent on the question of whether firms benefit symmetrically from geographic agglomeration (McCann and Folta, 2011). In this regard, this area can be extended and Sun Tzu theory may be utilized for this purpose.

In addition, Porter did not recommend long-distance operations of business by emphasizing the concentration of industries and local sourcing within a country, or more preferably a local cluster. However, some scholars (e.g., Davenport, 2005; Moon and Jung, 2010) argued that more firms actually source important resources internationally rather than from proximate areas. Other studies (e.g., Cohen and Levinthal, 1990; Drejer and Vinding, 2007) found that companies with higher absorptive capacity tend to be more connected globally instead of being restricted to local network.

Furthermore, Huggins (2015) claimed that under the rapid growth of knowledge-based global economy, both clusters and connectivity across clusters are important for sustained generation of competitiveness of both clusters and firms. In other words, a cluster should not be regarded as a separate island on its own, but rather it should be thought of being interconnected with other related clusters from a global scope. Such open networks and connectivity have become more important for economic growth. For example, according to UNCTAD (2014), Singapore, despite its small country size, was included in the list of MNCs' top prospective host economies from 2014 to 2016 because of its global connectivity with foreign countries. In fact, Singapore has shifted its economic goal from being "intelligent island," which emphasizes the technology development as the growth engine, to being "connected island," which aims to become a business hub connecting the multinationals to the global society.

Like Porter, Sun Tzu also focused on the location itself and ignored the connectivity across different terrains. Sun Tzu, for example, suggested that in the case of distant terrain, anyone who starts the battle will be in a disadvantageous situation, because the army has to travel a long distance which will make the army tired when they arrive at the destination. Thus the above extension of Porter's cluster by incorporating the linkage with neighboring and global clusters can also provide some useful implications for military strategy on exploiting the terrain advantages. A well-designed strategic linkage among different types of terrain along with a competent general can exploit even more advantages from the terrain. The following military case of Joseon navy's victory led by Admiral Yi against the Japanese fleet is a good example.

10.4   MILITARY CASE: ADMIRAL YI'S VICTORY IN THE BATTLE OF MYEONGNYANG

The battle took place between Joseon (Old Korea, 1392–1910) and Japan in the Myeongnyang Strait, near Jindo Island, off the southwest point of the Korean peninsula, on October 26, 1597, during the Japanese invasion of Korea (1592–1598).[4] After Joseon was defeated in the Battle of Chilchonryang, King Seonjo reappointed Admiral Yi Sun-shin as the commander of the Joseon fleet. However, Yi found that there were only twelve ships and around 200 men left from the Battle of Chilchonryang, where Joseon navy was brutally defeated. On the other hand, ecstatic from the victory at Chilchonryang, the Japanese troops were experiencing an exponential rise in confidence predicting another victory against the Joseon navy which was pitifully deprived of ships and men. Thus, Japan quickly put together the resources and sailed out of Busan harbor with more than 300 ships. Facing the second invasion from Japan, King Seonjo thought that the Joseon fleet had little likelihood to be restored, and thus asked Admiral Yi to abandon warships and take his soldiers to join the army general Gwon Yul. However, Admiral Yi responded by sending a letter which said, "...if we fight to the death, it is not impossible to defend against the enemy; I still have twelve warships under my command; as long as I live, the enemy will never look down on us."

---

[4]   The information of the Battle of Myeongnyang is abstracted and reorganized from web .newworldencyclopedia.org/entry/Japan%27s_Korea_War:_Second_Invasion_(1596-15 98), www.storiespreschool.com/battle_myeongnyang.html, and www.liquisearch.co m/yi_sun-sin/japanese_invasions_of_korea_1592%E2%80%931598/battle_of_ myeongnyang).

Admiral Yi conducted a thorough field investigation in order to find a suitable battlefield, where his navy could benefit the most, while the Japanese military strength could be largely nullified. Finally, Admiral Yi selected Myeongnyang Strait as the preferred location of battle. First of all, the entrance to the strait was narrow, and the Japanese could not enter with all their ships into the channel at a time. Hence, there was less room for maneuvering by the Japanese navy force. Second, the current was very strong and changed directions from one way to another in every three hours. Third, the deep shadows of the surrounding hillsides could generate an illusion of a large number of Admiral Yi's ships to make the enemy nervous.

On the morning of October 26, when a large number of Japanese ships advanced toward Admiral Yi, however, only the command-ship of Admiral Yi fought in the battle, while the other twelve ships were just standing in the back of the battlefield, seeking an opportunity to run away. Evidently and understandably, other Joseon officers were uncertain of their chances of winning and afraid of the numerous Japanese ships. Regardless, Admiral Yi then sent a fast warship toward the Japanese fleet, in order to lure the Japanese fleet into the Myeongnyang Strait. The Japanese then thought chasing the ship could lead them to the command-ship of Admiral Yi and kill him. However, the Japanese never imagined there would be a trap. They also did not know the characteristics of the strait that could drive them into a highly disadvantageous situation.

The Japanese moved toward the Joseon navy along the direction of the flowing water. However, the tide soon shifted to the opposite direction, and the Japanese ships began to drift backward and collide with each other; some sank outright while sailing through the strait. The Japanese ships that passed through the strait faced archers and cannon fire from Admiral Yi's warships. However, the Japanese could not see Admiral Yi's warships clearly because of the shadows of the surrounding hills. As a result, by taking advantage of the terrain (i.e., Myeongnyang Strait), the Joseon fleet led by Admiral Yi could defeat the Japanese fleet, which had a significantly larger number of ships than Admiral Yi's. Among the 333 Japanese ships, 133 were warships and the other 200 were logistical support ships. Among the warships, more than thirty ships which entered the strait were completely destroyed, and many others were also significantly damaged. In the end, the victory prevented the Japanese from entering the West Sea.

The victory of Admiral Yi proved how a leader could exploit the advantages of terrain, or sea in this case, while overcoming the disadvantages pertaining to the size of military force. Although Sun Tzu's tactics of terrain mostly discuss about the ground battles, instead of maritime conflicts, there are some similarities and important implications for battles on the sea. For example, the narrow channel of the Myeongnyang Strait can be compared to Sun Tzu's narrow terrain. In the case of narrow terrain, Sun Tzu advised that one should first occupy the strategic position and wait for the enemy. It is actually what Admiral Yi did. He first deployed his ships inside the strait and let one ship lure the Japanese fleet to enter the location which he had already planned.

The complete exploitation of the terrain would not be possible without a competent leader. Admiral Yi was one of the most respected heroes in Korean history, and the Battle of Myeongnyang is viewed as the most remarkable achievement of Admiral Yi. When the king asked Admiral Yi to give up the Joseon fleets, Admiral Yi rejected the king's order and decided to fight with the remaining forces and achieved a remarkable victory. This is a model case embodiment of Sun Tzu's principle in his eighth chapter in The Art of War ("Variation of Tactics"): "Even though the ruler has instructed that the combat should be avoided, one should engage in battle if it is appropriate to fight and win."

On the other hand, the Japanese defeat in the battle was because of their failure in understanding the environment, particularly the characteristics of terrain. The Japanese were well aware of the gap in internal strengths between Joseon navy and their own. However, the Japanese failed to understand that the location was not suitable for combat. This is what Sun Tzu said: "If one does not know the terrain, the possibility of victory is not complete." The Japanese navy was very competent in naval battle and also had experiences of sailing in rough tides. Nonetheless, they advanced by merely relying on their numerical advantages to break Admiral Yi's line, which turned to failure in the end. This is consistent with Sun Tzu's simple but deep insight stated in his chapter "Marching": "Numbers alone confer no advantage."

In this military case, the victory of the Joseon navy exploited not just one type of terrain, but the synergy effects of various terrains, such as the strong current and changes of its flow direction, the narrow strait, and the surrounding hillsides. More importantly, the success of Admiral Yi was due to the convergence and synergy effects of various factors, including the unique characteristic of the battleground, the advantageous structure of Admiral Yi's ships over the Japanese ships, timing of the tides, and most importantly the capability of Admiral Yi who designed all of these factors most effectively. This converged, synergistic effect is similar to the cluster effect of Porter.

IO.5 BUSINESS CASE: THE COMPETITIVENESS OF SILICON VALLEY

Silicon Valley is the most widely known cluster in the world. Until the 1950s, the region was just a farmland, famous for orange groves and plum trees. However, between the late 1950s and the early 1970s, this region underwent a dramatic transformation into the world's leading center of silicon chip manufacturing, thanks to university-based research and postwar government military spending. Such transition and development gained it the current name, Silicon Valley, which refers to the Santa Clara Valley, the southern part of San Francisco Bay. Since the 2000s, policy makers also included the wider Bay Area of California by including San Francisco and Oakland into the region (Huggins, 2015). Historically, Silicon Valley suffered two crises – one in the early 1980s because of the emerging Japanese competitors and the other in the early 2000s because of the dotcom bubble burst. However, Silicon Valley successfully overcame these difficulties and evolved into an even more successful cluster, which inspired numerous foreign policy makers to learn from its success model. In the following section, I will discuss and analyze Silicon Valley's success using Porter's cluster theory.

As Porter pointed out, clusters do not arise from a vacuum; instead they have a sequence of historical events leading up to the cluster formation. The birth of Silicon Valley is a good example to show how locational advantages can be proactively created and exploited instead of being passively bestowed. The origin can be traced back to the establishment of Federal Telegraph in 1908, which contributed to the development of wireless technology in this region. The government's defense spending and Stanford University played an important role in the formation of this industrial cluster. Professionals and technicians promoted the businesses in the beginning, and this later attracted a large number of engineers from the eastern United States. In addition, the interlinkage or network among firms and organizations also played an important role for further development of the cluster. The informal cooperation among individuals and entrepreneurs promoted the spread of technology and knowhow in the region (Saxenian, 1990).

According to Porter (1998), easier access to the needed resources such as capital, talents, technology, and information helps firms improve their productivity. Silicon Valley accounts for more than 20 percent of the total venture capital investment in the United States (Zhang, 2007). The vast pool of venture capital has especially benefited many start-ups at the founding stage. Since many venture capitalist investors have previous entrepreneurial experiences, they tend to be better at evaluating and monitoring the start-ups. Moreover, due to the early and better access to venture capital, start-ups in Silicon Valley can quickly transform their ideas into outputs and introduce them into the market (Zhang, 2007).

The second advantage of clusters emphasized by Porter (1998) is the effects of innovation inducement. Piscione (2013) claimed that a worthier name for Silicon Valley is "innovation valley." The claim was likely to have been inspired by the fact that every five to ten years, someone in Silicon Valley creates something which is followed or imitated by others elsewhere (Piscione, 2013). However, if the so-called innovation created in Silicon Valley is analyzed, one will find a curious characteristic: the successful firms of Silicon Valley are not always the inventors of some super-advanced or state-of-the-art technology. Rather, firms in this region have competitive advantages in commercializing the already existing technologies into the market.

Porter's cluster concept particularly emphasized the interaction between cooperation and competition for innovation. Competition pressures firms to continuously innovate in order to survive, and cooperation facilitates innovation by providing the complementing resources. In Silicon Valley, although the industrial system is rather decentralized and fragmented, it is well integrated through formal and informal cooperative practices and institutions (Saxenian, 2000). On the other hand, Route 128, another famous industrial cluster in the East of the United States, was characterized by a more separate and self-sufficient organizational structure, which actually hindered its adaptation to the environmental changes. The different organizational structures of the two clusters became one of the key reasons why Silicon Valley survived and shifted to next generation successfully, while Route 128 faced continuous downturns during the 1980s.

The third benefit of clusters is that they encourage the creation of new businesses. The flow rate of ideas, capital, and talent is very slow for the large firms or incumbent firms which have a top-down organizational structure. They have to pass a long bureaucratic process before they reach the top executive. In Silicon Valley, a venture-capital firm usually receives thousands of unsolicited business plans in a single year. In an average large firm, thousands of business plans will take a very long time to process. However, because Silicon Valley firms have flat organizational structure and diffusion of power, the employees can all actively contribute to creating new business models and thus expedite the process.

Hence, Hamel (1999) pointed out the critical difference between the way of doing business in large firms and start-ups in Silicon Valley.

The former type of firms adopts the method of resource allocation, while the latter type employs resource attraction. There is always the limit of complicated financial analysis for creating a new business for the large firms. However, for those firms in Silicon Valley, a good idea can more easily attract the resources in the region, and have a greater chance of turning into reality. It is common for several venture capitals to jointly invest in a start-up, and there may be less consideration of capital budget. In fact, the risk embedded in a project launched by a start-up is often lower than that by a large firm, because the projects of start-ups do not need a large amount of initial investment compared to large firms.

Although Porter's cluster theory is useful for explaining the competitiveness of Silicon Valley compared to other regional clusters, it does not fully capture the success factors behind Silicon Valley's superior performance. Its broad global linkage with other clusters should also be considered, and such interregional or intercluster linkage becomes more important for sustainable growth in the increasing scale and scope of globalization. On one hand, there has been an increasing collaboration between Silicon Valley and other foreign clusters, such as Bangaluru, Shanghai, and Helsinki since 2001 (Joint Venture, 2007). On the other hand, a large number of engineers and entrepreneurs from emerging Asian countries build networks in order to acquire knowledge, skills, and technology from Silicon Valley; and many Asian engineers and technicians also move to Silicon Valley and thus provide a large pool of young and low-cost talent for Silicon Valley.

Porter well explained the different performance between firms inside and outside the clusters. For example, the start-ups located in Silicon Valley are normally performing better than those located elsewhere. Hence, Porter's cluster concept sees that the benefits of clusters diffuse equally among firms within the cluster. However, in reality not all firms in Silicon Valley are equally competitive. Annually, 3,000 start-ups opened or moved into Silicon Valley, but 2,500 closed or moved out of the region (SVLG and SVCF, 2015). This implies that in addition to the environmental influences, the internal capability differences among firms should also be taken into consideration to explain individual firms' performance differences in the same environment of Silicon Valley. In this respect, Sun Tzu's strategy of dealing with different positions within the same terrains can provide useful implications.

10.6 CONCLUSION AND IMPLICATIONS

For military strategy, this chapter highlighted the importance of terrain for gaining an advantageous position in the battlefield. The geographic terrain itself is a fixed, uncontrollable factor, but a capable general can make it controllable and regard the terrain as an aid to his own army. Controlling terrain requires a high level of skill as one must be able to bend the environment to accommodate one's needs, instead of adjusting one's own needs or goals to the set conditions of the environment. Therefore, what is more important is the general's capabilities, which may often be very flexible as seen from Han Xin's deployment strategy near the river. The general must be able to accurately understand the intentions of the enemy and even control the enemy by enticing or discouraging them. To employ these strategies, however, the most important point of Sun Tzu is that one has to thoroughly investigate oneself, the enemy, and the terrain. The military case study (the Battle of Myeongnyang) illustrates many of the useful strategies suggested by Sun Tzu.

For comparing and contrasting with Sun Tzu, this chapter examined Porter's cluster theory, which is particularly important compared to other preceding cluster studies in that Porter's cluster is not just a region of improving the business efficiency but that of encouraging innovation. Throughout many of his publications, Porter emphasized the importance of innovation as a major source of corporate and national competitiveness and he argued that cluster is a particularly effective tool for promoting firms' innovation. It is also interesting to note that Porter stressed the role of geographical concentration (i.e., cluster) for gaining competitive advantages when business activities are increasingly dispersed across the globe. Government policymakers and business managers must have a comprehensive understanding of clusters before making decisions.

Both Sun Tzu and Porter emphasized the role of location in achieving victory in military campaign and business. Another similarity between the two theories is that the location advantage does not occur automatically, but requires additional efforts by leaders and other participants. In military, Sun Tzu emphasized the role of general. On the other hand, in business Porter argued that the development or decline of a cluster depends on the efforts and investment by firms and governments. However, Porter's cluster theory shows limitations when it comes to explaining the phenomenon of interconnections among global clusters, such as the connection between Silicon Valley and some emerging Asian clusters. His cluster concept also overlooks the differences in performance among firms within the cluster. The second limitation can be complemented by Sun Tzu's strategies of dealing with terrains. In turn, Sun Tzu's theory can also be improved as it limits the exploitation of advantages to a single terrain, instead of a cluster of various terrains.

11 International Strategy

Sun Tzu: Strategic guidelines for expeditionary operations
Porter: Configuration-coordination model for firms' internationalization

While Sun Tzu had already introduced the significance of terrain in the chapter "Terrain" of *The Art of War*, he reintroduced the idea as the main topic with detailed strategic guidelines in his eleventh chapter. The literal meaning of the title of Sun Tzu's chapter 11, *Jiu Di*, is nine terrains. However, the nine terrains of Sun Tzu's chapter 11 are quite different from the six terrains of his chapter 10. The discussion on terrains in Sun Tzu's chapter 10 primarily concerned the types of natural layout and geographical features of the land. In *Jiu Di*, Sun Tzu presented a different approach to terrains by organizing them according to their strategic – not geographic – position in war (Kim, 1999). For example, Sun Tzu suggested appropriate strategies depending on the three criteria: relative distance from the home territory, accessibility, and risks involved. Sun Tzu in the chapter of *Jiu Di* introduced nine situations and the tactical suggestions for operating in these battlefield situations.

In addition to the nine specific situations, Sun Tzu provided useful guidelines for launching an expeditionary attack. These strategic guidelines are important because expedition combat is often the most difficult of offenses, and sometimes the strategic goal cannot be attained without effective expedition efforts (Kim, 1999). Regarding the strategic guidelines for the expeditionary attack, Sun Tzu placed particular emphasis on the control of the soldiers' psychological condition and the importance of cooperative relationships with neighboring countries.

"Nine Situations" or *Jiu Di* is the longest among the thirteen chapters in *The Art of War*, accounting for about one-fifth of the entire length of the book. Sawyer (2005) commented that this chapter only reiterates several crucial, loosely integrated principles as a part of its continuing examination of topographical implications. On the other hand, some scholars (e.g., Wu and Yu, 1993) said that this chapter is not inferior to the chapters such as "Laying Plans," "Strategic Attack," or "Weaknesses and Strengths." I would say that the chapter "Nine Situations" is at least as important as other chapters, because in this chapter Sun Tzu suggested very practical terrain strategies by integrating and extending other related strategies of the preceding chapters.

Comparable to Sun Tzu's idea of sending expeditionary combat units is Porter's framework of firms' international strategy, focusing on the international expansion of firms' business activities for achieving higher competitiveness. Sun Tzu's emphasis on both locational advantage and coordination among units within the troops as well as other neighboring countries can be linked to Porter's two determinants of configuration and coordination of his framework for categorizing various types of international strategy of firms.

In the first two sections, I will explain the two connectable theories of Sun Tzu and Michael Porter. I will first introduce Sun Tzu's specific tactics in different situations and the principles for an effective expeditionary operation. Then, I will explain Porter's (1986) Configuration-Coordination framework. Following the analyses, I will examine the linkage between the two theories. For case studies, I will show the military case of the Battle of Incheon and the business case of Starbucks' entry into China to help readers understand and utilize these strategic linkages between war and business.

11.1   SUN TZU: STRATEGIC GUIDELINES FOR EXPEDITIONARY OPERATIONS

11.1.1   Operational Tactics in Nine Situations

The nine terrains can be categorized by three criteria – relative distance from the home territory, accessibility, and risks

Table 11.1 *Comparison of terrains in Sun Tzu's chapters 8, 10, and 11*

Chapter 11 (9 Types)	Chapter 10 (6 Types)	Chapter 8 (5 Types)
Dispersive terrain (散地)		
Light terrain (輕地)		
Heavy terrain (重地)		
Contentious terrain (爭地)	Precipitous terrain (險形)	
Accessible terrain (交地)	Accessible terrain (通形)	
Focal terrain (衢地)		Focal terrain (衢地)
Treacherous terrain (圮地)		Entrapping terrain (圮地)
Constricted terrain (圍地)	Narrow terrain (隘形)	Encircled terrain (圍地)
Fatal terrain (死地)		Fatal terrain (死地)
	Entangling terrain (挂形)	
	Temporizing terrain (支形)	
	Distant terrain (遠形)	
		Desolate terrain (絕地)

Source: Wee et al. (1991).

involved.[1] Dispersive terrain, light terrain, and heavy terrain are categorized by each terrain's relative distance from home territory. Contentious terrain, accessible terrain, and focal terrain are categorized according to their accessibility levels. Treacherous terrain, constricted terrain, and fatal terrain concern the risks involved in a situation. As some of these types of terrain have been introduced in the previous chapters of Sun Tzu's book (e.g., chapters 8 and 10 of *The Art of War*), here they have been reorganized for comparison in Table 11.1 based on the explanation of Wee et al. (1991). In the following, I will illustrate the characteristics of each situation and the operational tactics for each situation.

[1]   Some related information can be found in Wee et al. (1991), Kim (1999), and Minford (2008).

Dispersive Terrain This terrain is where the army is fighting in its own territory. If soldiers are near their home, they will be anxious to see their wives and children, forget their mission, and wish to return home. Therefore, they are likely to look for an escape from fighting and scatter in every direction. In this situation, Sun Tzu proposed that the army should not fight in dispersive terrain and that the general should be particularly attentive to unifying the determination of the army.

Light Terrain This terrain is where an army has made a shallow penetration into the enemy's territory. As it is a shallow penetration into the enemy's territory, it is relatively easy to retreat backward. Therefore, Sun Tzu proposed not to stop into the light terrain. He then suggested a general should keep the forces closely linked so that the soldiers do not break away from their affiliated troops.

Contentious Terrain This terrain is where it is equally advantageous to both one's enemy and oneself. Due to the significance of this type of terrain, both sides are likely to fight bitterly for it. Therefore, Sun Tzu said, "Do not attack an enemy who has occupied the contentious terrain." In contrast, if the enemy has not yet arrived at the desired location, Sun Tzu suggested that the general should rush all his rear forces, so that the head and tail both reach the destination.

Accessible Terrain This terrain is open and equally accessible to the enemy and oneself. In such situation, the enemy can traverse the terrain easily. Due to this nature of accessible terrain, Sun Tzu said, "Do not allow one's formations to be separated." He then asserted that a general should keep an eye on defense, particularly the supply and communication lines.

Focal Terrain This terrain is surrounded by several other countries. If a country is located in a focal terrain, one is always under the threat of being captured by other neighboring countries. Thus, for those in a focal terrain, Sun Tzu recommended forming and maintaining a good relationship with the neighboring countries and strengthening the ties with allies.

Heavy Terrain[2] This terrain is where the army has penetrated deep into the enemy territory, and has advanced into many of the enemy's fortified cities and towns. As the return route is filled with enemy's fortified towns and cities, far away from one's own territory, one is at the risk of unstable supply lines. Hence, the way to ensure the survival in this situation is to take the enemy resources and protect one's own supply routes to ensure a continuous flow of provisions.

Treacherous Terrain This terrain is where travel is difficult, such as the mountainous areas, deep forests, dangerous passes, and marshy swamps. When an army is confronted with this terrain, Sun Tzu suggested to leave the place as swiftly as possible, in case one is trapped in the passive situation.

Constricted Terrain This refers to terrain where the access route is narrow and the retreat route is tortuous. Thus, in such terrain, getting in is as difficult as getting out of the situation; so the terrain allows a smaller army to strike the larger army with ease through ambushes. Hence, Sun Tzu suggested devising strategies to avoid danger.

Fatal Terrain This terrain is where the army can survive only by mustering the courage to fight out of extreme desperation. When soldiers are surrounded and there are no other alternatives, they fight to the death. Therefore, Sun Tzu suggested that in a fatal terrain, the general should plainly and clearly let his men know that their only chance of survival is fighting one's way out of it.

11.1.2 Principles of Expeditionary Operations

Raid Strategy

In addition to the specific tactics in different strategic situations, Sun Tzu proposed the principles of operations and the way to control the army when an expeditionary force penetrates into the enemy territory. In particular, he stressed the importance of the raid strategy when penetrating into the enemy territory. According to Sun Tzu, the main

---

[2]   This may be better positioned in the third place right after the light terrain.

objective of the raid strategy is to separate the enemy both physically and psychologically. Sun Tzu then proposed several principles for the successful operation of raid strategy: to stress the speed of operations; to take advantage of enemy's absence; to travel unanticipated roads; and to attack when the enemy is not prepared. "Speed" in the first principle is referring to the speed of the operation; whereas the second principle is about avoiding the enemy's strengths and attacking their weaknesses, and the third and fourth are about utilizing *Chi* strategy. These principles, in fact, were already mentioned in the previous chapters. Specifically, speed has been discussed in Sun Tzu's chapters 2 and 7. In his chapter 2, Sun Tzu advised avoiding a long campaign, and in his chapter 7 he asserted the significance of speed, or timely arrival at the destination, for successful maneuvering of the troops. Avoiding the enemy's strengths and attacking their weaknesses are the core themes of his chapter 6. Also, in his chapter 5, Sun Tzu stressed the importance of combining *Cheng* and *Chi* strategies to attain a strategic advantage in war.

Troop Cohesion and Commitment

In addition to the raid strategy, troop cohesion and battlefield commitment are seen as important factors for obtaining a decisive victory when an army penetrates into the enemy territory. The essence of troop cohesion is the cooperation among different divisions of the army, while the battlefield commitment requires the commitment of individual soldiers. The definition of troop cohesion can be explained by the following two perspectives. One is the cohesion in thinking and the other is the cohesion in action.[3] Cohesion in thinking refers to soldiers' sharing of the same objective, attitude, and mind-set. Sun Tzu said, "Even people who dislike each other, if they are in the same boat, they will help each other in order to get out of the trouble."

Sun Tzu referred to a highly cohesive army as *shuai ran*, a legendary snake in Mountain Chang. The distinctive characteristic

---

[3]   More information can be found in Bei (2012).

of this snake is that if one strikes its head, the tail will attack; if one strikes its tail, the head will attack; if one strikes the middle, both the head and tail will attack.[4] If the army moves like this snake, their efforts to rescue each other will be like the cooperation between left and right hands. Sun Tzu said when the army achieves the highest level of cooperation, the task of directing the army can be as easy as that of directing a single individual.

For the cohesion of action, Sun Tzu emphasized the importance of knowing the soldiers' psychological condition by thoroughly examining how human feelings and emotions are processed. Psychological status of soldiers is crucial in military operation (Bei, 2012). If the psychological condition of soldiers is stable, they will make all their efforts to prepare for war. In contrast, if soldiers' psychological condition is not stable, they will easily feel reluctant or fearful of going to war. Therefore, without psychological stability, even with a large number of military forces and advanced equipment, the army may not achieve the desired victory. The US failure in the Vietnam War is a good example.

Then how can one stabilize soldiers' psychological status and maximize their commitment to war? Sun Tzu provided a general rule of operations as follows. When there is no alternative, soldiers will fight. Therefore, put them in positions where there is nowhere else to go; then they will fight to their death without retreating (e.g., fatal terrain). The specific way of operation for an invading force is that the deeper one's army penetrates into the enemy territory (e.g., heavy terrain), the greater the cohesion of one's army will be; the shallower the penetration (e.g., light terrain), the looser and more dispersive one's army will become.

However, Sun Tzu said fettering the horses and burying the chariot wheels are inadequate for preventing the soldiers from fleeing. In order to have the whole troop act in unison, both courage and

---

[4] What happens if one strikes both the head and the tail at the same time? The army which can do both is so strong that they do not need strategy. Strategy is particularly useful and important when one is not so strong.

strong administration along with education are necessary, so that all soldiers may cooperate in one mind, focused on a single goal. Therefore, the efficient commanding and communication system for troop cohesion is particularly important. Even if individuals are strongly committed to the war, if the administration does not have an effective commanding and management system, the whole army will easily fall into chaos. Thus, the leader's ability to control the army is vital, as much as individual commitment, for maintaining an army's competitiveness.

11.2 PORTER: CONFIGURATION-COORDINATION MODEL FOR FIRMS' INTERNATIONALIZATION

Traditional concept of comparative advantage derives from factor endowment (factor-cost or factor-quality differences) among different countries. Therefore, firms gaining these advantages in a particular country will export the product made in their home countries to elsewhere in the world. However, in the new pattern of international competition, instead of locating all the activities in the home country, firms locate some of their activities where they can be performed most efficiently anywhere in the world. Therefore, global firms can gain their competitive advantages through global operations of appropriate configuration and coordination. As local circumstances change, however, they need to adjust their value chain and relocate activities. The case of Nike serves as a good example. Once China lost its comparative advantage in wage level, Vietnam became the biggest production base for the company in 2010. Even in Vietnam, however, labor will not stay cheap forever. Thus, CEOs are already looking into prospective future investment candidates, as an article from Economist (2012) speculated "Myanmar looks tempting, provided that reforms there continue."

A firm competing internationally must decide where and how to spread the activities in the value chain among countries. To better explain the different patterns of international competition, Porter (1986) introduced two dimensions of how firms compete

High	High foreign investment with extensive coordination among subsidiaries		Simple global strategy
Coordination of Activities			
Low	Country-centered strategy by multinationals or domestic firms operating in only one country		Export-based strategy with decentralized marketing
	Geographically dispersed		Geographically concentrated

Configuration of Activities

FIGURE 11.1 The dimensions of international strategy
Source: Porter (1986).

internationally. The first is configuration, which is related to the location in the world and in how many places the firm's activities in the value chain are performed. Configuration options range from *concentrated* (i.e., performing all activities in one location and serving the world from it) to *dispersed* (i.e., performing the activities in various locations). The second dimension is coordination, which refers to how tightly the activities performed in different countries are coordinated with each other. Coordination level ranges from *low* (i.e., operations in each country are in autonomy) to *high* (i.e., operations of each country are tightly coordinated by sharing the same information, production process, parts, and so on). There can be many different variations of international strategies within this frame of configuration and coordination quadrants. Figure 11.1 shows some of the possible variations in international strategies.

Low Coordination If a firm employs a dispersed configuration (i.e., placing the entire value chain in each country) and coordinates little among themselves, the firm is regarded as pursuing a *country-centered strategy*. GM often uses this country-centered strategy with separate brand names and production facilities for each market.

If the firm only operates in one country, Porter calls it the *export-based strategy*. This is the case for many luxury brands. For example, Gucci from Florence in Italy, produces in one location and serves the global market only through exports.

High Coordination As the firm's strategy moves from the lower left-hand corner of Figure 11.1 up or to the right, its strategy becomes increasingly global. The simplest global strategy is to concentrate as many activities as possible in one country, serving the world from this home base and tightly coordinating the activities conducted all over the world. Many Japanese firms adopted the simple global strategy in the 1960s and 1970s. The other case is high coordination in combination with geographical dispersion. The case can be seen in the European Aeronautic Defense and Space Company (EADS), a global leader in aerospace, defense, and related services. This company has sites in Germany, France, Spain, Singapore, and Russia, which foster technological excellence through the sharing (i.e., coordination) of competences and means between various partners of the EADS Group.

11.3   THE INTEGRATION OF SUN TZU AND PORTER

In general, it is not recommended for an army to travel a long distance and engage in a war with the enemy, as explained by Sun Tzu in the distant terrain in the chapter "Terrain." However, in some cases, expeditionary combat may be preferred or even be necessary, when no other alternatives can achieve the expected political/military goals. The US attacks on Iraq and Afghanistan can be good examples. Similarly, in business a firm will tend to globalize, extending the business activities from home to foreign countries, when there are no good alternatives in its home country. The following will examine the linkages between Sun Tzu and Michael Porter.

11.3.1   The Importance of Locational Advantage

Both Sun Tzu and Porter emphasized the importance of geographic location to gain advantages. In military, Sun Tzu preferred fighting in heavy terrain over light terrain when one's expeditionary forces are invading the enemy territory. In this case, Sun Tzu emphasized the importance of securing provisions from the enemy territory. He said that the army requires a large amount of human and physical resources to wage war, and in order to achieve victory at the minimum cost, one should utilize enemy or local resources as much as possible. Sun Tzu referred to this strategy as "conquering the enemy and growing stronger."

Similarly, in business, Porter said that gaining a competitive advantage is affected by where the firms locate their activities in the value chain for international competition. This idea falls into the dimension of configuration of Configuration-Coordination (C-C) framework. By spreading the activities in the value chain to the preferred locations on a worldwide basis, one can exploit local country-specific advantages to enhance the competitiveness of each activity, thereby improving the efficiency of the entire value chain. The firm can then become stronger as it becomes more internationalized.

According to Porter, the configuration of business activities is influenced by four elements: economies of scale in the activity, a proprietary learning curve in the activity, comparative advantage of one or a few locations for performing the activity, and coordination advantage of colocating linked activities such as R&D and production. Therefore, firms can select "an ideal location" depending on the characteristics of the activities, and the comparative advantage of the location. In addition, Porter introduced the concept of "global platform." Rather than just serving consumers where the activity is located, the location can function as the base for serving a larger region or even the global market. Porter suggested two determinants for choosing a global platform. The first is the factor endowment of the country and the second determinant is the feature of the country's demand and local operating environment.

However, there is a critical difference between Sun Tzu's military and Porter's business strategy in choosing the location. Sun Tzu emphasized that when soldiers are placed into the positions where there is nowhere to retreat or escape, they will fight to the death for survival. This implies that soldiers' individual commitments should be forcefully induced, rather than left to their free will. In business, however, firms expand their business from domestic to global scope when the benefits outweigh the costs of globalization. Thus in business, the motivation is either voluntary or driven by incentives, rather than by unavoidable pressure. CEOs have more freedom than military generals in choosing the location.

11.3.2   The Importance of Coordination

Sun Tzu highlighted the importance of troop cohesion for an expeditionary force invading the enemy territory. As mentioned earlier, Sun Tzu compared a well-coordinated troop to the snake, *shuai ran*. When one military unit is in danger, the other unit should come to rescue. In addition to the emphasis on the internal coordination within the army, Sun Tzu also pointed out the importance of relationship with the external parties, such as the neighboring countries. The possibility of coordination depends on whether they have shared interests. Sun Tzu said, "The people of Wu and Yue have conflicts with each other, but if they encounter severe wind when passing a river in the same boat, they are likely to combine efforts to rescue each other to ensure their survival." However, Sun Tzu also warned that one should not form the alliances without knowing the intensions of the partner countries, and that one should make sure that the enemy is isolated from the support of its neighboring countries before starting a war.

Likewise, in business, Porter emphasized cohesion or coordination among different activities located in different countries. Coordination among dispersed activities improves the ability of firms to gain the economies of scale and scope in activities. Porter's work and other empirical studies (e.g., Taggart, 1998) show that the more specialized and interdependent foreign subsidiaries are, the more likely they will coordinate with each other. However, high coordination is also accompanied by high risk, because each party plays an important role in completing the whole value chain. Thus, if a problem occurs in any activity, the whole value chain and thereby the competitiveness of the firm will be disrupted. The supply chain crisis of Toyota incurred by the March 11 earthquakes in 2011 is a good example.

However, one factor Porter overlooked is the coordination with other independent firms or organizations (including the host country governments).[5] The competitiveness of multinational firms is determined not by a single firm itself, but by the capability of all of the involved parties and the synergistic linkage created within the business ecosystem. The government is also a powerful actor that influences multinational firms' configuration and coordination strategies. With the multinational firms' growing investment in developing countries, developing country governments prefer multinational firms to allow more partnership with local firms through joint venture or other forms. Compared to the multi-domestic strategy, the global strategy has a lesser degree of local integration (Hansen, Pedersen, and Petersen, 2009). Therefore, it is also critical for multinational firms to consider local economic benefits in order to sustain their business in the long run.

However, there is still a major difference between troop cohesion in military and activity coordination in business. The military highlights the concept of "help." When one military unit is in difficulty, other units will help without calculating the risk and dangers they may be confronted with. Therefore, "helping" an endangered division is likely to be a zero-sum, as one is pouring resources to mend for a hole rather than to create something new. It is most definitely better than a negative sum outcome, but certainly not the most desirable expenditure of one's limited resources. However, coordination in business is more closely connected to creating synergy and co-development. Coordination potentially allows the sharing and accumulation of know-how and expertise among dispersed activities in the global scope (Porter, 1986).

[5]   Similar arguments have been discussed in Chapter 2 of this book, when assessing Porter's value chain framework.

Therefore, both sides will benefit from coordination, not simply transferring the resources at one's expense to "help" the other side. Hence, it is more of a positive-sum game.

11.4 MILITARY CASE: THE UNITED NATIONS FORCES' VICTORY IN THE BATTLE OF INCHEON

The Battle of Incheon broke out on September 15, 1950, and ended on September 19, resulting in a decisive victory and strategic reversal of the tides in favor of the United Nations (UN) forces.[6] By early September of 1950, the entire Korean Peninsula except for Busan was occupied by the North Korean army. Douglas MacArthur, the commander-in-chief of the UN army, thought that the only way to reverse the unfavorable situation was to conduct a surprise landing attack on Incheon, located in the middle-left of the peninsula that was already heavily occupied by the North Korean army.

However, Incheon might have been the worst place to attack. Omar Bradley, one of the most famous American generals during World War II, saw Incheon as "the worst possible place ever selected for an amphibious landing" (Pearlman, 2008: 87). This analysis might be true because Incheon's 30-foot tides were so severe that there were only two days out of the entire month of September that allowed the port to be accessible to the landing craft. The daily fluctuations of tides further limited the time appropriate for conducting the operation. Any delay or unexpected resistance from the North Koreans could cause a serious problem. In addition, Incheon was far behind the front lines. If the North Koreans could keep the existing UN forces inside the battle frontier at Busan, they could isolate and overwhelm the UN forces at Incheon (Kinni and Kinni, 2005). Thus, when MacArthur proposed this plan, many were negative, calling his plan suicidal. Instead, other navy leaders favored the landing at Gunsan, but MacArthur overrode them as he did not think other options would be decisive enough for victory.

---

[6] Information of the battle of Incheon is abstracted and reorganized from militaryhistory .about.com/od/battleswars1900s/p/Inchon.htm.

On September 15, 1950, the UN forces under the command of general MacArthur, successfully and dramatically landed in Incheon. The Battle of Incheon lasted for only five days. In the morning of September 15, the UN fleet moved to their respective positions. Around 6:30 am, the first UN troops came ashore at "Green Beach" on Wolmi-do. Supported by nine tanks from the 1st Tank Battalion, the Marines successfully captured the island by noon, suffering only fourteen casualties from the operation. Until the afternoon, they defended the causeway to Incheon harbor, while awaiting reinforcements. Due to the extreme tides in the harbor, the reinforcements did not arrive until 5:30 pm. And at 5:31pm, the 1st Marines landed and scaled the sea wall at "Red Beach." Located just above the Wolmi-do causeway, the Marines on Red Beach quickly reduced the North Korean army opposition, allowing forces from Green Beach to enter the battle.

Pressing into Incheon, the forces from Green and Red Beaches were able to take the city and compelled the North Korean defenders to surrender. As these events were unfolding, the 1st Marine Regiment was landing on "Blue Beach" to the south. Although one landing ship tank (LST) was sunk while approaching the beach, the Marines met little opposition. The landings at Incheon caught the North Korean command by surprise. Believing that Gunsan would be the main location of attack, the North Korean army had sent only a small force for the protection of Incheon. Hence, the North Koreans were unprepared as well as outnumbered and unable to call in quick reinforcements. Furthermore, they were in danger of being split up between Incheon and Busan and eventually had to retreat northward. The victory in this battle led to the recapture of the South Korean capital Seoul about one week later. UN casualties during the Incheon landings and subsequent battles for the city were 566 killed and 2,713 wounded. On the other hand, during the actual battle, more than 35,000 North Korean soldiers were killed or captured.

MacArthur's selection of Incheon as the battleground was key to winning the decisive victory, which led to the recovery of South Korean territory. MacArthur's raid strategy and its outcome reflect all of Sun Tzu's principles laid out in this Chapter. First, the amazing speed at which the forces were built up and the timely and accurate intelligence information contributed to the success. Second, the North Koreans had decisively committed all of their forces at the extreme southern end of the Korean peninsula, against the army at the Busan Perimeter, but appeared unaware of the risk of their extended and vulnerable lines of communication. Incheon was a proper place to cut the North Korean army's supply and communication lines, thereby allowing the breakout of the Busan Perimeter. Third, MacArthur said, "In war, surprise should be decisive." Because of the tough geographical conditions, it was difficult for North Korea to imagine and prepare for an attack in Incheon, and thus the UN army could succeed in landing at Incheon by surprise.

In addition, Sun Tzu said if soldiers are put in a life or death situation, they will fully commit themselves to the battle in order to secure their own survival. The Incheon case is similar to Sun Tzu's definition of heavy terrain: a port with treacherous conditions, located at the heart of the Peninsula, surrounded and occupied by the enemy. General MacArthur insisted on the Battle of Incheon, which involved the risk of deploying the major force into the ground occupied by the enemy. However, with this strategy of fatal terrain, soldiers of UN forces fought to the death, leading to victory.

On the other hand, the two axes of Porter's C-C framework can be applied to understanding the outcome of Incheon landing. For the first component of the C-C framework, "configuration," firms choose to locate activities to take advantage of local factor endowments. Therefore, selecting an appropriate location will allow firms to maximize their competitive advantage. In the beginning, the UN saw Gunsan as a good location for landing, but MacArthur favored Incheon due to its strategic significance. This insightful decision led to a great success and moreover minimized the cost of victory. For the second element "coordination," the UN forces succeeded because of their efficient cooperation among different divisions through timely and accurate intelligence information. On the other hand, the capture of Incheon severed North Korean army's supply lines, which prevented North Korean army from coordinating with the rest of their forces. Thus, the significance of coordination is fully revealed in this military case.

11.5   BUSINESS CASE: STARBUCKS' SUCCESS IN CHINA

In 1971, Seattle saw the opening of its first-ever Starbucks store.[7] In the following decades, the company extended its product portfolio and expanded its business to the rest of the United States and eventually to the world. By now, the company operates about 20,000 stores in more than sixty countries, and about 60 percent of the stores are located in the United States. As for business strategy, Starbucks is well known for the standardization strategy of its stores. Once you enter a Starbucks, unless you look at the souvenir corner with special cups or mugs, it is difficult to tell in which city the store is located. Visitors are welcomed by an almost perfectly uniform atmosphere that is unique to Starbucks brand, regardless of whether they are in Seattle, Seoul, or Shanghai.

Meanwhile, Starbucks' success in China is a noteworthy case. Starbucks viewed China as a strategic market, and made it a clear priority for accomplishing growth outside the United States. Starbucks entered China in 1999 by opening a coffee shop in Beijing. Twelve years after Starbucks' entry, the coffee shop has opened more than 570 stores in forty-eight Chinese cities. The average profit per store in China turned out to be higher than that in the United States. Starbucks' success was not guaranteed in the beginning, since China is a country with a strong consumer preference for tea, rather than coffee; coffee was an uncommon and rather unpopular commodity. Then how could the Seattle-based coffee company make such a big success in China? Forbes (Wang, 2012) discussed the success factors of

---

[7]   The case of Starbucks is abstracted and modified from Forbes (Wang, 2012) and Rein (2012).

Starbucks' entry into China by drawing upon some lessons to learn from Starbucks.[8]

First, Position Smart

Traditionally, tea has been the national delicacy and specialty of China. Hence it seemed to be impossible for an American franchise coffee maker to sell this Western beverage to the Chinese people. However, China's middle class was growing at an exponential rate, and with that, there was a change in consumer attitudes. To this consumer group, Western products, such as Starbucks, gained strong attention (Atsmon, Dixit, and Wu, 2011). Starbucks well targeted and accommodated the demand. Therefore, Starbucks not only established a prominent presence in major cities like Beijing, Shanghai, and Guangzhou, but also established its stores in the second- and third-tier cities, where there was a relatively high percentage of middle-class people due to the increasing rate of urbanization.

In addition, Starbucks did not promote any advertising that could be regarded as a challenge to the Chinese tradition of tea-drinking culture. Instead, it chose high-visibility and high-traffic locations to project its brand image. Starbucks then capitalized on the tea-drinking culture of Chinese consumers by introducing beverages made from using popular local ingredients such as green tea. This strategy effectively turned potential obstacles into Starbucks' advantage encouraging the Chinese consumers to quickly develop a taste for Starbucks' coffee as well as tea.

Second, Brand Global

As Starbucks well understood the value of global branding, it took a series of steps to maintain brand integrity. One of the best practices that Starbucks adopted was to dispatch its best baristas

---

[8]   Forbes (Wang, 2012) introduced five points of explaining the success strategy of Starbucks' operation in China – think different, position smart, brand global, partner local, and commit long term. As the first success factor is the effect of the other four factors, this book illustrates only the other four factors for the case study.

from established markets to new markets to train the new employees. These baristas thus not only helped build Starbucks culture in the new stores but also made sure that all the local stores could follow Starbucks' global standards. While branding globally, in order to tailor to Chinese consumers' tastes, Starbucks also introduced highly localized menus after an extensive market survey and analysis of consumer tastes. Starbucks even gave each store the flexibility to select different beverage portfolios that fit the local customers' tastes at its particular location.

Third, Partner Local

China proved not to be a homogeneous market. For example, the culture of northern provinces of China is much different from that of the eastern provinces. Consumer purchasing powers are also substantially different among different regions (e.g., inland versus coastal cities). Considering this complexity of the Chinese market, Starbucks formed partnerships with three regional companies for expanding its business across the country. In the north, Starbucks established a joint venture with Beijing Mei Da coffee company. In the east, the company made an alliance with the Taiwan-based Uni-President. In the south, it cooperated with Hong Kong-based Maxim's Caterers. Each partner brought different strengths and local expertise that helped Starbucks gain insights into the characteristics and trends of local Chinese markets.

Fourth, Commit Long Term

China was not an easy market to penetrate, requiring special long-term efforts. As an important long-term strategy, therefore, Starbucks invested in employees. Starbucks excelled in hiring, educating, and training its workers. The company believed that employees play an important role in delivering the unique Starbucks' experience to customers. A long-term commitment, however, requires patience. It took time to educate the market and gain customer loyalty, but the long-term investment paid off in the end.

According to Porter (1986), location can be a source of potential advantage for global firms as they can flexibly select the best location for realizing maximum efficiency in their value chain activities. In the beginning, Starbucks focused on the first-tier cities of China, because an average Chinese person, at that time, was unlikely to pay for a cup of coffee that cost almost as much as his or her one-day income. As the Chinese economic situation improved, Starbucks began to open more franchises in the second- and third-tier cities, thereby increasing the market presence. Besides the configuration of activities, Starbucks also paid great attention to the coordination of activities, by sharing its best barista-training program. This high-coordination strategy ensured the quality of service at each local store to meet its global standards. According to Porter, within the value chain, the downstream activities tend to be appropriate for the localization strategy, while upstream and supporting activities tend to be more appropriate for standardization strategy. Starbucks employed a hybrid strategy of combining these seemingly conflicting strategies in an efficient manner. For example, the supporting activities such as human resource management were highly standardized, while marketing and sales activities such as menus of different regional outlets were quite customized to local needs.

Sun Tzu's military thoughts introduced in this chapter can further provide some useful implications for the Starbucks case. Sun Tzu highlighted utilizing different tactics in different situations. Similarly, Starbucks achieved success due to its flexible business model which is different from the typical strategy of Western firms, thereby making it easier to enter the Chinese market, while suffering less hostility. For example, rather than using active advertising and promotions that could be perceived as a threat to China's traditional tea-drinking culture, Starbucks focused on selecting high-visibility and high-traffic locations to spread and market its own brand image. Sun Tzu also emphasized the alliances with local guides when penetrating into the enemy territory, saying, "Those who do not employ local guides will not secure advantages of terrain." This idea is also applicable to the business cases. Because of the differences in the way of doing business, Starbucks formed joint ventures with local firms when penetrating different markets in China in order to reduce the liability of foreignness.

However, there are still some differences between military and business strategies which can be found in the case of Starbucks. In military, Sun Tzu emphasized placing the soldiers in the fatal situation so that they will fight with all their might. Therefore, the victory in war may be obtained at the expense of the life of individual soldiers. However, in business, firms employ opposite strategy in order to raise the commitment of the employees. Rather than exploiting employees' energy and time (putting them in a desperate situation, in Sun Tzu's terms), firms tend to invest more on educating and training to build up their skills, which not only benefit the employees themselves but also the company in the long run.

In addition, although Sun Tzu's raid strategy may not be directly relevant to the business case, its underlying principles can provide insights to understanding Starbucks' successful entry into the Chinese market. To reiterate, Sun Tzu's first principle for a successful raid operation is that the force must advance in a swift manner. The swiftness in advancement is what Starbucks excelled at when managing its activities in the Chinese market. The second principle is that a force must take advantage of the enemy's absence. Starbucks satisfied this requirement by being the first multinational coffee company in the Chinese market, which allowed Starbucks to obtain a strong first-mover advantage. Third, Sun Tzu stated that in a raid strategy, a force must travel the unanticipated roads. Starbucks took an unexpected road to China – a country with a strong tea-drinking culture, where coffee was more or less unknown. Although Porter's C-C framework provides a useful tool for analyzing the degree of the firm's globalization, Sun Tzu's strategy can complement some unexplained portions of the business model.

11.6 CONCLUSION AND IMPLICATIONS

Earlier in *The Art of War*, Sun Tzu advised that an army should make low altitude land its foreground, and high altitude land its background in position along with another warning that the army should not stay near the river. From this perspective, Han Xin's decision to position his army in front of the river in the battle of Jingxing could be a questionable choice. However, it is now clear that Han Xin deployed his army in the fatal terrain from a different strategic purpose. This thus shows why the chapter, "Nine Situations," is important, as I stressed at the beginning of this chapter. Although Sun Tzu suggested many general principles of strategy in his book, one can skillfully integrate them and realistically illustrate the power of flexibility, while staying consistent with the general guidelines of his preceding chapters. Therefore, readers need to thoroughly understand Sun Tzu from a holistic point of view, in order to fully utilize Sun Tzu's strategies for the relevant situations.

In business, Porter's C-C model has a special significance. During the 1980s when business was becoming more and more internationalized than ever before, people realized the need for more active internationalization, but the problem was that they did not know where and how to internationalize. At that time, Porter introduced a systematic model to measure the level of internationalization and provide strategic guidelines for expanding the scope of internationalization. The two dimensions, configuration and coordination, are powerful in distinguishing different types of international strategies such as export strategy, foreign investment strategy, and simple global strategy. Although some modified and extended models have been developed (e.g., Moon, 1994; 2010), Porter's C-C model provided the foundation for analyzing the degree of firms' internationalization.

By comparing Sun Tzu's core ideas in the chapter *Jiu Di* and Porter's C-C framework, some important similarities and differences were found. One key difference is that while Sun Tzu analyzed the environmental factors more intensively, Porter focused more on the firm's internal strategic preference for internationalization. For example, Porter explained different patterns of international strategies of GM, Ford, and Toyota, but he did not intensively analyze how efficiently these firms utilized the location advantages of foreign countries for enhancing their competitiveness. In this regard, Sun Tzu's detailed guidelines on terrain strategy can be useful for extending Porter's theory on firms' international strategy, as shown in the Starbucks case. On the other hand, Sun Tzu's expeditionary strategy can also be enriched with a more consideration of coordination (of Porter's C-C model) between expeditionary forces.

12 Superior Power

Sun Tzu: The fire attack
Porter: Created and sustainable advantage through innovation

The fire attack had a special place among military operations in ancient warfare. As technological breakthroughs were scarce and rather dragging, utilizing fire in battles remained one of the most sophisticated war strategies for a long time. However, Sun Tzu coupled the discussion of the unparalleled powerfulness of fire attack with a warning against its destructiveness. According to Sun Tzu, while both fire and water are powerful, water is less destructive than fire because water can isolate an enemy but cannot deprive them of their supplies or equipment. This is the main reason why Sun Tzu added a separate chapter to discuss the issues on the fire attack. Sun Tzu's discussion of the fire attack in *The Art of War* is the first-known theoretical articulation of warfare using fire, and it provides the basis for the later contemplations on this subject (Sawyer, 2005).

The chapter "The Attack with Fire" (chapter 12 in *The Art of War*) can be divided into two main topics: the general principles of the fire attack and the warnings on its risks. For the general principles, Sun Tzu discussed the types, conditions, and methods of fire attack. Then, Sun Tzu used a considerable portion to illustrate the potential huge damages that can be inflicted by the fire attack and the cautions in executing fire attacks. Su Shi in Song dynasty said that Sun Tzu considered the fire attack as the most powerful yet dangerous tactic. Zhao Benxue in Ming Dynasty also shared a similar thought, noting the potential destructiveness of the fire attack to caution against undiscriminating usage. The second issue essentially reiterates the central philosophy and the theme of *The Art of War*, being cautious about war, as stated clearly in the first chapter

("Laying Plans"), and is also regarded as the overarching message throughout the chapters from 1 to 12 (Kim, 1999).

The superiority of the fire attack can be compared to the creation of competitive advantage through innovation, and Sun Tzu's emphasis on the consideration of postwar effects can be compared to Porter's concept of sustainable competitive advantage (i.e., long-term growth) in business. As a leading scholar of industrial organization, Porter emphasized the role of external environment in creating firms' competitiveness and he argued that firms' competitiveness is highly influenced by the business environment of their home countries, which is determined by the four factors of the diamond model (Porter, 1990). He further claimed that the maintenance of firms' high productivity depends on continuous investment and innovation by firms and other related organizations. However, Porter's statement on sustainable growth is more concerned with the production side, and overlooks the interests of other stakeholders. To amend this limitation in Porter's theory, I will introduce other scholars' extensions on the sources of sustainable advantages and show how Sun Tzu's military thinking can complement the shortcomings of Porter's theory on sustaining competitive advantage.

This chapter begins with Sun Tzu's principles regarding effective control of the fire attack and postwar consideration. I will then introduce Porter's concept of created advantage, discussing its definition, effects, and methods. Following the introduction of military and business theories, I will explain in more detail the linkage between Sun Tzu's and Porter's theories. For case studies, I will present the analyses of the military case of the Battle of Red Cliffs and the business case of Nobel Brothers' business in Azerbaijan.

12.1 SUN TZU: THE FIRE ATTACK

12.1.1 The Fire Attack: Types, Conditions, and Methods

In the chaotic period of Spring and Autumn that led numerous war lords to arise from all over China, the major form of operation in the battlefield was direct confrontation of physical forces as weapons were not sophisticated by today's standards. This battling method incurred a huge cost that hurt not only the loser but also the winner; the reward for the winner was rather meager. Thus, using fire to attack and reap victory in a short span of time was seen as an effective method of winning at a low cost (Wu and Yu, 1993). Its impact can be compared to that of nuclear weapons in modern times (Moran, 2010). Sun Tzu mainly discussed three issues on the fire attack: targets, conditions, and ways of attacking the enemy with fire. In the following, I will explain each in detail.

When conducting a fire attack, the targeted spot must be selected with particular care to effectively weaken the enemy's combat power. Sun Tzu listed five potential targets. The first is to burn the enemy's soldiers in their camp. The second is to burn food and forage. The third is to burn the wagons and equipment. The fourth is to burn the warehouses. The last is to burn the supply routes. The first is a direct method of destroying the enemy's combat power, while the other four types are indirect ways of weakening the enemy's power by demolishing their supply chains.

On the other hand, the success of fire attack depends on whether or not the proper conditions to conduct fire attack are present and the materials for raising fire are readily available. There are particular seasons and days appropriate for igniting fire and launching the attack. Sun Tzu said the proper season is when the weather is dry. The days are when the moon is in the constellations of the Sieve, Wall, Wing, or Crossbar.[1] All of these four are days of rising wind. Since the appropriate days for igniting fire are very limited, one should thoroughly prepare for the fire attack.

In Sun Tzu's period, the fire attack was far from being a light gesture of harassment. At that time, various tactics of implementing a fire attack were developed. Sun Tzu proposed the following five methods. First, if fire starts inside the enemy's camp, one should

---

[1]   These are respectively the 7th, 14th, 27th, and 28th of the twenty-eight stellar mansions which are part of the Chinese constellations system.

immediately launch an attack from outside the enemy's camp. As the enemy will most likely be in a state of panic when fire breaks out, this chaos can be exploited by mobilizing the outside troops, and thus one can easily defeat the enemy.

Second, if fire is ignited, but the enemy remains quiet, one should not take any action, as the enemy might have prepared an ambush. Instead, one should watch and wait until the force of flame has reached its height, and then decide whether to attack or withdraw according to the situation. Cao Cao commented that if one sees a possible way to attack, then advance; but if one finds great difficulties, then retreat.

Third, the fire attack can also be launched from outside the enemy's camp if conditions are met. When one sets fire from outside, one does not have to wait for the enemy's reaction from inside. The only thing one should do is to choose the proper time to ignite flame.

Fourth, when fire is set upwind, do not attack from downwind. For example, if wind blows from the east, one should not attack from the west, as one may suffer from the fire. Therefore, calculating the direction of wind is critical as it may backfire against oneself.

Fifth, a wind that rises in the daytime lasts long, but a night breeze subsides quickly. Although the wind blows persistently during the day, it will probably be weakened at night. Therefore, one should launch a fire attack during the daytime not at night.

The fire attack and the water attack are the two important special operations in ancient military tactics. Sun Tzu emphasized that both are useful to reduce the enemy's strengths before the actual engagement in combat. However, Sun Tzu valued the fire attack more. He said, "Those who use fire in their attacks are wise; those who use water in their attacks are powerful." His preference of fire over water attack is due to the greater resources required to carry out water attack in comparison to its limited effectiveness (Wee et al., 1991). In addition, water can only cut off the enemy's advance or temporally have them in trouble, but may not seriously destroy their belongings, such as the supplies and equipment. On the other hand, successful fire attack guarantees annihilation of the enemy's resources at less cost.

12.1.2 Postwar Consideration

In the second part of this chapter, Sun Tzu reiterated the fundamental objectives of going to war and the consequences of war. Ultimately, he emphasized the need to be cautious before committing to war. Based on Sun Tzu's definition, the only valid reasons for going into a war are either when it is needed to protect the country or to obtain some interests for the country. Here, Sun Tzu warned about the catastrophic effects of recklessly engaging in war due to momentary anger or other emotional impulses. He said, "A ruler should not start a war out of anger, and a general should not fight a battle out of resentment." This is because if one's country perishes, it cannot be brought back into existence, and those who are dead cannot come back to life. Sun Tzu frequently warned of the potential large cost of war in earlier chapters of his book. For example, in the beginning of his first chapter, Sun Tzu emphasized that warfare is of vital importance to the country and that it is a matter of life and death, and a road either to safety or to ruin. Also in his second chapter, Sun Tzu said that the cost of raising an army of 100,000 men is a thousand ounces of gold per day. Therefore, a wise ruler and generals should not go to war when the objective is not clearly justifiable.

Accordingly, Sun Tzu suggested the following principles of going to war: do not move unless there is an advantage; do not use the troop unless there is a gain; and do not fight unless there is a danger.[2] These general principles highlight Sun Tzu's cautious attitude toward engaging in war. In addition, Sun Tzu in this chapter particularly directed the readers' attention to the aftermath of war. Even if one wins a war and seizes the enemy's land, if one cannot consolidate the accomplishments, the victory will drain one's resources. Therefore, winning a war is not the final goal for an army, but consolidating the victory is more important.

---

[2]   The Chinese characters are: 非利不動, 非得不用, 非危不戰.

12.2 PORTER: CREATED AND SUSTAINABLE ADVANTAGE THROUGH INNOVATION

12.2.1 Diamond Model for Analyzing Created and Sustainable Advantage

Classical economists, whose origins date back to Adam Smith, argued that national prosperity grows out of a country's natural resource endowments, its labor pool, interest rates, or currency's value. However, Porter (1990) proposed a new argument that national prosperity is created, not inherited. Therefore, he argued that national competitiveness should be regarded as competitive advantage, not comparative advantage. Here, it is important to clarify the difference between the two concepts, *comparative advantage* and *competitive advantage*. Comparative advantage is largely based on the inherited resource endowments, whereas competitive advantage is created through innovation.

Some evidences can be found from the real world. Most economically advanced countries (e.g., Western Europe) account for a large share of the global wealth despite their lack in natural resources and population. Japan, which was well known for its scarce resources, became the first Asian country successfully entering the advanced countries' club. Moreover, the four Asian tigers (i.e., Singapore, Hong Kong, Taiwan, and South Korea) achieved substantial economic success in the late twentieth century, although all of them are very poor in natural resources. In contrast, the other countries, particularly the resource-abundant countries, such as BRICS (i.e., Brazil, Russia, India, China, and South Africa), still remain in the category of developing countries.

Statistical evidences for this argument can also be found in Cho and Moon (2013b). This study classified the countries of the world into four groups by their degree of created advantage and inherited advantage. They found that countries with high created advantage are mostly distributed in the country group whose GDP per capita is higher than $20,000. In contrast, countries with low created advantage are mostly distributed in the group whose GDP per capita is lower than $20,000. These findings also proved that a country's wealth does not depend on its inherited resources, but on how much it creates new advantages. The above findings are consistent with the economic phenomenon of "Dutch disease" or "resource curse," implying that inherited resources may turn into more a curse than a blessing.

Porter said a nation's competitiveness depends on the capacity of its industries to innovate and upgrade, and the firm is the main actor of competition in an industry. Firms achieve competitive advantage through a series of innovations. The scope of innovation is very broad, including both new technologies and new ways of doing things such as a new production process, a new marketing approach, or a new way of training the workforce. Innovation is often the result of unusual efforts, and the successful innovation is usually preceded by high pressure and even adversity.

However, almost any newly created advantage can be imitated. Sometimes the first-mover advantages such as good customer relationships and efficient distribution channels may allow a firm to retain its position for some time. However, some competitors will ultimately find a way to innovate around these advantages or create a better way of doing similar activities. Therefore, if firms stop improving and innovating, they will inevitably be overtaken by their rivals and followers. The only way to sustain competitive advantage is to continuously upgrade, moving to more sophisticated types of advantage.

Then, what contributes to firms' capability to consistently innovate? The answer lies in four broad attributes of a nation, each of which constitutes one of the four determinants of Porter's diamond model for national competitiveness: factor conditions; demand conditions; related and supporting industries; and firm strategy, structure, and rivalry. The four corners of the diamond model are self-reinforcing, which means an increase in the capability of any determinant will reinforce the upgrade of capability of other determinants and resultantly the improvement of the whole system. Porter said domestic rivalry especially has great power to promote improvement in other factors of the diamond model because it elevates and magnifies the interaction among the four attributes.[3] I have introduced Porter's diamond model in Chapter 1 to compare it with Sun Tzu's five elements model for evaluating general competitiveness. In this chapter, I reiterate the diamond model to explain the sources of creating and sustaining competitive advantages. Porter's diamond model is a highly useful model for analyzing various issues in economics, business, and other areas of competitiveness (Cho and Moon, 2013a).

12.2.2 The Arguments of Other Business Scholars for Sustainable Advantages

Porter's (1980, 1985, and 1990) sustainable advantage emphasizes a firm's or nation's relative position against its rivals. Firms should always maintain their advantages ahead of the competitors and the sustainability of their competitive advantages depends on the inimitability of their superior positioning. Another popular theory in the field of strategic management, the resource-based view of the firm (e.g., Wernerfelt, 1984; Barney, 1986, 1991; Prahalad and Hamel, 1990; Peteraf, 1993), attributes four characteristics to resources – valuable, rare, inimitable, and nonsubstitutable – as the drivers of sustainable competitive advantage (Barney, 1991). Despite their different perspectives on achieving sustainable advantages, Adner and Zemsky (2006) argued that both theories primarily concern firms' supply-side interactions while neglecting the interactions with the demand side or firms' capability to create value for consumers. For example, the problem faced by Intel in the late 1990s was not from the threats of imitation of its rival of AMD, but its lack of ability to create higher value for consumers, or the decreasing marginal utility of its product, which led to reducing consumers' willingness to pay for products or services (Adner and Zemsky, 2006).

---

[3] Domestic rivalry falls under firm strategy, structure, and rivalry of the diamond model.

On the other hand, Hall and Vredenburg (2003) stressed that successful innovation for sustainable growth of a firm should concern the impact of secondary stakeholders, particularly in the highly complex and uncertain business environment. Traditional approaches are mainly concerned with the primary stakeholders who are directly involved in the value chain, such as suppliers, customers, and other partners. However, Hall and Vredenburg argued that the traditional approach is often insufficient to fully explain how sustainable growth is achieved because the secondary stakeholders – including safety advocates, local communities, and activists for various issues (e.g., anti-globalization, animal rights, and environmental issues) – have been imposing increasing influences on the firms' sustainable development. For example, Monsanto, a US chemical company, developed genetically modified crops which could contribute to the reduction of the usage of pesticides and herbicides. The new crops successfully avoided the opposition of customers and partners, because the processing was much the same as the regular crops. However, Monsanto encountered opposition from environmental groups, who argued that the newly developed crops would impose negative influences on the wild plant species, increase pest resistance, and worsen developing countries' overdependence on the seed companies.

Another important implication suggested by this article is that radical innovation (e.g., Joseph Schumpeter's (1942) creative destruction) does not always guarantee a success. Because such kind of innovation implies the demise of or threats to existing businesses, strong opposition from these businesses may arise. Moreover, the radical technology requires the support of different organizations and infrastructures. Therefore, disruptive innovation is less likely to be achieved by a single company's own efforts, but the collection of a wider scope of stakeholders.

Along with Hall and Vredenburg's (2003) argument for integrating wider stakeholders in order to achieve sustainable growth, Chesbrough (2007) recommended an open business model. This business model incorporates at least two different companies, unlike the traditional model which is usually run by a single company. For example, Qualcommn used to produce its own mobile phones until the 1990s, but currently it focuses on making chips, while licensing its technologies to other mobile phone makers. This business model is called "open" when one company develops an idea but forms a partnership with another firm or sells the idea to another firm. Therefore, an open business model requires more specialization for partner companies. Chesbrough (2007) claimed that when the invention takes more time and cost, and the life cycle of products becomes shorter, the open business model or outsourcing for some value chain activities of business is often more efficient.

12.3 THE INTEGRATION OF SUN TZU AND PORTER

12.3.1 Creating Competitive Advantage in War and Business

Successful operation of the fire attack in a battle and creating competitive advantage in business may seem to be different concepts. A close analysis, however, reveals surprising commonalities in their fundamental working principles. For one, both refer to advantages "created" rather than "inherited," and for another, both advantages are deeply affected by the interaction with surrounding environmental conditions. Fire is an effective way of attacking the enemy. Fire's massive power is effective because it can disrupt the enemy forces and supplies without inflicting great damage to one's own army. Similarly, in business, although companies that have achieved international leadership employ different strategies and modes of operation, the characteristic of all successful companies is fundamentally the same. All of them achieved competitive advantage through innovation. Some innovations can help create competitive advantage by developing an entire new market (e.g., smartphone industry) and others may do so by serving a neglected market (e.g., Japanese small-sized cars in the United States in 1980s and 1990s).

Despite the great power of fire, the condition of launching the fire attack is very limited to conditions of the external environment. Sun Tzu explained launching a fire attack requires dry seasons. In addition, the daily weather needs to be observed before igniting the fire; sufficient strength of wind in appropriate directions is a necessary condition. Unless these conditions are satisfied, one should not conduct the fire attack. Similarly, in business, the creation of competitive advantage depends on the conditions of national environment, which Porter summarized as four attributes of a nation (i.e., the four determinants of the diamond model).

However, there is a critical difference between the fire attack in war and the creation of competitive advantage in business. The proper condition of launching the fire attack is highly uncontrollable, which relies much on the *heaven* condition. In contrast, the conditions of creating competitive advantages in business can be developed by human efforts. In addition, Sun Tzu said that fire is an aid to the attack, which should be accompanied by the attack through the main military force. However, in business, the created advantage is the core source of competitiveness of successful companies. The inherited advantages (e.g., natural resource and cheap labor) are becoming less important because they can be easily accessed in the increasingly global economy, and also less sustainable because they can be easily substituted by advanced technology (e.g., automation system leading to the reduced demand for labor input).

12.3.2 Sustaining Competitive Advantages in War and Business

Sun Tzu singled out consolidation of the victory as the most important part of conducting war, implying that an ineffectively managed victory is no more than a useless, expensive trophy that is bestowed without prize money. If one cannot integrate the power and material gains from war with the level of one's current competitiveness, the gains will turn into a burden instead. This is the case when one has to spend large amounts of resources to protect the seized land or city from the enemy, but without obtaining any benefit from them. This is consistent with the principle Sun Tzu suggested in his eighth chapter, which states, "There are fortified cities that one should not assault and there are terrains one should not contend." In addition, if one lacks the ability to consolidate the achievement, the enemy will come back and reclaim it. In business, Porter also argued that the only way to sustain competitive advantage is to upgrade it because if a firm's competitive advantage is not sophisticated enough, it will be easily taken over by its competitors who could come up with a better or cheaper way of providing the same goods or services. Therefore, creating new advantages is not the final goal for a company, but how to maintain one's competitive position is more important.

While Sun Tzu warned about the potential costs of consolidating the achievement or reconstruction after war, Porter placed a greater emphasis on the necessity of sustaining competitive advantages, but overlooked the cost of creating such sustained advantages. Sun Tzu discouraged hastily joining a war and strongly advocated taking extra cautions before committing to a war. Therefore, it is wise to avoid war if the costs are calculated to be larger than the benefits. The same considerations must be given to starting a new enterprise or developing technology in business as well; if the estimated cost of developing a new advantage outweighs the potential profitability, the firm should forego the plan.

In addition, Porter focused more on the interests of the primary stakeholders, instead of the secondary stakeholders who play increasing roles in the growing globalized and interconnected business environment. This implies that a firm can invent a breakthrough technology; however, if it cannot satisfy the interests of a wider range of stakeholders, it will ultimately encounter difficulties from the opposing parties. Hence, companies should reach beyond the limited traditional model of value creation. In this regard, Sun Tzu's grand strategy, considering costs of prewar preparations, supporting the ongoing war efforts, and dealing with the postwar aftermath for a sustainable military operation can provide a useful implication for business practices. Creating a single superior technology ahead of the rivals in business may produce profits for a short period, but attaining long-term success requires the consideration of more factors as discussed above.

12.4 MILITARY CASE: WU AND SHU'S VICTORY IN THE BATTLE OF RED CLIFFS

The Battle of Red Cliffs took place in 208 A.D. between the allied forces of the southern warlords Liu Bei (the country of Shu) and Sun Quan (the country of Wu), and the northern warlord, Cao Cao (the country of Wei).[4] This battle was a very important one at the end of the Han Dynasty that led to the formation of the Three Kingdoms. While this case exemplifies how a smaller army can defeat the larger and better-equipped army by using effective strategy, it also demonstrates the efficiency of the fire attack.

After establishing the control over the northern area of China, Cao Cao with his army started to move southward and first defeated the country of Shu. As the city of Jingzhou was captured by Cao Cao, the Shu army was forced to retreat to Jiangxia. In order to defeat both Shu and Wu, Cao Cao led his 200,000 soldiers and continued to move southward to Yangtze River, near the border of Wu. Facing the strong army of Wei, Shu and Wu made an alliance to defend against Cao Cao's army. However, there were only 50,000 allied forces: 30,000 trained naval soldiers from Wu, plus 20,000 from Shu.

Since Cao Cao's troops were already exhausted by motion sickness (due to the river's current) as they lacked in naval training and experiences, they lost control and had to camp in the north of the Yangtze River, while the Wu and Shu troops stayed in the south. Later, Cao Cao ordered to bind his entire fleet all together with strong iron chains to consolidate the navy. However, this in fact turned out to be a strategy born of complete ignorance of naval warfare; the connected fleet, intended to help the soldiers cope with motion sickness, became

[4] Information of this case study is abstracted and modified from history.cultural-china .com/en/34History359.html, and english.cri.cn/1702/2005-4-29/121@232802.htm.

a critical disadvantage which the Wu and Shu allies later took full advantage of. Observing this, Zhou Yu (the general of Wu) and Zhu Geliang (the chancellor of Shu) developed a stratagem to use fire to burn Cao Cao's fleet. First, Huang Gai, a veteran general of Wu, made a feigned surrender to Cao Cao. Huang Gai purposely challenged Zhou Yu, who responded as planned, by brutally whipping and humiliating the old general. After this incident, Huang Gai went over to Cao Cao's camp, claiming that in his humiliation and sense of betrayal he decided to convert sides with his whole fleet of warships. Cunning though he was, Cao Cao fully believed Huang Gai.

As Cao Cao was waiting for Huang Gai to come along with his fleet, warships of Wu followed behind. When Wu's warships, laden with kindling and fish oil, closely approached Cao Cao's fleet, they suddenly burst into flames. Supported by a brisk southeasterly wind, they soon turned Cao Cao's warships into a living hell consumed by roaring flames. Taken completely by surprise, Cao Cao's fleet was severely damaged, if not completely destroyed. The flames then spread onto the northern bank to the camping area of Cao Cao's army, destroying his troops there as well. After this battle, Cao Cao retreated to Luoyang, a city in Henan Province today. Wu secured its sovereignty in southeast China, and Shu took back Jingzhou, and later expanded into Sichuan Province in western China. Accordingly, China was separated into three independent kingdoms and the period of the Three Kingdoms started since then.

Sun Tzu' guidelines for the fire attack were well illustrated and utilized in the Battle of Red Cliffs. Wu and Shu allies directly burned Cao Cao's ships and soldiers, and thus significantly weakened Cao Cao's military capacity. In order to carry out the fire attack, Wu and Shu allies made various preparations. First, they prepared warships, kindling materials, and other devices. These are necessary for the fire attack. Second, in order to get as close as possible to maximize the power of the fire attack, they devised a feigned surrender of Huang Gai and managed to convince Cao Cao of this trick. It provided an opportunity to make a surprise attack on Cao Cao's forces. Third is the weather condition. The direction of the wind changed from northwest to southeast. This is consistent with Sun Tzu's principle that when the fire is set upwind, one should not attack from downwind. Without taking advantage of appropriate weather condition, the fire attack would not have been possible. Because of this favorable wind direction, combined with the above reasons, Wu and Shu achieved a great success with minimum damage and costs, while Cao Cao's army suffered from a huge loss.

Porter's concept of created advantage can enrich the analysis of this military case, as he argued that competitiveness is created, not inherited. In fact, the military success factors explained above are almost all newly created factors by Wu and Shu, including the needed kindling materials and devices, the deception strategy, and even the knowledge of the local weather condition. Therefore, the advantages of Wu and Shu compared to those of their adversary were all created by their extra innovative efforts, most of which did not exist in the beginning of the battle. In addition, Porter said that one's disadvantage could be turned into an advantage. In the Battle of Red Cliffs, Wu and Shu's disadvantageous conditions (e.g., smaller size of the combined military forces, which is one-fourth of the Wei's army) pressed them to devise a very innovative way of creating advantage, which was a well-designed fire attack to achieve a victory with low cost.

12.5   BUSINESS CASE: NOBEL BROTHERS' BUSINESS IN AZERBAIJAN

When the name Nobel is mentioned, many people would first think of the well-known Nobel Prize and the invention of dynamite by Alfred Nobel. However, Alfred was not only a brilliant inventor and philanthropist but also a daring entrepreneur and shrewd industrialist. To one's surprise, a significant portion of funding for the Prize traces back to Azerbaijan.[5] Alfred and his brothers, Robert and Ludvig, owned the Nobel Brothers' Petroleum Company at the time when Azerbaijan

[5]   Information of this case study is abstracted and modified from Moon (2016b) and www .azer.com/aiweb/categories/magazine/23_folder/23_articles/23_oilbarons.html.

was producing more than 50 percent of the world's oil. Alfred was the major shareholder in the company and the withdrawal of his shares from the company enabled the awards to be established.

Nobel Brothers' business in Azerbaijan started when Robert Nobel stopped by Baku, the capital of Azerbaijan in 1873, searching for high-quality wood for gun production in Russia. Because it was expensive and also not easy to procure wood from Western European countries, he came to the virgin forests in the southern area of Azerbaijan, looking for other types of timbers. When he passed through Baku, he witnessed the beginning of the hype for oil. He instantly saw the potential opportunity of making money from oil and boldly purchased a refinery and a kerosene-producing plant. It took several years, however, to convince his brothers to establish the Nobel Brothers' Oil Producing Company together in 1879. This decision resulted in the Nobel Brothers' presence in Baku for more than forty years; and over that time their company became the largest oil producer in the region. The company became the major supplier of oil and oil-related products for the regions of Europe, China, India, and Iran, and by 1990 it accounted for almost a half the world's oil production (Frantz, 2001).

The Nobel family introduced many innovations in oil extraction, refining, and transportation. They developed the first pipelines, first railway oil tankers, first storage tanks, and many other firsts. Within a short period, a new industrial suburb was developed around the Nobel-owned refineries. At that time, the view of chimneys and pipes represented the advancement and historical achievements of mankind. Unfortunately, no one considered the side effects on environment and ecology back then.

The oil refineries generated massive clouds of smoke, and travelers often described that they were like being enclosed inside a chimney. Consequently, the idea of developing a park emerged in recognition of such pollution problem. Starting from 1882 to 1883, the Nobel Brothers began to order all of their empty ships returning from Iran and Lankaran (the southern part of Azerbaijan) to collect and deliver the best fertile soils. With this richer soil, they began to cultivate an area of more than 10 hectares (about 25 acres). After laying down fertile soil, they began importing various plants and trees, mainly from the neighboring country, Georgia. In the end, they were able to cultivate a huge number of plants and trees, including fruit trees, and many of them had never been grown in Baku.

However, they later recognized that they had to solve another critical problem. They needed freshwater to irrigate such a large-scale park. They then utilized tankers and ordered them to return with fresh water from the Volga River. Later, they created a new way of irrigating the area with condensed steam generated in their refineries, which they routed to the park through special pipelines. The park soon developed into the landmark of the city. Within the park, the Nobel family built their mansion, their workers' houses, administrative offices, hospitals, and other entertainment facilities. Their success in oil production businesses later attracted many foreign investors.[6]

The Nobel Brothers' investments were not limited to natural resources of oil and gas. Enhancing the competitiveness of their businesses required favorable business determinants, or the four elements of the diamond model. Therefore, the Nobel Brothers invested a large amount of resources in improving the related fields, such as the technical revolution in oil extraction, refining, and transportation, which in turn benefited them by increasing their firm's productivity. The continuous improvement in the firm's productivity ultimately contributed to long-term growth for almost half a century. Historically, Baku was not an attractive place for foreign investors, despite its rich endowment of oil and gas. However, the early development of oil, technical inventiveness, and modernization of infrastructure at the end of nineteenth century allowed Baku to assume the leading position in oil production in 1900 (Adams et al., 2002).

The Nobel Brothers' business success aptly depicts how one can make money through exploiting inherited advantages, but sustain

[6]   However, in 1917, the Nobels and other foreign companies were forced to shut down and leave because of the Bolshevik Revolution.

one's competitive advantages only though continuously creating new advantages. In addition to the development of numerous inventions to directly improve firm productivity, the Nobels also considered the environmental issues and the interests of a wider scope of stakeholders, including the local communities. Although Porter emphasized the social issues in his later work on corporate social responsibility (see Chapter 7), until the early 1990s, his works on firms' and national competitiveness had mainly focused on the buildup of competitiveness through innovation, which is directly involved in the firm's value chain. In this respect, Sun Tzu's philosophy of the grand strategy, considering before, during, and after war, provides the legitimacy for consideration of a broader strategy of sustainable competitive advantages.

12.6 CONCLUSION AND IMPLICATIONS

The fire attack was a very innovative way of attacking the enemy in Sun Tzu's time. He listed the conditions of using the fire attack, including certain seasons, days, and time. They appear to be somewhat superstitious by today's standard, but worked well as seen in the Battle of Red Cliffs. Although Sun Tzu's strategy was focused on the fire attack, his thought can be usefully applied to contemporary war and business. More importantly, Sun Tzu repeated his warning of being cautious of war, which emphasizes the importance of considering the aftermaths of war. Hence, consolidating the victory is the ultimate goal, not the victory itself. This is a critical difference from other militarists, such as Clausewitz, who primarily focused on winning the war without counting the postwar effects. This is why scholars (e.g., Liddell Hart) regard Sun Tzu's strategy as the most comprehensive, finest classic among numerous military strategies.

In business, Porter introduced the concept of created advantage as a counterargument to the conventional economics on comparative advantage of nations. In fact, the core sources of competitiveness of advanced countries or more sophisticated industries of a country are more related to the created advantages rather than inherited ones.

Porter further demonstrated that the national environment, which is described as the four attributes of the diamond model, affects the capability of creating advantages of firms. However, Porter's concept of business sustainability relies more on the innovation of production side, and recently many scholars argued that the continuous creation of high value for consumers and consideration of a wider scope of stakeholders' interests are also critical for creating and maintaining a strong competitive position. Furthermore, the open business model also helps companies reduce risks and save resources, thereby efficiently creating and sustaining their competitiveness.

This chapter linked Sun Tzu's fire attack and Porter's concept of created advantage, and showed that there are both similarities and differences. An important similarity is that both fire attack and created advantages produce great power in war and business. As shown in the military case of the Battle of Red Cliffs, the success factors by Wu and Shu are almost all created factors which produced greater impacts on the result of the battle. In addition, both are heavily dependent on external conditions. Just as the appropriate weather and material conditions are necessary to make fire attack effective, appropriate environmental conditions as mapped out in the diamond model are required for firms to create new advantages. Moreover, both require the consideration of long-term consequences and the sustainability aspect. For warfare, Sun Tzu emphasized the postwar effects; on a similar ground, for business, Porter argued that the ultimate goal of a firm is not to create short-run advantage, but to constantly upgrade its competitiveness. However, Porter emphasized more the benefits of creating and sustaining competitive advantages than costs of doing so. The Nobel Brothers case demonstrated that Sun Tzu's philosophy of the grand strategy, considering a broader scope of stakeholders, can complement Porter's innovation strategy. On the other hand, the military case of the Battle of Red Cliffs showed that Sun Tzu's strategy can also be further improved by adopting Porter's innovation strategy.

13 Information Advantage

Sun Tzu: Foreknowledge through the use of spies
Porter: Understanding information technology versus core competence

The last chapter of Sun Tzu's book is about spies: the importance, types, characteristics, and principles of using spies. Sun Tzu proposed active utilization of spies because an effective usage of spies can significantly reduce the cost of war and sometimes even prevent war from occurring in the first place. Given the cost-reduction effects, employing a spy can be seen as a relatively cheap, but high-return investment. According to Sun Tzu, spies can be used not just to acquire information about the enemy, but also to spread wrong information and make the enemy misjudge. However, due to the highly difficult and complicated operations of spying, Sun Tzu said unless one is wise, benevolent, righteous, and subtle, one cannot properly manage spies and benefit from using spies.

There is a coherent military thought throughout the thirteen chapters of *The Art of War*: the importance of knowing the enemy and oneself. On the other hand, among the Western military theorists, the significance of intelligence was not as strongly emphasized. Although Clausewitz admitted that intelligence could magnify strength by reducing uncertainty, he did not attribute as much significance to intelligence as Sun Tzu did. This is because Clausewitz thought that many intelligence reports in war are contradictory, filled with uncertainty, and frequently false (Clausewitz, 1968[1832]). Some ancient Chinese scholars also denigrated spying activities and argued that the use of spies is the worst policy and should be restricted because false information could actually damage entire military operation (Kim, 1999). However, the majority of researchers on Sun Tzu's military strategy agree that this chapter is no less important than other chapters, especially given that spies were the only way to obtain inside, highly secretive information on the enemy during Sun Tzu's time (Kim, 1999).

On the other hand, in business, information technology (IT) plays a significant role for acquiring useful information; thus some emphasized that IT can be a source of competitive advantage of firms. However, Porter (1985) argued that IT cannot replace the traditional sources of a firm's unique competitive advantages, but can only complement traditional sources of competitive advantage. Although the combination of IT and a firm's core competence is critical for achieving a firm's competitiveness, simply the advancement in IT cannot sufficiently explain a firm's competitiveness as demonstrated in the case of Google's failure in China, which will be explained later in this chapter. Other factors, such as local business environment, also play vital roles. I will demonstrate that understanding customers' real needs and adapting to local regulations and laws, particularly for the multinational firms operating in foreign countries, are also necessary.

In this chapter, I will first introduce Sun Tzu's guidelines for using spies to acquire the enemy's information. Then, I will explain Porter's concept of IT and discuss how it affects the industry structure and firms' competitive advantages. Following the analyses, I will analyze the linkage between Sun Tzu's and Porter's theories. For case studies, I will examine the military case of Mata Hari, a spy for Germany and France during World War I, and the business case of Google in China to demonstrate the application of these strategic linkages between war and business.

13.1   SUN TZU: FOREKNOWLEDGE THROUGH THE USE OF SPIES

Any military general engaging in warfare must understand that every time he mobilizes the army – whether to move to a particular location, build a defense wall, or fight in a battle – he is exhausting enormous resources, including human lives, food, and weapons. Therefore, a general should always take every precaution possible when he makes a decision concerning the movement of the army. Unfortunately, however, military leaders are often paralyzed by what is called the "fog of war" – uncertainty about the conditions under which they will be fighting, as well as uncertainty about how the enemy will respond to their actions. In this regard, throughout *The Art of War*, Sun Tzu emphasized the vitality of obtaining information, especially before an action is executed.

A thorough preparation – such as securing reliable information on the enemy – should always precede the devising of any military strategy. When it comes to the reliability of information, the open-source information, which can be obtained by diplomats, traders, and other observers, is often limited and potentially erroneous (Sawyer, 2005). Therefore, using spies is an effective way to gain access to the information on the enemy's true situation and intentions. In this manner, the successful use of spies is an important part for winning a victory in warfare. One may argue that using spies is immoral and shameful, but Sun Tzu said that there is nothing which can be more shameful than waging a war without knowing the enemy and exposing the army to a dangerous situation, thereby resulting in unnecessary casualties. Therefore, instead of shying away from using spies, Sun Tzu pronounced that there is nothing more central to the art of war than intelligence operations, and none deserves higher rewards than spies who bring quality information about the enemy.

13.1.1 Five Types of Spies

Sun Tzu categorized spies into five types. They are local spies, inside spies, converted spies, doomed spies, and surviving spies.[1]

Local spies are ordinary people in the enemy's country who can provide basic information on the characteristics of their home country. These spies are useful because they are easy to hire, but their roles are limited to providing only rudimentary level information.

---

[1] The Chinese characters are: 鄉間, 內間, 反間, 死間, 生間.

Inside spies are those with high positions in the enemy's army or government who can provide high-level intelligence about the enemy's strategies and operations.

Converted spies are those who have been sent by the enemy, but are turned to work for one's own army. These spies are hard to hire, but if one can manage to make an enemy spy a converted spy and use him effectively, the results can be substantially valuable.

Doomed spies are those who are sent to the enemy to deliberately spread false information in order to direct their military strategies to one's intention. These spies are often intentionally captured by the enemy, confess the false information, and thus are mostly doomed to death.

Surviving spies are those who are sent into the enemy camp, but with a mission that requires them to return home safely with acquired information. These spies are able to embed themselves into the enemy's organization and obtain useful information. Since they require highly sophisticated skills, they must be specially selected and trained.

Among the five types of spies, the first three (local, inside, and converted spies) come from the enemy's side, while the other two (doomed and surviving spies) belong to one's own country. Among the five types of spies, converted spies are the most valuable, because they can help and create synergy effects with the other four types of spies. With the help of converted spies, one can more easily hire local and inside spies, send the doomed spies deep into the enemy's organization, and protect the security of surviving spies when they conduct their tasks. Therefore, Sun Tzu said generals should seek out the enemy spies and turn them into converted spies by bribing them with generous rewards and treating them well. However, converted spies have the disadvantage that they are hardly to be fully trusted, because their mission is to deceive one's army in the first place. Due to this problem, Sun Tzu suggested to use not just one type, but all five types of spies.

13.1.2   The Principles of the Use of Spies

The Requirements for the Treatment of Spies

Spies can play a critical role enough to change the winner of the war. In order to successfully use the spies, the most important task is to be highly secretive when using the spies. If plans related to secret operations are prematurely disclosed, Sun Tzu warned that the spy and all other relevant persons will face the risks of being put to death. Because of the nature of the activity, which requires the maintenance of top-level confidentiality, the control and management of spies must be conducted seamlessly and strictly. When selecting spies, trustworthiness should be valued as the most esteemed quality. In other words, the military leader should possess good knowledge of the spy's character and choose one he can trust and control with ease.

On the other hand, spies should also be loyal to the general or ruler even when personal safety is threatened. Sun Tzu said among all military matters, none can be compared to the intimate relations to be maintained with spies. In addition, spying is highly risky and the spies can lose their lives at any time. In order to encourage people to get involved in such dangerous operations, and also not to be bribed by the enemy, they should be rewarded as generously as possible in return for their contributions to the country. Therefore, Sun Tzu said none can be more liberally rewarded than spies.

The Requirements for the Leader's Capability of Using Spies

The use of spies is not an easy matter; not all generals can successfully employ spies and benefit from using spies. The success requires superior wisdom to devise a strategic plan of sending the spies deep into the enemy's organization and obtain useful information without being discovered. One's spies can also be utilized by the enemy as converted spies or the enemy may deliberately release false information so that the spies could mistakenly deliver it to their home country. Sun Tzu said that only those who are detailed and subtle can obtain and decipher the truth from spy activities. Therefore, Sun Tzu said only those who are wise can benefit from using spies.

In addition, in order to obtain true loyalty from one's spies, one should treat them with absolute sincerity. Although appealing to them with generous rewards is important, the enemy can also offer the same level of rewards to the spies, thus only trust built upon sincerity from the bottom of one's heart can really move the mind of the spies. Therefore, Sun Tzu said only those with personal attractiveness and strong ethics can effectively manage spies.

13.2   PORTER: INFORMATION TECHNOLOGY VERSUS CORE COMPETENCE

Over the past fifty years, there have been three waves of IT-driven transformation. The first wave in the 1960s and 1970s promoted the automation of value chain activities, operating through manual, paper, and verbal communications, thereby substantially improving operational efficiency of activities. The second wave driven by the rise of the Internet during the 1980s and 1990s facilitated the coordination and integration of individual activities within a firm and with outside independent firms across national boundaries. Unlike the previous two waves which only transformed the value chain, in the third wave driven by the "Internet of Things (IoT)" since 2000s, IT was incorporated directly as an integral part of the product, thereby transforming the products significantly (Porter and Heppelmann, 2014). For each wave of IT-driven transformation, Porter examined the truth of the phenomenon and its influences on gaining firms' competitive advantages. The following explains Porter's two articles, published in 1985 and 2001, regarding the role of IT and Internet in creating competitive advantages.

13.2.1   Porter and Millar (1985): IT and Competitive Advantage

IT has changed the nature of products, processes, companies, industries, and even competition itself. According to Porter and Millar

(1985), IT means more than just computers. It should be considered broadly as a phenomenon that encompasses the information produced and consumed by businesses and a wide spectrum of increasingly convergent and linked technologies that process information. In addition to computers, it includes data recognition equipment, communications technologies, factory automation, and other related hardware and software.

IT affects a firm's operation through its value chain. Each activity in the value chain is composed of a different ratio mix of physical and information-processing components.[2] Before the information revolution, technological progress mostly affected the advancement of physical components, while information processing remained to be done manually with lagging technological development. However, since the age of information dawned, the development speed of IT has become faster than that of physical processing, and the scope of possible information processing is expanding.[3]

Overall, IT affects each of Porter's five forces for industry attractiveness, thereby influencing the industry structure either by eroding or improving the industry attractiveness. For example, because of readily available and easier access to information, consumers now possess the power to compare the costs of similar (or substitutable) products offered by different firms. Thus, the bargaining power of

---

[2]   *Physical* component refers to all physical tasks when performing the activity. *Information-processing* component refers to the steps required to capture, manipulate, and channel the data for performing the activity.

[3]   The information technology affects the nine types of activities in the value chain through the following ways. First, information technology substitutes machines for human effort in information processing. In the beginning, information technology was mainly applied in the accounting and record-keeping functions. But nowadays, it involves all activities in the value chain. Second, information technology helps firms collect information, which was not possible before. For example, the number of variables which firms can analyze and control increases substantially. Third, information technology transforms the physical processing component. For instance, the computer-controlled machines make manufacturing faster, more accurate, and more flexible than manually operated machines. Fourth, information technology enhances the linkages between activities, both within and outside the company, by creating new linkages between activities and coordinating a firm's activities more closely with those of buyers and suppliers (Porter and Millar, 1985).

buyers increases due to IT development. On the other hand, by utilizing IT, firms can flexibly modify or add the latest and better features to existing products, thereby increasing the threat of substitution.

Nevertheless, the fact that IT can deteriorate the industry structure (i.e., eroding industry attractiveness) does not mean technology only poses harm without benefits. The development of IT can improve industry attractiveness by lowering the threats of potential entrants (i.e., raising the barriers), for instance, by creating complex software systems and new technologies that require large capital investments. In addition, an effective management of IT can replace some tasks of suppliers, thereby reducing the bargaining power of suppliers.

IT also creates great effects on competitive advantage by lowering cost or enhancing differentiation of the value chain activities. The enhanced capability of information processing can play a large role in reducing the production costs through automation and increasing the economies of scale. In addition, IT can change the cost drivers of activities in ways that can improve a company's relative cost position. On the other hand, for the effects on differentiation, IT can affect a company's capability of differentiation by adding information systems to the physical products or to the activities in the value chain.

13.2.2   Porter (2001): Internet and Competitive Advantage

In contrast to many arguments that the Internet nullifies the usefulness of management strategy, Porter (2001) argued that the Internet is not the source of competitive advantage. Instead of becoming obsolete, with the introduction of the Internet, strategy in business has become even more important as it distinguishes firms from other rivals, while the simultaneous introduction of the Internet by the competing firms makes their uniqueness blurry. The Internet, in fact, tends to weaken the industry attractiveness, as firms pursue similar strategies and engage in destructive price competition. What is even worse, some firms employ the Internet technology as the basis of competition, which leads to the shift from their extant differentiation to price strategy, and it becomes harder to earn higher profits. Thus, the two fundamentals of generating profits should be still the industry structure which determines the average profits of firms within the industry, and the competitive position which allows firms to earn higher profits than their competitors.

Although the Internet can enhance the overall efficiency of an industry, in general it leads to deteriorating profits of the industry. However, the negative effects do not mean that firms should simply avoid adopting the Internet technology; it means that firms should be careful about how they deploy the Internet technology, because the Internet is no longer an optional accessory to business but a necessary condition for firms to maintain competitive advantages and survive the fierce market competition. Some may assume that the Internet would provide first-mover advantages by increasing switching costs and creating strong networks. However, Porter argued that the switching costs will be lower in reality than the traditional ways of doing business, and that the formation of networks through partnering with complements or outsourcing is also not enough to keep the entry barriers high. This is because the increased open access through the IT development will make competitors more similar and erode their distinctiveness.

Therefore, according to Porter (2001), the appropriate view of the relationship between the Internet and competitive advantage is that the Internet does not replace the conventional sources of competitive advantage, but complements the traditional ones. In other words, firms should integrate the Internet with other existing competitive advantages such as skilled talents, proprietary technology, or efficient logistical systems to further enhance their competitive advantages. For example, Walgreens, a pharmacy chain in the United States, introduced an online ordering system that actually required the company to open more stores, because customers preferred to pick up their prescriptions at the nearby stores rather than receiving them through the mail. The Internet system helped the company increase its sales, but the extensive network of stores was still maintained as the core competence of the company rather than being replaced by the Internet.

Porter's views have been supported by other scholars studying the role of IT in achieving competitive advantages. For example, Powell and Dent-Micallef (1997) found that although IT itself does not help firms produce sustained performance, firms which combined IT with their existing critical resources such as human and business resources gain superior performance. On a similar note, many scholars (e.g., Clemons and Row, 1991; Mata, Fuerst, and Barney, 1995; Breznik, 2012) denied the view that IT can be the source of competitive advantage. Referring to the resource-based view of the firms, they argued that IT itself does not satisfy the four qualifications of competitive resources: valuable, rare, inimitable, and nonsubstitutable, or VRIN (Barney, 1991).

13.3 THE INTEGRATION OF SUN TZU AND PORTER

13.3.1 *Acquiring Foreknowledge on Rivals in War and Business*

Obtaining information about the enemy is a crucial determinant for winning a war. Sun Tzu said, "Whether the objective is to strike the army, to attack the city, or to assassinate an individual, it is always necessary to begin by finding out the proper information of the enemy commander, his assistants, staff, door guards, and attendants." Sun Tzu emphasized the unquestionable significance of conducting high-quality preliminary research to acquire foreknowledge on the enemy before going to war.

Similarly, in business, firms have to thoroughly study their rivals' competitiveness. McNeilly (1996) argued that firms should know what the competitors are capable of and what their current plan of attack is. Moreover, one must also be able to predict how the leaders of the competing firms may react to one's actions. However, since the ecosystem of business competition is complicated, a firm not only has to confront the competition against its direct rivals, but also consider all the competitive factors – such as suppliers, buyers, substitutes, extant rivals, and potential rivals – that compose the five forces of industry structure (Porter, 1980).

Then, how do we acquire foreknowledge? Sun Tzu said, "Foreknowledge cannot be acquired from ghosts or spirits, nor obtained inductively from experiences, nor by any deductive guess. It must be obtained from men who know the enemy and their situation." For this purpose, he claimed that the role of spies is to obtain the needed information of the enemy. In modern days, besides the use of spies, IT (e.g., cyber hacking) is widely applied in military to obtain the needed information from the enemy. On the other hand, IT also allows its users to spread information among the targeted audience. The Islamic States' strategy provides a good example for this case. Islamic State has attracted and recruited foreign fighters by using the SNS such as Facebook and Twitter, online magazine (e.g., Dabiq), and radio broadcast, as propaganda tools. The number of foreign fighters doubled to a total of 27,000–31,000 during the period of June 2014 and the end of 2015 (Economist, 2015).

In business, before the information revolution, the access to information mainly depended on the human efforts. However, since the rapid development of IT, manual jobs have been replaced by machines for gathering and processing information. This technology has made it faster and more accurate than manual operations. In addition, before the information revolution, the process for competitive analysis was very weak, but due to the development of advanced IT, firms can conduct more sophisticated analysis with a greater number of variables, scenarios, and alternative strategies than before.

13.3.2 The Role of Spies and IT in War and Business

Despite their importance in obtaining critical information from the enemy, spies are no more than a supplementary tool – far from being the main means of winning a victory. Although Sun Tzu did stress the noncombat victory in defeating the enemy's stratagem or their alliances, in many cases, a victory is gained by head-to-head fighting. Therefore, even if one has a capable spy and information network, they cannot replace a competitive, physical military force. For instance, even if one obtains foreknowledge that the enemy will attack soon, the information will have no use if one does not have an army that can effectively react against the enemy attack.

In business, Porter and Miller (1985) also argued that although IT has a great effect on creating firm's competitive advantages, it is not the main source of competitive advantage. According to Porter (1980), there are only two sources of competitive advantage: low cost and differentiation. IT is a tool for achieving competitive advantage by either lowering cost or enhancing differentiation levels as it influences each activity in the firm's value chain. While acknowledging that the Internet is very powerful as it can influence the value chains of an entire industry, Porter (2001) argued that the Internet is not the fundamental source of competitive advantage but a useful conduit in achieving extraordinary performance. Firms should use it in a manner that complements traditional activities with Internet applications, thereby strengthening their existing unique position in an industry, rather than thinking of IT as a substitute for firms' strategic positioning.

Clear differences exist between the objectives of employing spies for military missions and implementing IT for gaining competitive advantage in business. In military, spies are used to obtain the information of the enemy particularly to find their weaknesses, so that one can attack the enemy's weaknesses and avoid their strengths. Another objective of using the spies is to spread wrong information to evoke the enemy to make a wrong decision. However, in business, IT is used to enhance one's competitive advantage, without directly incurring benefits or costs to one's competitors. In military, one's victory is achieved by exploiting the enemy's weaknesses toward one's advantageous position, but in business, success is based on the fundamental enhancement of one's competitiveness, while the rivals' strengths may be unchanged. This is because military espionage is considered necessary, normal, and acceptable, while business espionage is frowned upon and many people condemn it as unethical and unacceptable (Wee et al., 1991). McNeilly (1996) suggested that in business, most competitor data and information can be obtained from public sources where no trickery is required. Hence, the activity of industrial espionage is restricted, and companies' intellectual properties are protected by law. For example, employment contracts are often designed in a way to prevent employees of a company from moving to another company, especially a direct competitor, within a certain timeframe to protect the firm's proprietary knowledge from its rivals.

13.4 MILITARY CASE: MATA HARI, A SPY FOR GERMANY AND FRANCE

Mata Hari was a Dutch dancer and courtesan executed for alleged espionage for Germany during World War I.[4] She is often portrayed as the most famous female spy of the twentieth century. Mata Hari was her stage name, and her original name was Margaretha Geertruida Zelle (1876–1917). She was born in Leeuwarden of the Netherlands in 1876. At age nineteen, she married a Dutch army officer and accompanied him to Indonesia where she experienced an unhappy marriage due to her violent and unfaithful husband. In this exotic world, on the other hand, she encountered the dances that later inspired her to become a dancer. In 1902, the couple moved back to Amsterdam and were soon separated. She decided to go to Paris for a new start in 1903.

Without a husband, not professionally trained in any career, and without any money, she used her experiences in Indonesia to create a new personal character, one who put on jewels, smelled of perfume, sometimes spoke in Malay, and danced seductively. She first debuted

---

[4] Information of this case study is abstracted and modified from history1900s.about.co m/od/1910s/p/MataHari.htm, www.wisegeek.com/who-is-mata-hari.htm, www.inde pendent.co.uk/news/world/europe/was-mata-hari-framed-9245320.html, and www.s kygaze.com/content/mysteries/MataHari.shtml.

as a dancer in a salon and achieved an instantaneous success. In order to make herself more exotic, she also used "Mata Hari" as her stage name, which means the "eye of the day" in Malay. Not surprisingly, the sensual dancer had scores of admirers who willingly paid for her. In the spring of 1914, she accepted a very attractive contract from the Berlin Metropole. At the time, however, the world was on a fast track to war and it was soon to engulf her. Penniless and adrift, she had no option but to return to her native Netherlands. In the fall of 1915, she was approached by a German consul. He told her that he was recruiting spies and offered her 50,000 francs and the code name H21, if she would spy for Germany. She agreed and took the cash.[5]

She visited France two times in 1915 and 1916, and during both times she was closely tracked by the French counterintelligence. However, there was no evidence that she was working for Germany. On her second trip to France, the French counterintelligence chief, Georges Ladoux, contacted her and tried to persuade her to spy for his side to seduce the German officers and that in return they would give her a million francs. At that time, she fell in love with a young Russian officer; the relationship with him seemed to be one true love in her life. She needed the money to settle down with the young officer. Eventually she accepted the offer from the French.

She was sent to Spain to seduce a German military attaché in Madrid via the sea lanes. However, the British forced the ship ashore at Falmouth, a city on the southern coast of England, and arrested Mata Hari, believing that she was a German spy named Clara Bendix. She was released after convincing the British that she was actually working for France. Mata Hari continued her journey to Madrid; she soon quickly formed liaisons with Germany's naval and military attachés in Madrid, and succeeded in seducing the German attachés. However, what exactly was the nature of her duties to the German officers remains part of the mystery surrounding Mata Hari.

---

[5]   See Lichfield (2001) for more information about this.

At the end of 1916, Berlin advised the two German attachés in Madrid that they were paying too much for the routine information provided by "Agent H-21" and sent Mata Hari back to Paris. On the other hand, the Germans then deliberately sent a telegram to Berlin which was intended for the French to intercept. As expected, the French decoded it and used it to prove that she was still working for the German intelligence service. Mata Hari returned to Paris on February 12, 1917 and stayed at the elegant Hotel Plaza. The next day, however, she was captured and was executed by the firing squad on October 15, 1917, at the age of 41.

According to Sun Tzu's classification of spy, Mata Hari can be classified as converted spy, because she first worked for Germany and then was utilized by the French. Mata Hari was employed as a spy because she had relationships with many prominent political figures, including military officers and other influential men in Russia, France, and Germany. She was also smart and could speak several languages. Moreover, as a citizen of the Netherlands, a neutral country during the war, Mata Hari was allowed to travel across national borders easily.

Sun Tzu said in order to obtain the spy's loyalty, the employer of the spy should treat the spy with sincerity. However, there was no such relationship between the employers (Germany and French) and Mata Hari. Their relationship was established based on taking advantage of each side and lacked in sincerity. Germany and France preferred Mata Hari's several competitive advantages and intentionally used them. Mata Hari's main goal was to earn money rather than to faithfully serve any particular country. This is why she was also easily persuaded to accept the French offer, although she was already working for Germany. Therefore, their relationship was bound to be very short term and volatile.

On the other hand, Germany arranged the whole process to make its adversary (France) directly punish Mata Hari, by sending her to France and sending the telegram to betray her to France. The French arrested and executed Mata Hari without even obtaining enough evidence that she had released important secrets to Germany. At that time the French claimed that she released top secrets to Germany about the information of the French weapons such as the tanks, which led to the deaths of thousands of French soldiers on the battle. However, after decades following Mata Hari's death, one report by the UK government wrote that there was in fact no evidence that Mata Hari delivered any secrets to Germany. Leon Schirmann, who spent ten years studying the case of Mata Hari, also admitted that she was the "perfect victim" who became the scapegoat for the French.

If we use Porter's view on the information advantage, we can easily see the mistake of French execution of Mata Hari. According to Porter, information is not the main source of competitive advantage, but just an aid to efficiently achieving a strategic goal. Therefore, the French did not have to execute Mata Hari as the execution did not aid France at all. Furthermore, the French already knew that Mata Hari was a converted spy from Germany. As the war was still going on, the French should have thought how to use Mata Hari more effectively rather than just to execute her. Germany also made a similar mistake as it had intentionally released the information of Mata Hari to have France kill her.

13.5 BUSINESS CASE: GOOGLE'S FAILURE IN CHINA

Google was founded in California, U.S.A., in 1998, by two graduate students of Stanford University, providing the Internet search services; currently it has become the global leading provider of the Internet search services. The mission of Google is "to organize the world's information and make it universally accessible and useful." In order to increase its international market, Google launched a Chinese-language version of google.com in 2000, hosted in the United States. Although the company secured a dominant position in the overall global market, its market share in China remained secondary to Baidu, a Chinese IT company. The problem was mainly due to the fact that the censorship by the Chinese government had reduced the speed of Google's search engine substantially.

In order to solve this problem, Google launched Google.cn in January 2006. To make it as "Chinese" as possible, the company hired Chinese employees and partnered with the Chinese technology firms. According to CEO Eric Schmidt, one of Google's "big projects" during 2007 was to grant greater autonomy to Google's local management in China. Google tried to make Google.cn as distinctly Chinese by adopting the local Chinese name of *Guge*, which roughly translates to "harvest song" but this name choice has been widely mocked by the Chinese users. Despite all these efforts, however, Google decided to leave the Chinese market in 2010, and moved its headquarters from China to Hong Kong. What are the main reasons that caused Google's failure in China, despite its superior global position in its field?

The Censorship by the Local Government

Since 2000, the US-based Google.com has been available to Chinese users. However, in September 2004, the Internet users in China suddenly could not access the site. Only two weeks later, Google.com could be accessed. However, the message of strengthened government censorship, which made the search engine slower and less reliable, was clearly delivered to both Google and the users. Google was proud of providing a high-quality user experience. However, because of the Internet censorship by the Chinese government, the quality of Google search in China deteriorated. Google generated search results extremely slowly and it took a very long time to load search results compared to other search engines in China, such as Baidu. The difficulties Google faced can be seen in its performance during the period of 2003 to 2005: the share of Google in the Chinese market slightly increased from 24 to 27 percent, while Baidu's market share increased substantially from 3 to 46 percent (Raufflet and Mills, 2009).

When Google established the more localized, new search engine, google.cn, Google expected the firewall restriction to be lowered, which had slowed searching speed and constant dead-end results for online users in China. However, the Chinese government continued to censor

Google to filter out the information considered as inappropriate and harmful to China. Google executives were severely frustrated by the constant censoring of Google's local search engine. For example, the Chinese character for river, *jiang*, could cause an error message or a timeout on Google. This is because it is the surname of a former Chinese president *Jiang Zemin*. Hence, the names of many other leaders of China were also not allowed to be searched on Google in China. However, the government trusted Baidu's search service with any keywords, because their search system and contents were pre-examined and thoroughly censored – with potentially problematic pages deleted and prevented from appearing on the results – by the Chinese government before the service commenced (Raufflet and Mills, 2009).

Google's competitive advantage has always been offering a variety of specialized services, such as images, videos, maps, news, products, and phone numbers, but most of these services were restricted or blocked by China's censorship. As a result, in January 2010, Google decided to close the Chinese-language search engine, Google.cn in mainland China and moved the server to Hong Kong, claiming that the restricted activities in China are not consistent with Google's value of business.

Failure in Knowing China

The Internet activities in China are quite different from those in the United States and other developed countries. The most popular Internet activities in China are related to entertainment which include online chatting; downloading music, TV shows, and movies; and playing online games (Raufflet and Mills, 2009). In contrast, Americans and people in other developed countries use the Internet more for work-related tasks, such as reading the news, searching for information, and sending and receiving emails (New York Times, 2010). Ironically, however, Google did not provide the services of the highest demand in China. In contrast, Baidu, founded in 2000, increased its market share in the Internet by offering services that Google did not offer at first, such as easy links to download pirated songs, TV shows, and movies from Chinese websites. Baidu claimed this was legal in China because the media files were not in the users' own computers. Therefore, Google also introduced a free online music service in China in 2009, with the permission of the music labels, but it was too late to win back the lost ground.

Google relied just on its own strengths to tackle the huge Chinese market, but found later that their services were too far from meeting the demands of Chinese users. Porter said that the firm's strategy should be adapted to the industry structure, implying that one should know the competitive forces of the industry. However, Google ignored or underestimated the particular way of doing business in China (i.e., Chinese government censorship) and also failed to know the local industry (e.g., the real needs of Chinese consumers). In Sun Tzu's words, Google failed to obtain the foreknowledge before launching business in China.

An interesting point of discussion is the issue of downloading pirated media files. While absolutely prohibited in most of the developed countries of the Western Europe and North America, servicing pirated media files is not only legal but also a highly popular practice in China. What Google overlooked was the regional difference in standards of what is accepted or unaccepted. In order to compete with such companies as Baidu in China, Google should have been more knowledgeable of Chinese ways of doing business. It is ironic that the most successful IT company (i.e., Google) overlooked the importance of local information of the largest potential market. This basic information about the local market can be easily obtained even by the local spies, the most basic, not sophisticated spies, according to Sun Tzu.

As mentioned earlier, spying in the business world is not allowed, but the case of Google is a little different. It is not about spying and stealing information from other firms, but spying activities by the government on a firm with a strong political intent. Google claimed that the hacking by the Chinese government targeted Google's secure servers in the United States, thereby causing the sensitivity problem of data security. However, according to the Chinese government's position, in order to do business in China, both domestic and foreign firms must obey Chinese rules and laws.

13.6   CONCLUSION AND IMPLICATIONS

One of the consistent military thoughts that pierces the entire volumn of Sun Tzu is to know the enemy and oneself. The main idea to take from this chapter is the significance of knowing the enemy by using spies. Sun Tzu argued that the portion of expenses on employing spies is much smaller, but their roles and effects on achieving a victory in war are substantial. Therefore, Sun Tzu proposed an active utilization of spies in warfare to obtain highly sophisticated information about the enemy's status and their intentions. Sun Tzu's military thought on obtaining the enemy's information was very sophisticated compared to other military strategists living in Sun Tzu's period. At that time, people relied much on the superstitious ways of fortune telling when making important decisions such as waging war.

In the business world, information also plays an important role in determining a firm's competitive advantage. However, according to Porter, it can help firms increase operational efficiencies, but it is not the main source of competitive advantage. The practices of many companies in the 2000s supported Porter's concerns about the over-blown emphasis on the Internet and its impacts. The most successful companies were not those that just integrated the Internet into their strategies, but those that used the Internet as a tool to complement their existing sources of competitive advantage. A standardized technology such as the Internet cannot be a source of uniqueness. What is truly important is how to differentiate, specialize, and provide unique products and services to the customers, utilizing the Internet as a means to an end. Porter correctly pointed out the fundamental sources of competitive advantage.[6]

For the military case, if we use Porter's view on the limited role of information as a fundamental source of advantage, the French

---

[6]   See chapter 3 of Moon (2010) for more discussion on this issue.

should have utilized Mata Hari more efficiently rather than executed her because she was just a means of obtaining information, not a fundamental source of competitive advantage. The case of Google in China also needs to be reiterated to derive more important implications. Google executives and other people in developed countries did not correctly understand the unexpected and seemingly somewhat irrational behavior of the Chinese government. On the other hand, the Chinese government just as well did not understand Google. The problem arose because both Google and the Chinese government behaved based on their own predetermined philosophies and policies, which was detrimental to both parties. Google lost the great potential market; China lost the most innovative company and its potentially enormous spillover effects on the development of China's IT-related industries. This lose-lose result was caused by the misunderstandings and misevaluation of their potential business partners. From this perspective, business managers and policy makers can find useful implications from Sun Tzu's strategy of using the spies and Porter's strategy of using information technology.

Epilogue

In each chapter of this book, I compared and contrasted the military strategies of Sun Tzu with the business strategies of Michael Porter to derive useful implications and possible theoretical extensions for both the military and business fields. As I conclude this book, I would like to re-emphasize what is likely to be the most important lesson from Sun Tzu. The critical premise of Sun Tzu's strategies is that one can win even when one's army is equal to or weaker than the enemy's army in terms of absolute power of the army forces. This view is what strategy is truly about. If one has a military force superior to one's enemy's, there is no need to design a sophisticated strategy for defeating the enemy. Ironically, many military and business strategists argue that one should be stronger than one's opponent to win. However, it is extremely difficult and even unrealistic to maintain absolute superiority over the competitors at all times.

Strategy purports to maximize the utility of the existing resources. Thus, a skilled strategist can minimize waste and increase productivity. Sun Tzu's *Hsing* and *Shih* – the strategies for gaining decisive advantage over the enemy by exploiting geographical and psychological effects – are good examples of how a wise strategist may produce exponential strengths out of given available resources. A hundred soldiers may be no match for a thousand if they plainly fight fist to fist, but if aided with a good strategy, a difference of ten times the number can be overcome – and this is the beauty of strategy. The insights of Sun Tzu are compatible with the business world. From the strategic viewpoint, simply proposing to build more resources or to develop superior technologies is not always advisable, but carefully considering one's options to effectively utilize the resources one already has is a far wiser move.

As Sun Tzu's strategy mainly dealt with the confrontation between two military forces with similar strengths, he had to think of how to disperse the enemy forces and how to concentrate one's own forces. Many heroic strategists, the legendary winners of wars in history, were good students of Sun Tzu. The common secret behind their victories is that they won against a large army with a small army by finding the weaknesses of their enemies and attacking them with their strengths. In business, the equivalent of this strategy is finding a niche market and penetrating it with the firm's strengths. This strategy is more useful for the weaker firm or the latecomer than the stronger firm or the first mover. Examples include the Japanese firms' successful entry in the global market in the 1970s and 1980s, the Korean firms in the 1990s, and the Chinese firms in more recent years.

Sun Tzu's theory of military strategy is similar to the game theory of business strategy. As Sun Tzu assumed a similar level of intellectual capacity as well as physical capacity between one and one's enemy, one has to conceal one's strategic plan, often by cheating the enemy to lead them in the direction that one wants. Concealing and cheating thus work as the two important preconditions for successful implementation of one's military strategy. However, in business, concealing is not always possible, and cheating is not allowed. Then, how can a firm maintain its core competence without being imitated by its competitors? To this question, Michael Porter has provided a brilliant solution: strategic fit.

In the past, when the product was simple and based primarily on one major technology, it was relatively easy to emulate the industry leader. However, as the competitive product becomes more sophisticated and requires multiple technologies, firms realize that they cannot master all of the necessary technologies. In this new business environment, firms often develop and maintain the core technologies in-house, and outsource the noncore technologies to other firms. This is why in recent years the global leaders pursued open innovation and other cooperative strategies, without the risk of losing their core competences. Moreover, as the dispersion of firms' value chain activities across the globe (i.e., global value chain) is expanding, the competitiveness of firms increasingly depends on selecting the most appropriate partners, locating the value activities in the most suitable places, and coordinating these activities around the world. Competitors may try to copy some of these activities or competences, but it would be extremely difficult to copy the entire system of another firm that has a good strategic fit among related activities.

Strategic fit is just one case I reiterated and extended to exemplify how Sun Tzu's and Porter's strategies complement each other. There are still many cases in this book that the readers can look into for further useful implications, depending on their interests. Studying Sun Tzu's or Porter's strategies separately may not provide sufficiently deep insights. By comparing and contrasting the strategies of these two giants, we are able to understand not only their strategies in a more efficient way, but also find potential extensions for each theory, by borrowing complementary ideas from each other. Although Sun Tzu's book was written 2,500 years ago, it still provides many important lessons from which modern business can benefit.

I have taught this topic (Sun Tzu's military strategy and Michael Porter's business strategy) as a full-semester course at the Graduate School of International Studies, Seoul National University, for several years. I have enjoyed discussions with my students on how this topic can be applied to many other fields and how they can benefit from applying these strategies to their own lives. I want to thank both Sun Tzu and Michael Porter for their tremendous contributions to enhancing the wisdom on strategy, and hope this book will provide useful guidelines for future studies on the interdisciplinary approach and the cross-comparison between East and West strategic thinking.

References

Adams, S. 2015. The World's Most Influential Business Thinkers 2015. *Forbes.* November 9.

Adams, T., Mee, L. D., Emerson, M., and Vahl, M. (eds.) 2002. *Europe's Black Sea Dimension.* Brussels: Center for European Policy Studies.

Adner, R. and Zemsky, P. 2006. A Demand-Based Perspective on Sustainable Competitive Advantage. *Strategic Management Journal*, 27: 215–239.

Appliance Magazine. 2009. Haier's Recession Strategies. *Appliance Magazine.* www.appliancemagazine.com/editorial.php?article=2252&zone=1&first=1.

Atsmon, Y., Dixit, V., and Wu, C. 2011. Tapping China's Luxury-Goods Market. *McKinsey Quarterly*, April. www.mckinseyquarterly.com/Tapping_Chinas_luxury-goods_market_2779.

Barboza, D. and Stone, B. 2010. China, Where U.S. Internet Companies Often Fail. *New York Times.* January 15.

Barnes, M. 2010. The Mongol War Machine: How Were the Mongols Able to Forge the Largest Contiguous Land Empire in History? Presented by Publications in Contemporary Affairs (PiCA). www.thepicaproject.org/wp-content/uploads/2010/03/The-Mongol-War-Machine.pdf.

Barney, J. B. 1986. Organizational Culture: Can It Be a Source of Sustained Competitive Advantage? *Academy of Management Review*, 11(3): 656–665.

Barney, J. B. 1991. Firm Resources and Sustained Competitive Advantage. *Journal of Management*, 17(1): 99–120.

Barrett, G. 1989. *Archetypes in Japanese Film: The Sociopolitical and Religious Significance of the Principal Heroes and Heroines.* Selinsgrove, PA: Susquehanna University Press.

Bartholomees, Jr., J. B. 2008. The Tao of Deception: Unorthodox Warfare in Historic and Modern China. *Parameters*, 38(1): 113-114..

Bartlett, C. A. and Ghoshal, S. 1989. *Managing across Borders: The Transnational Solution.* Boston, MA: Harvard Business Press.

Bartley, C. M. 2005. The Art of Terrorism: What Sun Tzu Can Teach Us about International Terrorism. *Comparative Strategy*, 24(3): 237–251.

Bei, D. 2012. *The Art of War and Thirty-Six Principles.* Beijing: Zhongguohuaqiao Publishing. (in Chinese)

Bowen, J. K. 2007. Japanese Preparations for the Attack on Pearl Harbor. The Pacific War website. www.pacificwar.org.au/pearlharbor/prepsforattack.html.

Braun, J. V. 2008. Rising Food Prices: What Should Be Done? *IFPRI Policy Brief,* April. http://ebrary.ifpri.org/cdm/ref/collection/p15738coll2/id/9235.

Breznik, L. 2012. Can Information Technology Be a Source of Competitive Advantage? *Economic and Business Review,* 14(3): 251–269.

Burnes, B. 2004. *Managing Change in Organizations* (4th edn.). Harlow: Prentice Hall.

Business Wire India. 2017. Haier Tops Euromonitor's Major Appliances Global Brand Rankings for 8th Consecutive Year. February 6.

Center for Strategic and International Studies (CSIS). 2010. Record of North Korea's Major Conventional Provocations since 1960s. csis.org/files/publication/10 0525_North_Koreas_Provocations_60s_Present_0.pdf.

Chandler, A. D. Jr. 1962. *Strategy as Structure.* Cambridge, MA: MIT Press.

Chen, M. 1994. Sun Tzu's Strategic Thinking and Contemporary Business. *Business Horizons,* 37(2): 42–48.

Chen, Y. J. and Lu, B. S. 2006. *Appreciation of 'Sun Tzu's Art of War.'* Wuhan University Press. (in Chinese)

Cheng, D. 2013. Winning without Fighting: The Chinese Psychological Warfare Challenge. *Heritage Foundation.* July 12. www.heritage.org/research/repor ts/2013/07/winning-without-fighting-the-chinese-psychological-warfare -challenge.

Chesbrough, H. W. 2007. Why Companies Should Have Open Business Models. *MIT Sloan Management Review,* 48(2): 22–28.

Chhabara, R. 2015. Asia Column: Lessons from Nestlé's Crisis in India. July 8. www.ethicalcorp.com/stakeholder-engagement/asia-column-lessons-nes tles-crisis-india.

Cho, D. S. and Moon, H. C. (eds.) 2013a. *From Adam Smith to Michael Porter: Evolution of Competitiveness Theory* (extended edn.). Singapore: World Scientific Publishing.

Cho, D. S. and Moon, H. C. 2013b. *International Review of National Competitiveness.* Cheltenham, UK, and Northampton, USA: Edward Elgar.

Cho, D. S., Moon, H. C., and Kim, M. Y. 2008. Characterizing International Competitiveness in International Business Research: A MASI Approach to National Competitiveness. *Research in International Business and Finance,* 22(2): 175–192.

Clausewitz, C. 1968 [1832]. *On War*. Translated by Graham, C. J. J. New York, NY: Dorset Press.

Cleary, T. 1988. *The Art of War*. Boston and London: Shambhala Publications.

Clemons, E. and Row, M. 1991. Sustaining IT Advantage: The Role of Structural Differences. *MIS Quarterly*, 15(3): 275–292.

Cohen, W. M. and Levinthal, D. A. 1990. Absorptive Capacity: A New Perspective on Learning and Innovation. *Administrative Science Quarterly*, 35(1): 128–152.

Collins, J. M. 1978. Vietnam Postmortem: A Senseless Strategy. *Parameters: US Army War College Quarterly*, 8: 8–14.

ComScore. 2008. M:Metrics: iPhone Hype Holds Up. March 18. www.comscore.com/esl/Insights/Press-Releases/2008/03/iPhone-Hype-Holds-Up.

Dalton, C. M. 2008. From Battlefield to Boardroom. *Business Horizons*, 51(2): 79–83.

Danchev, P. 1998. Liddell Hart and Manoeuver. *RUSI Journal*, 143(6): 33–35.

Davenport, S. 2005. Exploring the Role of Proximity in SME Knowledge-Acquisition. *Research Policy*, 34: 683–701.

DeSutter, P. A. 1994. Sun Tzu, Clausewitz, and the Importance of Knowing Yourself and the Enemy. www.dtic.mil/cgi-bin/GetTRDoc?AD=ADA440962.

Douglas, M. A. and Strutton, D. 2009. Going 'Purple': Can Military Jointness Principles Provide a Key to More Successful Integration at the Marketing-Manufacturing Interface? *Business Horizons*, 52(3): 251–263.

Drejer, I. and Vinding, A. L. 2007. Searching Near and Far: Determinants of Innovative Firms' Propensities to Collaborate across Geographical Distances. *Industry and Innovation*, 14(3): 259–275.

Economist, 2004. Haier's Purpose: Haier Shows Why China Will Struggle to Build a Global Brand. March 18.

2011a. Oh, Mr Porter. March 10.

2011b. Sun Tzu and the Art of Soft Power. December 17.

2012. Comparative Advantage: The Boomerang Effect. April 21.

2015. Islamic State: Unfriended. December 12.

2016. Tata Group: Mistry's Elephant. September 24.

Forbes. 2014. What Has AirTran Done for Southwest Airlines? December 11.

Frantz, D. 2001. Baku Journal; How the Nobels Made a Prize of Baku. *New York Times*. February 3.

Gang, S. G. 2011. *The Art of War Read at the Age of 40*. Seoul: Hbooks. (in Korean)

Gartner. 2015. Gartner Says Smartphone Sales Surpassed One Billion Units in 2014. March 3. www.gartner.com/newsroom/id/2996817.

Gereffi, G., Humphrey, J., Kaplinsky, R., and Sturgeon, T. 2001. Introduction: Globalization, Value Chains and Development. *IDS Bulletin*, 32(3): 1–8.

Gertner, M. I. 2013. The Value Chain and Value Creation. *Advances in Management*, 6 (10):1–4.

Gilbert, B. A., McDougall, P. P., and Audretsch, D. B. 2008. Clusters, Knowledge Spillovers and New Venture Performance: An Empirical Examination. *Journal of Business Venturing*, 23: 405–422.

Griffith, E.. 2014. Why Startups Fail, According to Their Founders. *Fortune*. September 25.

Griffith, S. B. 1963. *The Art of War* (Trans.). Oxford: Oxford University Press.

Gunasekaran, A. 1998. Agile Manufacturing: Enablers and an Implementation Framework. *International Journal of Production Research*, 36(5): 1223–1247.

1999. Agile Manufacturing: A Framework for Research and Development. *International Journal of Production Research*, 62: 87–105.

Hacklin, F., Battistini, B., and von Krogh, G. 2013. Strategic Choices in Converging Industries. *MIT Sloan*, 55(1): 65–73.

Hall, J. and Vredenburg, H. 2003. The Challenges for Innovation for Sustainable Development. *MIT Sloan Management Review*, 45(1): 61–68.

Hamel, G. 1999. Bringing Silicon Valley Inside. *Harvard Business Review*, September/October: 71–84.

Handel, M. I. 2000. Corbett, Clausewitz, and Sun Tzu. *Naval War College Review*, 53 (4):106–124.

Hansen, M. W., Pedersen, T., and Petersen, B. 2009. MNC Strategies and Linkage Effects in Developing Countries. *Journal of World Business*, 44: 121–130.

Hart, L. 1954. *Strategy: The Indirect Approach*. New York, NY: Praeger, Paperbacks, Inc.

Harvard Business School homepage. www.hbs.edu/faculty/Pages/profile.aspx?facId= 6532.

Harvard Business Review. 2011. *Harvard Business Review on Greening Your Business Profitably*. Boston, MA: Harvard Business School Press.

Holstein, W. J. 2013. Hyundai's Capabilities Play. *Strategy-Business*. February 26. www.strategy-business.com/article/00162?gko=8346f.

Huggins, R. 2015. The Evolution of Knowledge Clusters: Progress and Policy. *Economic Development Quarterly*, 22(4): 277–289.

Hunt, L. 2005. Haier Group Company. www.marketbusting.com/casestudies/Hai er%20Report.pdf.

Jagannathan. R. 2011. Why a Gold-Plated Nano Will Do Little for Tata's Failing Car. *Firstpost*. www.firstpost.com/business/why-a-gold-plated-nano-will-do-little-for-tatas-failing-car-87924.html.

Jin, B. and Moon, H. C. 2006. The Diamond Approach to the Competitiveness of Korea's Apparel Industry. *Journal of Fashion Marketing and Management*, 10(2): 195–208.

Jo, H. J. and You, J. S. 2011. Transferring Production Systems: An Institutionalist Account of Hyundai Motor Company in the United States. *Journal of East Asian Studies*, 11: 41–73.

Joint Venture. 2007. *Index of Silicon Valley 2007*. Palo Alto, CA: Joint Venture.

Karnani, A. 2007. The Mirage of Marketing to the Bottom of the Pyramid: How the Private Sector Can Help Alleviate Poverty. *California Management Review*, 49(4): 90–111.

Ketels, C. H. M. 2011. Clusters and Competitiveness: Porter's Contribution. In Huggins, R. and Izushi, H. (eds.), *Competition, Competitive Advantage, and Clusters*. New York, NY: Oxford University Press.

Kim, G. S. 1999. *Military Classic 1: The Art of War*. Seoul: BKworld. (in Korean)

Kinni, T. and Kinni, D. 2005. Lessons in Strategy and Leadership: MacArthur at Inchon. *FT Press*. April 8.

Kiszely, J. P. 2000. Seizing the Advantage, Seizing the Initiative: New Opportunities, New Challenges. *RUSI Journal*, 145(4): 1–7.

Korb, L. J. and Rothman, A. 2011. Reasons to Keep Our Word – US Withdrawal from Iraq. September 13. www.americanprogress.org/issues/ext/2011/09/13/102 89/reasons-to-keep-our-word-u-s-withdrawal-from-iraq.

Kósa, S. and Porkoláb, I. 2009. What Should the Information Strategy Be in the Next Phase of the Terror War? *AARMS*, 8(1): 107–116.

Koste, L. L. and Malhotra, M. K. 2000. A Theoretical Framework for Analyzing the Dimensions of Manufacturing Flexibility. *Journal of Operations Management*, 18(1): 75–94.

Kothandaraman, P. and Wilson, D. 2001. The Future of Competition: Value-Creating Networks. *Industrial Marketing Management*, 33: 7–14.

Laugesen, J. and Yuan, Y. 2010. What Factors Contributed to the Success of Apple's iPhone? *2010 Ninth International Conference on Mobile Business*. ieeexplore.ieee.org/xpls/abs_all.jsp?arnumber=5494782&tag=1.

Lee, S. F., Roberts, P., Lau, W. S., and Bhattacharyya, S. K. 1998. Sun Tzu's The Art of War as Business and Management strategies for World Class Business Excellence Evaluation under QFD Methodology. *Business Process Management*, 4(2): 96–113.

Li, Y. 2011. Walmart Business Model Study. *International Journal of Advanced Economics and Business Management*, 1(2): 93–97.

Lichfield, J. 2001. Was Mata Hari Framed? *The Independent*, October 19.

Lin, T. W. 2005. Effective OEC Management Control at China Haier Group. *Strategic Finance*, 86(11): 39–45.

Liu, H. and Li, K. 2002. Strategic Implications of Emerging Chinese Multinationals: The Haier Case Study. *European Management Journal*, 20(6): 699–706.

Ludwig, C. 2015. Breaking Supply Chain Taboos in South Korea. *Automotive Logistics*. July15. automotivelogistics.media/intelligence/breaking-supply-chain-taboos-in-south-korea.

Lütolf-Carroll, C. 2009. *From Innovation to Cash Flows: Value Creation by Structuring High Technology Alliances*. Hoboken, NJ: John Wiley & Sons.

Ma, H. 2003. To Win without Fighting: An Integrative Framework. *Management Decision*, 41(1/2): 72–84.

MacDonald, J. B. and Neupert, K. E. 2005. Applying Sun Tzu's Terrain and Ground to the Study of Marketing Strategy. *Journal of Strategic Marketing*, 13(4): 293–304.

Machiavelli, N. 2007. *The Art of War: Two Perspectives*. Radford, VA: Wilder Publications.

MacMillan, I. C. 1982. Seizing Competitive Initiative. *Journal of Business Strategy*, 2(4):43–57.

Madslien, J. 2013. Hyundai and Kia Gain from European Crisis. *BBC*. March 7.

Mann, M. and Byun, S. E. 2011. Accessing Opportunities in Apparel Retail Sectors in India: Porter's Diamond Approach. *Journal of Fashion Marketing and Management*, 15(2): 194–210.

Margolis, J. D. and Walsh, J. P. 2003. Misery Loves Companies: Rethinking Social Initiatives by Business. *Administrative Science Quarterly*, 48: 268–305.

Marshall, A. 1890. *Principles of Economics*. London: Macmillan.

Martin, R. and Sunley, P. 2003. Deconstructing Clusters: Chaotic Concept or Policy Panacea? *Journal of Economic Geography*, 3: 5–35.

Mata, F. J., Fuerst, W. L., and Barney, J. B. 1995. Information Technology and Sustained Competitive Advantage: A Resource-Based Analysis. *MIS Quarterly*, 19(4): 487–505.

McCann, B. T. and Folta, T. B. 2011. Performance Differentials within Geographic Clusters. *Journal of Business Venturing*, 26: 104–123.

McCormick, B. 2001. Make Money, Not War: A Brief Critique of Sun Tzu's *The Art of War*. *Journal of Business Ethics*, 29: 285–286.

McCready, D. M. 2003. Learning from Sun Tzu. *Military Review*, 83(3): 85–88.

McNeilly, M. 1996. *Sun Tzu and the Art of Business: Six Strategic Principles for Managers*. New York, NY: Oxford University Press, Inc.

McPhee, W. and Wheeler, D. 2006. Making the Case for the Added-Value Chain. *Strategy and Leadership*, 34(4): 39–46.

Michaelson, G. and Michaelson, S. 2003. *Sun Tzu for Success*. Avon, MA: Adams Media.

Minford, J. 2008. *Sun Tzu's The Art of War*. North Clarendon, Tokyo, and Singapore: Tuttle Publishing.

Moon, H. C. 1993. The Dynamics of Porter's Three Generics in International Business Strategy. In Rugman, A. M. and Verbeke, A. (eds.), *Global Competition: Beyond the Three Generics. Research in Global StrategicMmanagement*, Vol. 4. London: Emerald Group Publishing, pp. 51–64.

1994. A Revised Framework of Global Strategy: Extending the Coordination-Configuration Framework, *The International Executive*, 36 (5): 557–574.

2010. *Global Business Strategy: Asian perspective*. Singapore: World Scientific Publishing.

2013. One Will Fail If One Is Satisfied with the Current Success and Ignores the Rivals. *Dong-A Business Review*, 139: 94–99. (in Korean)

2014a. Avoiding Strengths and Attacking Weaknesses to Achieve an Overwhelming Victory by Concentrating on the Competitive Advantage. *Dong-A Business Review*, 150: 88–93. (in Korean)

2014b. Sometimes the Devious Route Is the Short-cut, as Seen in Nestlé's Creation of Shared Value. *Dong-A Business Review*, 161: 106–111. (in Korean)

2016a. *Foreign Direct Investment: A Global Perspective*. Singapore: World Scientific Publishing.

2016b. *The Strategy for Korea's Economic Success*. New York, NY: Oxford University Press.

Moon, H. C., Hur, Y. K., Yin, W. Y., and Helm, C. 2014. Extending Porter's Generic Strategies: From Three to Eight. *European Journal of International Management*, 8(2): 205–225.

Moon, H. C. and Jung, J. S. 2010. Northeast Asian Cluster through Business and Cultural Cooperation. *Journal of Korea Trade*, 14(2): 29–53.

Moon, H. C. and Lee, D. 2004. The Competitiveness of Multinational Firms: A Case Study of Samsung Electronics and Sony. *Journal of International and Area Studies*, 11(1): 1–21.

Moon, H. C., Rugman, A. M., and Verbeke, A. 1995. The Generalized Double Diamond Approach to International Competitiveness. In Rugman, A. M., Broeck, J. V. D., and Verbeke, A. (eds.), *Research in Global Strategic*

Management: Beyond the Diamond (vol. 5). Greenwich, CT: JAI Press, pp. 97–114.

1998. A Generalized Double Diamond Approach to the Global Competitiveness of Korea and Singapore. *International Business Review*, 7(2): 135–150.

Moon, H. C. and Roehl, T. W. 2001. Unconventional Foreign Direct Investment and the Imbalance Theory. *International Business Review*, 10(2): 197–215.

Moore, J. F. 1996. *The Death of Competition: Leadership and Strategy in the Age of Business Ecosystems*. New York, NY: Harper Collins Publishers.

Moran, P. E. 2010. *Master Sun's Art of War: A Classic Text for the Modern Martial Artist*. Morrisville, NC: Lulu Enterprises Inc.

Morgan, D. 2009. The Decline and Fall of the Mongol Empire. *Journal of the Royal Asiatic Society*, 19(4): 427–437.

Mundy, S. 2013. Hyundai: Time to Abandon Caution and Push Overseas? *Financial Times*. May 3.

Nam, I. S. 2015. Hyundai Motor's Profit Falls Again. *Wall Street Journal*. April 23.

Nicas, J. and Carey, S. 2014. Southwest Airlines, Once a Brassy Upstart, Is Showing Its Age. *Wall Street Journal*. April 1.

Normann, R. and Ramirez, R. 1993. From Value Chain to Value Constellation: Designing Interactive Strategy. *Harvard Business Review*, July–August: 65–77.

Ocasio, W. and Joseph, J. 2008. Rise and Fall – or Transformation: The Evolution of Strategic Planning at the General Electric Company, 1940–2006. *Long Range Planning*, 41(3): 248–272.

O'Dowd, E. and Waldron, A. 1991. Sun Tzu for Strategists. *Comparative Strategy*, 10(1): 25–36.

Oliver, C. 2011. Hyundai Motor Seeks Steel-Making Advantage. *Financial Times*. November 3.

Pacific War homepage. Japanese Preparations for the Attack on Pearl Harbor. Retrieved from www.pacificwar.org.au/pearlharbor/prepsforattack.html.

Pearlman, M. D. 2008. *Truman & MacArthur: Policy, Politics, and the Hunger for Honor and Renown*. Bloomington, IN: Indiana University Press.

Peppard, J. and Rylander, A. 2006. From Value Chain to Value Network: Insights for Mobile Operators. *European Management Journal*, 24(2–3): 128–141.

Peteraf, M. A. 1993. The Cornerstones of Competitive Advantage: A Resource-Based View. *Strategic Management Journal*, 14(3): 179–191.

Phua, C. C. R. 2007. From the Gulf War to Global War on Terror: A Distorted Sun Tzu in US Strategic Thinking. *RUSI Journal*, 152(6): 46–52.

Piscione, D. P. 2013. *Secrets of Silicon Valley*. New York, NY: Palgrave Macmillan.

Porter, M. E. 1979. How Competitive Forces Shape Strategy. *Harvard Business Review*, March–April: 137–145.

1980. *Competitive Strategy: Techniques for Analyzing Industries and Competitors*. New York, NY: Free Press.

1985. *Competitive Advantage: Creating and Sustaining Superior Performance*. New York, NY: Free Press.

1986. *Competition in Global Industries*. Boston, MA: Harvard Business School Press.

1987. From Competitive Advantage to Corporate Strategy. *Harvard Business Review*, May–June: 43–59.

1990. *The Competitive Advantage of Nations*. New York, NY: Free Press.

1996. What Is Strategy? *Harvard Business Review*, 74(6): 61–78.

1997. Creating Tomorrow's Advantage. In Gibson, R. (ed.), *Rethinking the Future*. New York, NY: Free Press.

1998. *On Competition*. Boston, MA: Harvard Business School Press.

2001. Strategy and the Internet. *Harvard Business Review*, March: 63–78.

2008. *On Competition* (updated and expanded edition). Boston, MA: Harvard Business School Press.

Porter, M. E., Delgado, M., Ketels, C., and Stern, S. 2008. Moving to a New Global Competitiveness Index. In World Economic Forum (ed.), *The Global Competitiveness Report 2008–2009*. Geneva: World Economic Forum.

Porter, M. E. and Heppelmann, J. E. 2014. How Smart, Connected Products Are Transforming Competition. *Harvard Business Review*, November: 64–88.

Porter, M. E. and Kramer, M. R. 2002. The Competitive Advantage of Corporate Philanthropy. *Harvard Business Review*, 80(12): 56–68.

2006. Strategy & Society: The Link between Competitive Advantage and Corporate Social Responsibility. *Harvard Business Review*, 84(12): 78–92.

2011. Creating Shared Value. *Harvard Business Review*, 89(1/2): 62–77.

Porter, M. E. and Millar, V. E. 1985. How Information Gives You Competitive Advantage. *Harvard Business Review*, 63(4): 149–160.

Porter, M. E. and Rivkin, J. W. 2012. Choosing the United States. *Harvard Business Review*, 81(March): 81–93.

Powell, T. C. and Dent-Micallef, A. 1997. Information Technology as Competitive Advantage: The Role of Human, Business, and Technology Resources. *Strategic Management Journal*, 18(5): 375–405.

Prahalad, C. K. 2001. The Bottom of the Pyramid. *Siliconindia*, 5(10): 76–79.

2004a. *The Fortune at the Bottom of the Pyramid: Eradicating Poverty through Profits*. Upper Saddle River, NJ: Wharton School Publishing.

2004b. Why Selling to the Poor Markets Makes for Good Business. *Fortune*, 150 (10): 70–72.

Prahalad, C. K., and Hamel, G. 1990. The Core Competence of the Corporation. *Harvard Business Review*, 90(3): 79–91.

Prahalad, C. K. and Mashelkar, R. A. 2010. Innovation's Holy Grail. *Harvard Business Review*, July–August: 133–141.

Prasad, A. 2010. Strategy as "Inferior" Choice: A Re-interpretation of Porter's "What Is Strategy?" *Journal of Management Research*, 10(1): 15–24.

Rarick, C. A. 2009. The Historical Roots of Chinese Cultural Values and Managerial Practices. *Journal of International Business Research*, 8(2): 59–66.

Raufflet, E. and Mills, A. J. 2009. *The Dark Side: Critical Cases on the Downside of Business*. Sheffield: Greenleaf Publishing.

Record, J. 2009. Japan's Decision for War in 1941: Some Enduring Lesson. Retrieved from www.strategicstudiesinstitute.army.mil/pubs/display.cfm?pubID= 905.

Rein, S. 2012. Why Starbucks Succeeds in China. *Business Insider*. February 13.

Richey, R. G., Hilton, C. B., Harvey, M. G., Beitelspacher, L. S., Tokman, M., and Moeller, M. 2011. Aligning Operant Resources for Global Performance: An Assessment of Supply Chain Human Resource Management. *Journal of Management and Organization*, 17(3): 364–382.

Rugman, A. M. and D'Cruz, J. R. 1993. The Double Diamond Model of International Competitiveness: The Canadian Experience. *Management International Review*, 33(2): 17–39.

Rugman, A. M and Oh, C. H. 2008. The International Competitiveness of Asian Firms. *Journal of Strategy and Management*, 1(1): 57–71.

Sawyer, R. D. 1994. *The Art of War* (Trans.). Boulder, CO: Westview Press.

Sawyer, R. D. 2005. *The Essential Art of War*. New York, NY: Basic Books.

Saxenian, A. 1990. Regional Networks and the Resurgence of Silicon Valley. *California Management Review*, Fall: 89–112.

2000. *Regional Advantage: Culture and Competition in Silicon Valley and Route 128* (9th edn.). Cambridge, MA, and London: Harvard University Press. http://graphics8.nytimes.com/packages/pdf/technology/SVCI P_2015_PDFfinal.pdf.

Schmitt, J. F. 1990. Understanding Maneuver as the Basis for a Doctrine. *Marine Corps Gazette*, 74(8): 90–100.

Schumpeter, J. A. 1942. *Capitalism, Socialism and Democracy*. New York, NY: Harper and Row.

Shi, Z. H. 2000. *A New Interpretation on Sun Tzu's The Art of War*. Shanghai: Xuelin Publishing. (in Chinese)

Silicon Valley Leadership Group (SVLG) and Silicon Valley Community Foundation (SVCF). 2015. Silicon Valley Competitiveness and Innovation Project 2015. graphics8.nytimes.com/packages/pdf/technology/SVCI P_2015_PDFfinal.pdf.

Sledge, S. 2005. Does Porter's Diamond Hold in the Global Automotive Industry? *Advances in Competitiveness Research*, 13(1): 22–32.

Sleevi, N. M. 1998. Applying the Principles of War. *Military Review*, 78(3): 47–52.

Smith, A. 1937 [1776]. *An Inquiry into the Nature and Cause of the Wealth of Nations*. C. W. Eliot (ed.). New York, NY: P. F. Collier.

Southwest Airlines website. www.southwest.com.

Spanos, Y. E. and Lioukas, S. 2001. An Examination into the Causal Logic of Rent Generation: Contrasting Porter's Competitive Strategy Framework and the Resource-Based Perspective. *Strategic Management Journal*, 22(10): 907–934.

Sun, K. 1995. How to Overcome without Fighting: An Introduction to the Taoist Approach to Conflict Resolution. *Journal of Theoretical and Philosophical Psychology*, 15: 161–171.

Swafford, P. M., Ghosh, S., and Murthy, N. N. 2006. A Framework for Assessing Value Chain Agility. *International Journal of Operations and Production Management*, 26 (1/2): 118–140.

Taggart, J. H. 1998. Configuration and Coordination at Subsidiary Level: Foreign Manufacturing Affiliates in the UK. *British Journal of Management*, 9: 327–339.

Tata Motors. 2015. Tata Motors 70th Annual Report 2014–15.

Teece, D. J. 2007. Explicating Dynamic Capabilities: The Nature and Microfoundations of (Sustainable) Enterprise Performance. *Strategic Management Journal*, 28: 1319–1350.

Tully, S. 2015. Southwest Bets Big on Business Travelers. *Fortune*. September 23.

Teece, D.J., Pisano, G., and Shuen, A. 1997. Dynamic Capabilities and Strategic Management. *Strategic Management Journal*, 18: 509–533.

The Institute for Industrial Policy Studies. 2012. *IPS National Competitiveness Research 2012*. Seoul: IPS & IPS-NaC.

Toyota Motor Corporate website. www.toyota-global.com/company/vision_philo sophy/toyota_production_system/just-in-time.html.

Tung, R. L. 1994. Strategic Management Thought in East Asia. *Organizational Dynamics*, 22(4): 55–56.

UNCTAD. 2014. *World Investment Report 2014*. New York, NY, and Geneva: United Nations.

Verbeke, A. 2013. *International Business Strategy* (2nd edn). New York, NY: Cambridge University Press.

Wang, H. H. 2012. Five Things Starbucks Did to Get China Right. *Forbes*. August 10.

Wee, C. H. 1994. Managing Change: Perspectives from Sun Tzu's Art of War. *Journal of Strategic Change*, 3: 186–187.

Wee, C. H., Lee, K. S., and Hidajat, B. W. 1991. *Sun Tzu: War and Management: Application to Strategic Management and Thinking*. New York, NY: Addison-Wesley Publishing.

Wernerfelt, B. 1984. A Resource-based View of the Firm. *Strategic Management Journal*, 5(2): 171–180.

Womack, J. P., Jones, D. T., and Roos, D. 1990. *The Machine That Changed the World*. New York, NY: Free Press.

Wong, Y. Y., Maher, T. E., and Lee, G. 1998. The Strategy of an Ancient Warrior: An Inspiration for International Managers. *Multinational Business Review*, 6(1): 83–93.

Wu, R. S. and Yu, R. B. 1993. *Sunzibingfa Jieshuo*. Beijing: Jinmao Publishing.

Wu, W. Y., Chou, C. H., and Wu, Y. J. 2004. A Study of Strategy Implementation as Expressed through Sun Tzu's Principles of War. *Industrial Management & Data Systems*, 104(5): 396–408.

Youn, H., Strumsky, D., Bettencourt, L. M. A., and Lobo, J. 2015. Invention as a Combinatorial Process: Evidence from US Patents. *Journal of the Royal Society Interface*, 12(106): 1–8.

Yuen, D. M. C. 2008. Deciphering Sun Tzu. *Comparative Strategy*, 27(2): 183–200.

Zenith Management Consulting. 2005. How to Exploit Wal-Mart's Weaknesses. http://zenith-consulting.com/research/walMart/Wal-Mart-Strategy.pdf.

Zhang, J. 2007. Access to Venture Capital and the Performance of Venture-based Start-ups in Silicon Valley. *Economic Development Quarterly*, 21(2): 124–147.

Zhang, Q., Vonderembrse, M. A., and Lim, J. 2002. Value Chain Flexibility: A Dichotomy of Competence and Capability. *International Journal of Production Research*, 40(3): 561–583.

Zhang, W. M. 2016. The Great Significance and Far-Reaching Influence of the Long March of the Red Army. November 4. www.qstheory.cn/dukan/hqwg/2016-11/04/c_1119849325.htm. (in Chinese)

Index

Printed in the United States
by Baker & Taylor Publisher Services